Around the States in 90 days

ABOUT THE AUTHOR

Andy Moseley grew up in Walsall, and now lives in London. From his time in Walsall he picked up an unrelenting love of his local football club, an encyclopaedic knowledge of music trivia, and the beginnings of a very large record collection, none of which he has put to any practical use. From his time in London he picked up a desire to see America. He briefly achieved this in 2006, and did manage to put it to practical use by writing this, his first book, on his return.

Around the States in 90 days

3 Short Months - 1 Long Road

ANDY MOSELEY

NOLOGOPUBLICATIONS

First published in the UK by NoLogoPublications 2009

The author and publisher wishes to thank the following for permission to reprint
material:

The excerpt from *Big-Box Swindle* by Stacy Mitchell (Copyright © 2006 Stacy
Mitchell) on page 123 - reprinted by kind permission of Beacon Press, Boston.

The excerpt from the *Relocate to Sedona* page of the official tourism site of the
Sedona Chamber of Commerce on page 210 - reprinted by kind permission of
Sedona Chamber of Commerce

A CIP catalogue for this book is available from the British Library

ISBN 978-0-9561551-0-8

NoLogoPublications
Unit 5, 165 London Road
Kingston KT2 6NU
www.NoLogoPublications.co.uk

For Liz

Tour Itinerary

Introduction

Career breaks are often seen as voyages into the unknown or journeys of self discovery, where people head to remote locations for spiritually rewarding experiences. I knew myself well enough to know I wouldn't be spiritually rewarded by a voyage into the unknown, so, in 2006, when I decided there was more to life than work, I went to America. You see, while I wanted to escape the rat race, I didn't want to leave it behind completely, and while I wanted to observe rather than participate, I wanted to observe things I knew a bit about, rather than anything that might take me too far out of my own personal comfort zone. Liz, my girlfriend, felt the same. There was only thing we could do, cross the Atlantic and explore the land of the free.

The original plan was to sell the house, pocket the change, take a flight, and not come back until we had seen all of the country or ran out of money. First, we planned to go to small towns and big cities, then we planned to go to big towns and small cities, and then, just for good measure, we planned to go to places that were neither cities or towns but boasted some of the most spectacular and dramatic scenery known to man. Our aim, if we had one, was to find out whether America had survived the onslaught of shopping malls and chain motels or had become one vast country made up of indistinguishable places and indistinguishable people. However, if I'm being honest, we didn't really have an aim, all we had was a desire to see the country, which was enough for us to plan for a lifetime away from home, or a year long holiday at least.

Sadly, the American visa system ended our hopes of an exit to eternal summer slacking. As two people without jobs, houses, or friends in the States, the odds of getting a visa seemed limited to begin with, and became even more remote after I logged on to the US Embassy website and met with a system designed to thwart all but the most determined of would be travellers. Knowing that getting rejected for a visa would mean we wouldn't be let in on the visa waiver programme either, we changed our plans, and an unfocussed ramble around the country turned into a personal quest to cram as much as we could into ninety days before the small matter of a visa and our continuing right to be there became a problem.

If you've read the back cover and the tour itinerary, you'll already know where it began and where it ended, and you'll know that we went from one side of the country to the other. What more is there to say at the moment, other than perhaps to explain why we went from east to west and why we chose the places we did.

A trailfinders brochure and a love of music had a lot to do with it. The brochure helped someone as geographically challenged as me to work out just how close some places were to one another, and how far apart some classic road trips were. The love of music provided us with the most classic road trip of them all – Route 66. We had to go on that road. If nothing else it would take away the need for us to plan the route ourselves as we could just be lead by the song.

It didn't quite work out that way however. The route developed in weird and wonderful ways, almost like we were joining the dots in a badly drawn picture, with the start destination changing several times over, the middle being a loosely planned affair at best, and only the end forever being San Francisco. Some of the places that made it to the final itinerary were places we'd always known and always wanted to see, others were chance finds as we contemplated the various ways to get from A to B and then to E, skipping C and D because they didn't take our fancy.

When we came back, people said, "it doesn't seem that long since you went away," which was strange because at times the space from one weekend to another had seemed like a month at least to us. I guess that's a sign of how life is, you measure other people's time by your own, and the fewer places you are in, the shorter time can seem. But that's enough of the pseudo-philosophical, it's time to get on with the story.

Our journey took place in a time when George W. Bush was President of the United States of America and few people outside of that country had heard of Barack Obama, let alone guessed that he would one day be its leader.

On 11 July, we flew into Washington DC…

Part 1

East Side Story

1 – Washington

On 11 July we flew into Washington DC. To have flown out a week earlier, on Independence Day, and to have started in Philadelphia, the birthplace of the nation, may have seemed sensible to the outside observer, but somehow didn't occur to us. Perhaps this was an early indicator of what was to become a feature of the trip - finding out that things were happening either just as we were leaving or just before we arrived in a city. Alternatively, perhaps it was an indicator of our stupidity.

The day began in a hotel at Heathrow. The previous day we had put everything we owned into a storage unit. It should have been simple, and yet in the course of the day I had displayed further signs of stupidity, by managing to almost jam a six foot van under a five foot gate, and to lock myself into the said van as the door blew shut behind me, leaving me to hope against hope that Liz hadn't packed the phone when I called to ask her to release me.

In comparison, today should have been relaxing, but somehow it wasn't. We allowed three hours to check in for our flight, confident that we wouldn't really need it, and some two and a half hours later we made it to the gate as it was about to close.

Deciding to go for an upgrade was the problem. Had we just accepted the upgrade we may have been alright, but we hesitated and asked how much it was.

"Might be able to do two for the price of one, I'll just check" we were told by someone who disappeared before we could say "it's alright, don't worry if it will take time."

After ten minutes she reappeared, two for one was offered and accepted. We then lost another ten minutes as she revised our flight details on her computer, and sent us to the customer services desk to pay the balance, as she had no way of taking the payment herself.

Customer services looked at us with a bemused expression, clearly having no idea why we were there. We recounted the whole story, and after we'd done this, the clerk went away to check we weren't making it up. Eventually she returned and took my credit card, apologising for the delay. It was nearly an hour since we'd arrived at check-in.

We still had security to contend with. Taking a laptop on a plane for the first time I hadn't anticipated the scrutiny it would receive or the fact that it would be one of seemingly hundreds of laptops getting the same keen interest from the same machines and security guards. A further half an hour was spent queuing, unpacking and re-packing the laptop.

Hunger had now started to set in. To give an indication of just how bad it was, the dazzling array of food outlets - a Wetherspoons pub, a Garfunkels restaurant and assorted airport kiosks selling crap food at high prices - all had a certain appeal, and any of them could have taken the last of our English currency were it not for the fact that we had only fifteen minutes till the gate closed, and no idea where it was.

We made it just in time and boarded the plane ready for take off. It was delayed. As we sat patiently waiting for the plane to begin to move we heard an announcement, and realised that even now we could not begin to relax.

"We apologise for the delay to your flight today, this is because we are waiting for a passenger who has checked a bag in, but hasn't boarded the plane yet. We are trying to find the passenger. If we can't find him we will remove his baggage."

This was one of those pieces of information you'd rather not hear until after they've either got the person on the plane or got his luggage off. Everyone on the plane tried to look calm and not like people wondering whether a bomb was about to go off, but the anxious thoughts continued until, over half an hour later, the person turned up, greeted by scowls of hatred from an angry mob who would have lynched him if they still had the energy.

We arrived in Washington an hour later than expected. We stepped off the plane to a heat that felt somehow artificial in spite of being outside. Could we finally begin to relax? Not yet, as we still had to face an hour and a half in the queue at US customs, and my shoelace had come undone. Years ago doing up a shoelace was an activity that carried no risk whatsoever, but in these security conscious days I was too frightened to bend down and tie it up, for fear that someone would leap on me and try to disarm the latest would be shoe-bomber. I shuffled my way to the front of the queue, and out the other side of it, waiting until I had got a respectable distance away from customs before deciding no one would think anything of it if I dared to re-tie the lace.

Only then, outside the airport, in a taxi heading to the Washington Plaza Hotel, could I finally relax and feel that the trip was beginning.

We arrived at the hotel on Thomas Circle at half past six. We decided to have a walk around the local area. We didn't need a map thanks to the helpful system of numbered streets and avenues that mean you don't have to remember the order of the roads to know how to get to where you're going. The vertical streets are numerically ordered, the horizontal streets, with the exception of Constitution and Independence, are in alphabetical order. As long as you know the alphabet you're okay. For this reason it may be a good thing that George W. Bush had a chauffeur.

The hotel was at an intersection of about seven roads. The traffic lights there and in the rest of Washington helpfully tell you how many seconds you have to cross. This should help people make informed judgements about when to cross the road, but instead it just encourages them to play high speed chicken and lunge across with three seconds left.

We walked a few blocks looking for restaurants and bars. The valet parking outside most of the restaurants told us they were not cheap, but we still went up to the windows, looked at menus and reacted with horror at the prices. Eventually we settled on McCormick and Schmicks, the only restaurant that was open and didn't cost a fortune. The waiter spotted our English accents, and told us about an English bar a few blocks away. I was glad to know this, because an English bar is of course what you fly several thousand miles to the States for.

"It's got everything, there's beer and darts" he told us, without any sense that the two halves of the sentence were contradictory.

Notwithstanding this, we noted the directions, mainly because we hadn't seen any other bars that night, and went back to the hotel for a last drink. I felt relaxed.

July 12. I thought I had got away from all the stresses and strains of working life. Shortly after I woke up I realised that this was not the case. While I should have been thinking about being in the capitol city of the biggest country in the world, marvelling at the wonders that it and the next three months held for me, I instead spent the first part of the morning fretting over day to day things, like the non arrival of train tickets, and getting annoyed at the hotel staff's really understandable lack of knowledge of their whereabouts. In short, I was the same as I would have been at work. Can't run away from yourself, as they say.

The train ticket saga had begun shortly after checking in. We had booked the trains with a company called AllAmerica, who, as the name would suggest, are based in Lowestoft, and have a bit of a problem with grammar. They told us the tickets would be sent through to the hotel. When we asked at reception they told us they knew nothing about them, but admitted this did not necessarily mean they didn't have them as the manager may have left them somewhere and not told anyone. They asked us to come back the next morning.

I did. They had still not arrived, and the manager informed me he knew nothing about them. He suggested I ring the company. I bought a phone card from the hotel shop.

"Very good value. For 10 dollars you get 30 minutes to the UK" I was told. I rang AllAmerica. In a five minute call, they told me they would ring the Boston company they got the tickets from as soon as they opened and would ring me back. I ended the call. A polite pre-recorded American voice told me "you have ten minutes of call credit left." I checked my watch.

I rang my Mother to tell her we'd arrived and wish her a happy birthday. I was on the phone for about three minutes. At the end of the call the polite pre recorded voice came back to announce "you have one minute of call credit left." Time was flying and I wasn't even having fun. I headed back to the room feeling like the world had it in for me.

I put on the TV. The news was on, and the first item told me that Washington was in the middle of a crimewave and the Chief of Police was launching a state of emergency.

One British worker had had his throat slashed at the weekend in Georgetown, a fashionable area recommended for its nightlife, and two families of tourists were assaulted the night before on the National Mall. Initially, this being America, and not realising that Washington doesn't do shops, I thought the National Mall was a big shopping centre, but then the newsreader helpfully explained that it is the road where most of the museums and the Smithsonian Institute are. The basic thrust of the reporting was that the Georgetown incident in particular was rare - people are only normally killed in poorer areas. It was not clear whether it was an increase in the level of crime or the move to better off neighbourhoods that was responsible for the state of emergency. Either way it did not ease my mood, and I needed to rethink where to go that evening.

Being tourists in a new city, we did what tourists in a new city do and got tickets for the hop-on hop-off tourist bus. The trip began by heading round the major political sites. Our guide interspersed the sightseeing with little anecdotes, and bits of information. As a result we learned that the term lobbyist was born during President Ulysses Grant's time in office. Being partial to the odd drink and cigar he used to go to the nearby Willard Hotel. Local residents discovered this and went in to try to speak to him about whatever concerned them. Over time the numbers of people increased and action groups joined them in the lobby waiting to meet the president. They became known as Lobbyists, the term derived from where they where as opposed to what they did. If they had chosen a term that described what they did, they'd presumably be known as people who go on about their own problems while you're trying to have a quiet drink.

From the same fount of knowledge we learned that Ronald Reagan did not actually realise that any bullets had entered his body when John Hinckley shot him. He assumed the pain around his ribs was the result of a security man sitting on them to protect him. It may have been true, it may have been made up, either way it was better than just being told who lived in each building.

The next part of the tour took us to Georgetown, which didn't look like a place suffering from a crimewave. As we sat and had lunch by the river the weather was in the nineties for the second day running, so at least we could get tans before being murdered or assaulted.

We returned to the bus and went to the Ford's Theatre, which for the non-historians is where Lincoln was shot. Except the building itself isn't where he was shot, as it isn't actually the original theatre. It's a reconstruction on the same site and to the same dimensions. A bit of a shame that they have to admit it as my sense of seeing an important part of American history deserted me somewhat when I found out. Nonetheless the accompanying museum, which sets out the background and the plight of John Booth and his co-conspirators, was worth a visit.

The house where Lincoln spent his last hours is still there in its original location and form. Sadly, it had been forced to close for the day. It's the smallest house in Washington and, as a place without air

9

conditioning, is deemed unsafe for people to be inside when the temperature is too high. The exact time when it was first closed possibly marks some landmark moment in global warming.

In the evening we ate in the Post Bar, where Bob Woodward used to drink when he was investigating the story that became known as Watergate. The bar is one of the places on the Watergate trail, and probably the only one that sells alcohol.

As you might expect from a capital city, Washington is alive with politics. As you might not expect from a capital city, outside of politics Washington isn't alive with much else. The population is just 750,000. The literature tells you 'it is not just the centre of US Federal Government, there is more to it than this,' and goes on to list galleries, shrines, churches, monuments, and parks, but stops short of theatres, clubs and nightlife. Visually stunning, the monuments and buildings have the grand feel of a proud nation, but on their own they don't make for a happening city.

For its place in world politics alone Washington is worth a visit, but anyone looking for an Oxford Street or 5th Avenue will leave disappointed. Washington's main shopping locations are Union Station and the Hard Rock Cafe. It's easy to see why New York is generally regarded as the unofficial capital of the States.

After leaving the Post Bar we tried to find the English bar, so desperate were we to find anywhere else that was open, lively, and not catering exclusively to people on six figure incomes. Heading off down M Street, we failed miserably in finding it, or anywhere else that looked exciting, until we reached 15th Avenue, which looked exciting but not for the right reasons. Being in the middle of a crimewave we decided to turn around and head back to the hotel. Too late in the day I learned that Celtic were in town to play DC United. There wasn't any Celtic presence which was probably just as well, it would have been a long journey, and the reward for making it would have been seeing their side lose 3-0.

Back at the hotel the train tickets had arrived. All was well apart from every train was at a different time from the ones we'd booked. Consequently we were now due to leave for Philadelphia at nine in the morning on the 14th. Nothing like a relaxed start to a day.

July 13. After breakfast in a little Deli - Washington has good Deli's - we went to the Amtrak station to join the Gray Line Interior of Public

Buildings tour. This was the only tour we had booked in advance. We did this as I wanted to go inside public buildings and the name suggested this was the tour that let you do this. It turned out that it shows you lots of exteriors, but only two interiors, and one of those was the Ford's Theatre, so it didn't really count. The other was the Capitol Building.

Like most key public buildings in America security at the Capitol Building has increased considerably since 9/11. We queued up for the security checks, emptied our pockets and removed our belts, before passing through scanners, on the other side of which we were told that in spite of all the checks large sections of the building were still out of bounds for security reasons. Either the checks are meaningless, or they really are paranoid about just how cunning attackers can be.

Although slightly truncated, the tour was still a good trip round the corridors of power, stopping off first at the Old Hall of the House, now the National Statutory Hall. Congress invited each state to contribute two statues of its most notable citizens for display in the Hall and around the building. Hawaii's donations do not make it into the Hall, allegedly because of their late acquisition of statehood. They reside somewhere further round the building. Having seen them I deny anyone to look at their bright colours and general elaborate design, in contrast to the austere and restrained statues of other states, and conclude that there isn't another reason for their exclusion.

We passed through the Rotunda where state funerals have been held from Lincoln onwards. Presidents lay in state in the centre of the Rotunda. Tourists get to walk over the exact spot where their coffins are placed, and look up and see a sight the ex-presidents would never see unless there had been a serious misdiagnosis somewhere along the way.

The Rotunda is also home to whispering point where at a certain height even a whisper can be heard by someone standing in a straight line from you, however near or far away they are. Sadly they say this to everyone on the tour and all politicians are also made aware of it, so the acoustic miracle has only ever caught people out in fiction. Not even George W Bush has whispered something he shouldn't have done.

In the afternoon we set off on the journey from the Capitol Building along Pennsylvania Avenue and up to the White House. Along the way the route passes between the FBI's home in J Edgar Hoover Building on one side of the road and the Justice Department on the other, residents of the two buildings keeping a watchful eye on the other out of a shared sense of paranoia and mistrust. This is the route that the presidential cavalcade takes following inauguration. The cavalcade should end with the president leaving the car and walking the last part of the journey to greet his public. Sadly while I felt I could do the walk in comparative safety even when the city was in the middle of a crimewave, George W Bush never felt safe enough, and instead completed the whole journey by car, which at least prevented him getting lost, or confused by the road numbering system.

The White House is now closed entirely to the public, you can only get inside if your local senator or representative invites you. The general tourist has to content themselves with the view from outside.

The official main entrance is on the south side, where the national Christmas tree is placed and probably where the photo for the president's Christmas card is taken. The north side has the Blair House, which isn't where Tony now lives in some strange kind of granny flat created by the Bush's, although, as the home where foreign leaders stay while visiting the White House, he will have stayed there in the past. Gordon Brown no doubt sees the irony every time he visits.

The north side entrance is closer to the building itself and, as a result, is also where you get the obligatory silent protestors with banners bemoaning various acts of injustice carried out against them. Government buildings just don't seem real without them these days.

In the evening we went to Stan's restaurant, which gives the impression of a quaint small eating house from the outside, but has an almost chain style interior downstairs. For no apparent reason it only serves wines by the glass, even though none of the customers look like they would see a bottle as a weapon to use in an argument, or indeed that they would have an argument there. Stan's feels more local than other places in Washington, and for eavesdropping on conversations it's a good venue although, sadly, you won't hear any scandals about the Government. The food was nothing special, but then you get what you pay for, and a meal at Stan's would be cheap in most places, let alone Washington.

Later on we headed back to the Post Bar. We sat down at the bar ready to order our drinks and instead had an experience that both flattered and ultimately frustrated us, as we were asked to show ID to prove we were old enough to drink. I can only think that the barmaid had had a bad night and wanted to take it out on someone who wasn't a local. Either that or she was as blind as a bat with a deluded sense that she herself still looked young so we had to be underage for that illusion to remain.

When you are hovering around forty anything that suggests you could be in your early twenties is flattering and rare to the point of unbelievable. As a result, with it being a question we never expected to have to answer, let alone provide documentary evidence for, we had no proof, and had to leave.

Amused and annoyed we headed off back to McCormick and Schmicks and a couple of other bars. A mixed note on which to end our last night, but then Washington as a whole had been a mixed place for us.

Perhaps it all goes back to George Washington, who chose a city built on a swamp as the centre of Government to make sure that anyone leading the country really did want to be a leader. An honourable ambition, but some would say that all that remains of it now is a former swampland overrun by career politicians.

2 – Philadelphia

July 14. We made it to Washington's Union Station early in the morning. The station is a grand building, it has the look of an iconic place with magnificent architecture and high ceilings. It was a last unexpected highlight of the city. Check-in time for the train was thirty minutes before its scheduled departure. Finding out that the American long distance rail network had check-in times came as a surprise to us, familiar as we were with the UK system of legging it on to a train as quickly as you can after it arrives and before someone blows a whistle to tell you that time's up and they're pulling off because they're already late. We imagined an efficient streamlined service run with military precision. The train left thirty minutes late, and picked up an extra thirty-minute delay on the way. It seems some things are the same the world over.

We reached Philadelphia about noon. We were staying at the Sheraton Society Hill Hotel, in the heart of the old city, and a short walk from the Delaware River. An excellent location and a fantastic hotel, it was also remarkably cheap and gave us a free upgrade for reasons unknown. We felt like we had bluffed our way into it.

The first song I heard on the radio in the hotel room was Elton John with Philadelphia Freedom. It was as if it was playing just for us, welcoming us to the city of brotherly love and freedom. The feeling of warmth and safety it created lasted until I read the hotel information and found out it was in a typhoon area and if an alarm sounded we should do pretty much as we would in a nuclear emergency and stay in the lower part of the building, away from glass if possible. Thankfully the information then added that this was highly unlikely to happen. We decided the odds had to be less than a crimewave in Washington, and it wasn't worth worrying about.

If the inevitable really did happen, the next sentence would read 'on leaving the hotel the sky turned black and the wind started to build ominously.' It isn't because it doesn't. We left the hotel, the temperature was in the nineties and the weather was as calm as it could be. We took the short walk round the corner into downtown.

Downtown Philadelphia has an ambience that Washington didn't have. The range of bars, cafes, restaurants and delis combined to create a bohemian atmosphere with a real community feel. We had lunch in a small bar that served large food. A Ruebens sandwich, consisting largely of corned beef and mayonnaise, was far bigger than the contents could ever suggest. After eating it I was ready for the afternoon.

First stop had to be the Liberty Bell, the most famous piece of badly completed workmanship this side of the new Wembley Stadium. The Bell, as made in England, developed a crack fairly early on in life, and cracked again almost a hundred years later. Either a flawed prediction on the odds of Americans ever being liberated from us, or a sign of a rushed job to meet a late deadline.

Preserving the status of the Bell as a symbol of freedom, you don't have to pay to see it. Preserving the more recent idea that freedom is under attack everywhere you turn, you do have to go through the usual belt removing safety checks to get to it and it's cracked glory. As the only attraction in a one-storey building, this seems excessive.

After a dose of America's past we caught up with America's present courtesy of a walk along Market Street to our first American shopping arcade. This being an inner city area it was not plush, sanitised and the size of a small town, but it did have the obligatory Starbucks, Virgin Records, Dunkin Donuts and Borders.

In Borders, Dorothy Goins, an author I'd never heard of was signing copies of A Woman Scorn'd, a book I'd never heard of. The lack of a queue suggested very few other people in Philadelphia had heard of her either. As if out of some strange sense of novelty value we bought a copy and chatted to the author. She asked us where we were from and how long we were staying. I don't know whether she began to regret the question when we started to recount our planned itinerary. She pulled off a convincing impression of being interested, and it wasn't as if she had anyone else to talk to anyway. She became the first of many people to tell us we'd be going to places she never had and would see more of her country than she had. As for her book, we lost it somewhere along the way, so I can't say whether it's worth reading or not.

In the evening we headed out down 3rd street and had a fantastic meal at the Plough and something or other, an Irish bar/restaurant on Walnut Street, before exploring the bars in the area, sitting outside in the late night heat and watching the local youth playing pranks on passers by. This consisted of dropping small change on the pavement and waiting until someone decided to pick it up regardless of its low financial worth. As soon as the person proudly clutched the new addition to their wealth, the shout of "Nickel" came forth in loud mocking tones to announce to the neighbourhood that here was someone picking up small change from the sidewalk. Such innocent fun, and so cheap to do. Nonetheless, we decided not to join in this new pastime, there are, after all, some things that really don't look as amusing when the protagonists are not teenagers.

July 15. We were being followed by Editors. Not journalists but the band Editors, who appeared to be a few days behind us everywhere we went. I'd have liked to have seen them. As a well known band at home playing in a country that knew little or nothing about them, I wanted to see what reaction they got. Sadly it was not to be. In Washington we saw their name on a poster advertising a gig the night we left, and in Philadelphia, as we walked down South Street and past the Theater of Living Arts, we saw their name again. They would be playing in three days time, one day after we were leaving. Good timing, it seems, is not only the secret of comedy, but also of journey planning.

South Street is described as having an eclectic mix of shops, cafes and nightlife. An oft trotted out phrase, but one that suits it. The bottom half of the street has restaurants of various nationalities and off-beat record and clothes shops that look as if you could get a bargain or a genuine musical find with comparative ease. Further up the road its charms start to fade and the eclectic and individual turn into cheap and run down with second hand places and junk shops dominating. We decided to come back to the bottom half that evening, and caught the tour bus round the city.

As the tour company couldn't work out what to do with the discount tickets we had they gave us over sixties tickets for a cheaper fare. We get on and off the bus without anyone questioning us about this. I felt nostalgic for that moment a few days earlier when we were asked to prove we were twenty-one.

The bus passed by the city hall building last seen in Ghostbusters, and the skyscrapers in a business district that lacked any atmosphere in the way that only business districts can. We headed off towards the outskirts of the city and the Rodin Museum, worth going to for The Thinker alone. Next stop was the Philadelphia Museum of Art, a draw for art enthusiasts, but more famous for Sylvester Stallone running up the stairs leading up to it in Rocky. Having started running before we went away I felt supremely confident of my ability to repeat the run and add it to the Washington inauguration route as a legendary journey I'd made. I managed it fairly easily which says more about the ability of cameras to make things seem challenging than it does about my level of fitness. Not that I'd say that to Sylvester Stallone.

We rejoined the bus and passed any number of blink and you'll miss them sights such as the home of Philadelphia Records and the street where Bruce Willis lived in the Sixth Sense. Leaving the bus we walked down the Benjamin Franklin Parkway.

The city commissioned Italian-trained architect Michael Rapuano to supervise the development of Eakins Oval and JFK Plaza, the two sides of the Parkway. We read in a guide that, just before they were built, the city invited Jacques Greber, an elderly man, to review the new development plans. The guide said 'Greber said that they were very good, indeed. He died soon thereafter.' Not sure if that was meant to suggest some sort of conspiracy, but I wouldn't praise the development too highly just in case.

JFK Plaza is better known as Love Square, courtesy of Robert Indiana's Love sculpture, one of the most iconic, and plagiarised, images of the Pop Art movement, which sits at the south-eastern end of the park. For anyone who doesn't know what it is, it is a big red sculpture of the word Love, with the L and O on top of the V and E. The O tilts, threatening to roll off the VE and break the square, implying the fragility and precarious aspects of the concept of love, according to Indiana who, with three marriages behind him, is well qualified to talk about fragile and precarious relationships.

Naming the plaza, or anything else, after Kennedy may not be unusual in most of America, but in Philadelphia it is a surprise. The reason for this is that when Philadelphia has anything new to name the default option appears to be to name it after Benjamin Franklin. The average landmark naming meeting in Philadelphia probably goes something like this;

"What is it you're building?"

"I'm building a park."

"What are you planning to call it?"

"I might name it after Benjamin Franklin, after all he is the most famous person who lived in our State."

"Isn't there already a Franklin Park?"

"Why sure, but it's never stopped us so far, I'll just call it Franklin green or Franklin arboretum or something like that."

"Okay, sounds good to me. I can't think of a better name."

"Neither can we."

And that is why, in addition to Benjamin Franklin Parkway, Philadelphia boasts Franklin Square, Franklin Plaza, Franklin Bridge, and the Ben Franklin Toll Bridge, to name but five.

In the evening we went back down South Street. After a drink in one of the bars we settled on a pizza for two at Pietro's Coal Oven Pizza. We figured a small pizza would be enough for one person only, so got a medium. This was the first food mistake of the holiday and another lesson in American portions. It was as massive as the salad that came with it. We knew there was no way we we're going to reach the end, and gave up early. The nice pool of oil under the bit we did eat suggested this was probably a good idea. It did not look the healthiest pizza ever.

After that we stopped at a bar where we were told on the door there was a ten-dollar cover charge for live music. It came down to five dollars when we said we'd give it a miss, and when we turned that down we were told we could get in for free. If we'd bartered a bit longer we may have got a free drink. We stayed for a couple of hours in which the live music failed to materialise, as the DJ played on, suggesting that the cover charge may not have gone further than the doorman. We stopped off at another bar, marvelling at the number of good drinking locations in the city, and rounded the night off in the hotel bar.

July 16. Did not wake up with a hangover. How did that happen?

Today was American history day. Not a national day in America, merely a day when we saw lots associated with American history beginning with a visit to Independence Square. These days the significance of the battle of Independence is obviously felt more by the Americans than it is by the British. Our tour guide, who had a copy of the Constitution on a wall in her house, thought that we'd be bitter about the loss of America, but after two hundred and thirty years we weren't holding a grudge.

After the usual slow journey through security we made it into the square and headed to Congress Hall, the meeting place of the US Congress from 1790 to 1800. We then moved on to Independence Hall where, in the Assembly Room, George Washington was appointed Commander in Chief of the Continental Army in 1775 and independence was declared on 2 July 1776, and not two days later as we, along with pretty much everyone else, believed. We were told the Lee Resolution was adopted and independence declared on 2 July. The wording of the final declaration was agreed on that day after much painstaking debate which lead to key paragraphs, including those on slavery, being added or removed. Franklin was not happy with the thought of the official signed declaration showing all the alterations and debates that had gone on, and between the 2nd and the 4th, he wrote a clean version. He brought it back for signing on the 4th of July, the date he added to the top of the declaration. Two days earlier, someone in the hall proclaimed that the 2nd of July 1776 would go down as a key date in history. This just goes to show that there in no such thing as a sure-fire bet.

Independence Hall, like Congress Hall, occupies a place as the site of key political and philosophical debates as the identity of the United States slowly developed. Standing in them and imagining the sort of conversations that would have gone on in the formative years of the nation gives you a real sense of American history, and the passion and determination that led to independence. The philosophy of the age was further demonstrated at the Princess and the Patriot exhibition, at the Museum of the American Philosophical Society. Focusing on the roles of Benjamin Franklin and the Russian Princess Ekaterina Dashkova, as two of the most fascinating minds in the enlightenment, it looked at the ideas of the age of reason, and the use of reason - the uniquely human ability to form ideas and act upon them.

The main conclusion I was forced to draw from all this was that even the greatest political minds of today would probably not be capable of thinking on anything approaching their level. I couldn't help but wonder what they would make of what has become of their noble aims if they saw society today. Was this a future they hoped for when they agreed the wording of the Declaration of Independence?

But enough of the philosophy, and on to the important things in life such as drinking and ghost tours. These formed the key parts of our final evening in Philadelphia. The Ghost Tour promised to be a candlelight walking tour through America's most historic and most haunted city. Little to challenge Philadelphia's status on the historic front, but on the haunted front it seems every major city around the world could lay equal claim, and normally do, with their own ghost tours. Philadelphia was about the fifth tour I've been on and one conclusion I've reached is that every major city has grave robbers who stole bodies from graves for use in scientific research only to come to a terrible end themselves. If only travel had been as easy in the 19th century as it is today, some of the later grave robbers may not have taken up the trade after hearing what happened to their counterparts from a ghost tour guide.

The tour was worth doing, both for the general entertainment and also for the opportunity to see some of the older parts of the city, including small streets with a remarkably large number of national flags hanging outside. We'd noticed this in Washington and now in Philadelphia. I'd always associated flag hanging with people from southern states who would love to bring back slavery, but here it seemed to signify a more dignified and historic form of patriotism. At least I hope it did.

After an Indian meal at the excellent Café Spice, the first non-historic thing we did all day, we went for a drink at the City Tavern on 2nd and Walnut Street. Like the Ford's Theatre, the City Tavern is an exact replica of the original. The original building burned down which is why the replica was needed. If you can momentarily forget this it feels like the real thing. Its place in history is not just as a drinking hole, but as the oldest drinking hole in America and more importantly, if true, a place where Franklin drank. To keep with tradition all the staff wear 18th century outfits, you can eat traditional food and there are specially named ales - the Franklin, the Washington and the Lincoln - brewed for the tavern alone. I went for the Franklin, it was Philadelphia after all.

Changing the mood entirely, our final drinking stop was the Eulogy Belgian Tavern on Chestnut Street. I was drawn to it by the promise of Belgian beer, and it didn't disappoint with over three hundred of them, not that I tasted more than four before we left.

And that was pretty much it for Philadelphia. A great eclectic mix of a place, historic and modern with almost every culture and nationality you can think of, and relaxed and laid back with it. Next up New York, which, I suspected, promised more of the same, except for the relaxed and laid-back bits of course.

3 - New York

July 17. 2006 was producing record-breaking temperatures in America. While the actual temperature was in the lower nineties they said that, with the humidity factor added in, the temperature was in the hundreds. This struck me as bizarre, in the same way it does when UK weather forecasters say the temperature is ten degrees but with the wind it will seem a lot colder. To me, the temperature with the humidity or wind is the actual temperature. After all, when it comes to deciding whether you need a coat or not, it's the one you use.

The record temperatures were not just in the east, in Dallas the temperature had been above a hundred degrees for days and in California forest fires, unusual for this time of year, were raging. Bizarre as the weather may have been it could not compete with ordinary day to day news however. A big story was about a woman on the outskirts of Philadelphia who had died from suffocation after falling into her own cesspit. I guess it's marginally better than suffocating in someone else's cesspit, but I was still alarmed at the fact that all her neighbours also had cesspits and were now considering what to do with them. I had visions of whole villages outside Philadelphia with open sewers under their gardens just waiting for people to take a wrong step. As last impressions of Philadelphia go, this was probably not the best one.

We left the hotel and went to the station to get the train to New York. No delays today. We reached New York around noon and caught a taxi to the W Hotel on Lexington Avenue. The room was the smallest of the three we'd had to date. Possibly indicative of the difference between New York and the rest of America, it was the first to have only one double bed and no tea and coffee making equipment, but it was also the artiest room and the artiest hotel. Needless to say, it was also the most expensive, illustrating how far New York has usurped Washington as the unofficial capital of the nation.

New York is the only place in the States we'd been to before. Our last visit was ten and a half years earlier for New Year 1995/6. We'd stayed at the Ameritania Hotel just off 5th Avenue and Broadway. On our first evening as we walked down the street we saw two guys arguing over something, or probably, to be more accurate, arguing over nothing. I thought it was bound to end with one of them being shot. It didn't, but given the city's reputation at the time it wouldn't have been a surprise if it had done. These days, following Mayor Guilliani, it is an entirely different city. It is cleaner, and murder and general crime rates have fallen. Which makes it a good time to become an unwitting petty criminal, which I did at the shop at the W Hotel.

The shop is not your average postcards and camera film place. It is primarily a designer clothes outlet. Shortly after we arrived at the hotel, a bag from the shop was brought up to our room. Without really thinking to check if it was for us, or to ask any questions about it, which might have been a wise option in such a security minded place, I accepted it, and took it into the room.

When I opened the bag, the first thing I saw was purple wrapping paper tied in a very long, very narrow, rectangular pattern. Something black was peeping out of it. It didn't seem like anything that would be delivered gratis to all guests, but that didn't make me think I shouldn't open it, so I slowly unwrapped it being careful not to disturb the contents. Actually that isn't quite true. I ripped open the paper with a complete disregard for any damage I may be doing to the unknown contents, which turned out to be a long sleek black dress. Not something we'd ordered and not something we thought we could risk keeping in the hope it didn't turn up on our room bill. So we took it back to the shop - anyone thinking that we kept it and that this was my petty crime should note that my crime was far more petty than this.

The assistant checked where the dress should have gone to and advised us that the woman in the room last night had bought it, and either forgot that she never received it, was too rich to care, or too stoned to remember buying it. While she told us this I was looking at the maps on the counter. I assumed they were free for guests and took the midtown and NYC maps before strolling out of the store. As we sat in a cafe eating lunch I noticed the $6 price tags on them, and realised my crime. I didn't feel compelled to take them back and admit what I'd done, after all this was not enough to trigger a Washington DC style state of emergency let alone a return to the dark days of New York's past.

The rest of the afternoon was taken up with a stroll along 5th Avenue, stopping at St Patrick's Cathedral, and then heading towards the Museum of Modern Art on East 53rd. By the time we got there it was nearly four o'clock and we were told to go away and come back another day as there were no cheap admissions for the last hour. The American Folk Art Museum next door closes on Mondays so any plans to go there and get out of the heat for a while were abandoned and we headed in to Central Park. Last time we were there, there had been heavy snow. Only a few people had braved the cold winter weather to wander round it. We found Strawberry Fields, the Lennon memorial, by accident, not even knowing it was there. Strawberry Fields would look beautiful in any weather but covered with snow it was even more evocative, and the whole park seemed a scenic and beautiful place, albeit one that you wouldn't go out in late at night.   In summer, however, with one hundred degree plus temperatures and more people than you could fit into some small cities, the intimacy of a cold winter's day disappears.

The heat in the park felt more oppressive than the heat outside the park. Contrasted with the freshness of Philadelphia it provided proof of why the temperature with added humidity is the one to note. You have to force yourself to relax on a day like this, and frankly the heat left us with too little energy to make the effort.

Taking refuge in our room we put on the TV. Summer is the dead time of year on US TV. Re-runs and programmes that are either too new or too quirky to cut it in the main season are all there is at prime time, while earlier in the evening all you can watch is the phenomenon that is the celebrity news show. These run for an hour somewhere between six and eight on all the major networks, and are the ultimate in padded TV. Each programme begins with a list of the big entertainment stories they'll be running and a couple of exclusive snippets from an interview or exposé that will be on the show later. After the near ten minute opening, the presenters appear and tell you just what is coming up today, in case you'd forgotten what you'd just seen, and remind you of what you heard about the stories on the show the day before.

Just as you think you're about to get an in-depth story you reach an ad break, which is proceeded with a list of what you can see when they come back. This is the same as the list that began the programme, so you make it to the break without any story at all. The second part begins by repeating the first half of the first part, and then finally moves on to a story which turns out to be little more than what you've already seen with a few more quotes thrown in for good measure. Then there is the 'still to come' section, which is all the stories bar the one you've just seen, and from there it's back to the adverts. The pattern repeats itself over the hour ending when the last story gets its minute long exposé and you get a summary of today's stories, the same summary you got at the start of the programme. In the course of an hour you get twenty minutes of adverts, half an hour of clips, and about five minutes of entertainment news. The big stories this day were the disenfranchisement of Tori Spelling in Aaron Spelling's will and Christie Brinkley's latest divorce. Other than finding out that Tori got little or nothing in her dad's will, and Christie was getting divorced, I learned nothing much about either of them.

We left the hotel and went to Connoly's Irish Pub for something to eat. Inexpensive, reasonably good food, not five star stuff but served with the levels of care, pride and enthusiasm that seem to be standard in American bars. Back at the hotel the main bar and club appeared to have switched into 'smart, young, after work' mode. Feeling excluded on every level, we headed back out, walked around and found another Irish bar to round off the evening. I wondered what America did for bars before the Irish arrived.

July 18. The heatwave continued with ninety-nine degree pre-humidity temperatures and energy company officials, worried about systems overloading, asking people to conserve energy. Their suggestions on how to do this ranged from the obvious to the socially irresponsible. First off was the request to turn off air conditioning when out. I'd have thought the cost of air conditioning would automatically make it something you left to come on just before you returned, but I suppose that's just me speaking as a man from a country where private air conditioning is both a rarity and seldom needed. Next request was to make limited use of washer dryers. Surely not good advice, when the heat is in the upper nineties the last thing you want is people heading on to crowded tubes wearing clothes they have worn for several days. The final recommendation showed that America does get irony, as from a brightly lit news studio with banks of TV's in the background, we were asked to use lights and TV's sparingly. Let he is who is without sin cast

24

the first stone, as someone once said.

We left the hotel into the searing heat to take the first of the obligatory bus tours around the city. The pace of New York is apparent wherever you go, there is the traffic congestion around Times Square, the large numbers of people looking impatient in Central Park, and there is also the way water sellers operate. While in other cities you just get off the bus and get a drink at pre-designated stops, in New York they throw bottles of water up to you and you throw the money down to them. The buses don't stop long enough for any more refined transactions, the water sellers know where the buses are, they know how hot it is, and off they go. Occasionally you might get the time to actually walk down and pay, but that's a luxury that just doesn't have the same feel to it. The level of trust in the financial exchange is also good to see, although this may be more to do with the possible consequences of not rewarding water with money than a sign of community spirit.

We got the downtown bus. The tour went past Ground Zero, the former site of the World Trade Centre. Memento selling has become a popular past time amongst the dubious street traders in the area. Our tour guide made an impassioned plea that people did not buy from them, particularly if they claimed that the money was going to families of victims, as the money doesn't go anywhere near them. That this was even happening in the city only five years after the collapse of the Twin Towers, says a lot about the way anything can be used for financial gain by some people. I would like to think that even the most unscrupulous street vendor would have more dignity than to do this.

Whilst there was something very mawkish about the sight of a major tragedy becoming a tourist attraction, as a result of what used to be there, what happened on 11 September 2001, and what that came to signify, it was perhaps inevitable that it would happen. The empty spaces and absence of large buildings served not so much as a reminder of the lessons of history, as some sites in Berlin do, but more as an explanation for all the increased security measures we were witnessing everywhere. Although they were irritating, and possibly unnecessary, we could suddenly understand the scale of shock and fear that had led to them being introduced.

Moving on from Ground Zero, we got the boat from Battery Park to Liberty Island. Last time we came was in the Clinton era and a budget dispute meant that there were no boats so all you could do was look at the statue from a distance. This time we at least got on the Island but sadly all passes for the observatory tour inside the Statue of Liberty had gone for the day, and we had to content ourselves with an outside view. Having discovered the view looks different depending on how you face it we took a lot of photos from all angles only to discover later that the views aren't that different on a six by four picture. Proving that I am a tourist, I did the standard Statue of Liberty imitation pose, with an ice cream where a torch should be, before getting back on the boat for Ellis Island and back to Battery Park.

Last time here we'd also been unable to get to Brooklyn, although that was caused by too many tour bus operators having a holiday rather than a major budgetary dispute. This time round the Brooklyn bus was running from Pier 17, and I had the chance to fulfil another ambition, to cross the Brooklyn Bridge. The opening credits of Taxi, the 70s sitcom that brought Danny DeVito to fame, was where this ambition stemmed from. Sadly it remained unfulfilled as buses are prohibited from using the Brooklyn Bridge due to the roadway's maximum height - 11 feet - and weight - 6,000 lb. We had to go over the next bridge instead. This was the first disappointing thing about Brooklyn, but not the last.

The whole place was somewhat lacking. It has precious few landmarks compared to the rest of New York, and those we saw paled in comparison to them. Our tour guide tried to make the place seem appealing and interesting, but we just ended up thinking 'so what if there's a nice church or an old row of houses to look at, there are hundreds of them the other side of the river and things actually happened in them.' His valiant attempts were not helped by a fire in the city that meant main roads were closed and traffic was blocked. Consequently we missed two key sites - although one of them was only an arch - and spent ages looking at others, or, to be more precise, the absence of others, on rundown streets.

We were told that Brooklyn is an upcoming area, which may explain the building site feel to it. In a few years time it may have its first stadium since Ebbets Field Ballpark, the home of the Brooklyn Dodgers Baseball team, was demolished in 1960. This could suggest both a glorious future and a glorious past for Brooklyn, although its claim to having previously had a stadium does rather depend on your definition of the word, as Ebbets Field would not warrant the description today. Cramped and decrepit by the end of its life, the demolition was inevitable as the Brooklyn Dodgers stopped playing there in 1958, following an early example of un-sporting franchising, later adopted in the UK by the people of Milton Keynes when they couldn't be bothered to make a football team of their own, which saw club owner Walter O'Malley, fed up with the lack of interest the borough had shown in a new stadium, moving the team lock stock and barrel to Los Angeles.

The pre-demolition demise of the ground says a lot. Not replacing the ground with anything of grandeur or status immediately after demolition says more. Even now, several decades later, the regeneration has run into opposition from Brooklyn politicians and community activists, who say its scale could ruin the neighbourhood's character. It is hard to see what character there is that could be worth saving from such ruin. The view of the Brooklyn Bridge on the way in had been impressive but, as we crossed back, the best view was the one welcoming us back to Manhattan.

In the evening we returned to traditional tourist activities with a trip up the Empire State Building. The queue outside was deceptively small, a larger and longer queue lurked inside. It took about an hour to slowly wind our way towards the woefully understaffed ticket desks and on to the incredibly well staffed security checks. This time the level of security was understandable, given the height, location and symbolism of the building. On our last visit we'd seen the daytime view, but at night New York is a different city with all the buildings lit up. I took copious photos, knowing that most of them would either not come out, or would just be a few dark lights with nothing to suggest what they were. Not for the first time I wished I had watched the video that came with my camera telling me how to use flash photography.

After a drink in a nearby bar, it was back towards the hotel and on to The Press, another Irish bar with a relaxed atmosphere. Even though it was around eleven o'clock there were still a few small post work drinks going on, and they still served us a bowl of chilli and nachos, a cheap starter for one which stretched easily into a full late night meal for two.

Outside the temperature was still warm in spite of it being early the next morning. Back in the room Liz decided, as she had done most evenings, that the air conditioning made the room too cold, and adjusted it by ten degrees. I woke up sweating at four in the morning, convinced I was going to be the first person ever to die of heat exhaustion in an air conditioned room.

July 19. Took the uptown bus tour and went into Harlem. Harlem

27

contrasts splendidly with Brooklyn. We'd been here before. The city we saw ten years ago was run down and had several no go areas, but it had a character and a certain charm which Brooklyn lacked, mainly as the people had stayed rather than moved out en-masse. As a result, whilst it has changed remarkably in the last ten years, it still retains a community feel to it. The landmark sites like the Harlem Apollo - where stars are born and legends are made - are instantly recognisable, and the surrounding area felt refreshed and revitalised compared to 1996.

Prices have gone up so that houses that were worth between fifty and a hundred thousand then are worth nearer a million now. Grandparents who bought houses for next to nothing are now millionaires, which is all very good, but the miracle of Harlem does have its downside, which is that these new found riches can't really be realised that easily. Owners can't sell their houses, unless they want to move away from New York or revert to living in a run down area. If they leave their houses to their children, who are now struggling to get on the housing ladder, the money will be spread over numerous offspring and won't fill the gap between the mortgages they can afford and the cost of the properties they want to buy. In spite of this, a sign protesting about million dollar condos was the only indication that some resentment to the gentrification was building up, so perhaps miracles do happen after all.

In the afternoon we went to the Guggenheim Museum. The design of the gallery would make it worth a visit even if the building were empty. It has no floors as such, instead a wide ramp slowly winds up the edges of the wall to the top of the building with a few rooms coming off along the way. This lends itself well to unfolding exhibitions like the one we saw showing the work of the architect Zaha Hadid. Looking at all her designs for buildings that showed a status of 'not commissioned' the easy conclusion to reach was that Hadid has had a spectacular lack of success. Even her proposed add on structure to the gallery for the exhibition was not commissioned. From the early drawings for each design, it was easy to see why. It would take a brave person to look at the strange lines and blocks shooting up in all directions and say "oh yes I see what you're intending and it would fit in well in our city centre." They were excellent art, but as good architectural designs, the end game isn't easy to see. When we reached the scale model stages the designs became easier to understand and visualise, but we still couldn't manage to look at the early drawings and recognise them as one and the same idea.

We left noting that she seemed to have got a few more commissions recently, but still thought here was someone who probably should diversify rather than try to make a living from architecture and design. In the following year, back in the UK, we noticed her name more, and almost every time it was prefaced by a word such as visionary and followed by a description of a recently completed work by the ever more prolific and successful Ms Hadid. We really can spot winners sometimes.

From the Guggenheim we cut into Central Park heading past the reservoir. The reservoir and the views across towards the direction of the Hudson are spectacular so it was no surprise that this coincided with the camera running out of film, and me cursing myself for not buying a digital camera before we went away. We decided to come back tomorrow, and for now I went for a run round part of the reservoir just to say that I'd done it even though I wasn't sure which scene from which film I was trying to imitate.

Heading down the west side of the park we went into Tavern on The Green. The weather was looking up with predictions of showers later to freshen things up and, as we sat out eating more meal sized snacks, all seemed well in the world. Little did we know what dire eventualities lay behind that innocuous weather forecast.

We went into Grenwich Village for a meal on Bleecker Street in the evening. Bleecker Street was recommended on the previous day's tour as one of the places New Yorkers go to eat. The direction away from tourist areas to local places seems to be a common thing with tour guides, and yet it is perhaps misguided. If they succeeded in getting everyone to eat where the locals eat, the locals would probably go elsewhere complaining that their neighbourhood restaurants had turned into tourist attractions, and the guides would have to find other places to direct tourists to. For this reason it's probably just as well most people don't venture too far from their hotels for a meal.

We took the subway using directions from the concierge at the hotel. They were crap. Bleecker Street is a long street. At one end there are a variety of restaurants, bars and clubs including CBGB's, the legendary venue, which was still open at the time. At the other end there is a long walk to all of the above, and nothing else. The concierge's directions began with a long walk from the hotel and ended with an equally long walk to the wrong end of the street. Just up the road from the hotel was another stop from which there was a route that led to the heart of the

29

street. Clearly the concierge didn't eat where the locals eat.

We walked some distance, as a mild rain began, and stopped at a Mexican restaurant. In a street famed for good restaurants we managed to find the exception to the rule. Just as we were nearing the end of fajitas served without vegetables and little in the way of sauce, the weather took a decided turn for the worse. It wasn't just raining, it was heavy rain wrapped up in wind, and it wasn't just wind. It was a swirling wind from all directions that picked up buckets of rain and, rather than put them down, added them to new rain to give a very wet slap to anyone who ventured out.

The canopy on the outside of the restaurant billowed up whilst wave after wave of rain came off it. When each wave eventually found its way to the ground it joined others in a sea flowing down the street. Thunder and lightning joined in as the sea became a river and the only traffic was the occasional taxi whose driver had been fortunate enough to come out just before the rain and find punters who had been unfortunate enough to come out at exactly the same time. If light showers alone would freshen things up, tomorrow would be the cleanest, freshest day New York had ever seen.

We stayed in the restaurant drinking until the rain slowed. We had a lot to drink. When it seemed safe to leave we ventured outside and almost immediately the rain seemed to increase speed once more. We abandoned plans to go anywhere else on Bleecker Street, and then abandoned plans to walk to the station as a taxi approached. We missed the opportunity of going to the comedy club we went to on our last visit where the comedians outnumbered the rest of the audience. On this night I'd guess that even the comics had stayed away. We also missed the chance to see CBGB's, which makes me sadder still now that it has closed.

We returned to The Press. The barman remembered our drinks. I felt a sense of pride at being a local at a New York Bar. I also felt a bit drunk. We didn't stay there too long. Wouldn't want to fall asleep in the local.

July 20. With the humidity factor suitably reduced following last nights storms we headed out into the slightly fresher air, stopping at the Museum of Modern Art before returning to Central Park where we foolishly believed it would be easy to find the reservoir again. Sadly, Central Park is a massive place and the sign posts and maps can easily lead you in the wrong direction. One wrong turn and you are heading completely the wrong way. If you don't realise this, your next turn takes you further away, and if you carry on for a few more turns you end up out of the park quicker than you can say "bugger, we're lost." As you can guess, we didn't find the reservoir. We found the zoo, we found a lake, we found a radio station setting up for the evening, but we didn't find the reservoir. We found directions for it near the lake, and that was when we found that we had been heading away from it for the best part of the day and decided just to rely on our memory of it rather than go back.

After leaving the park we looked for other landmarks from our first visit. The Ameritania Hotel was still there, looking pretty much like I remembered it, but the bar over the road, where we spent several hours getting served beer in two pint glasses for reasons I never understood, was now gone. Also gone was Legz Diamond's which, from the outside, had the feel of an old time New York strip bar with links to the Mafia. It was no surprise that sometime in the last ten years the legz had closed, so to speak. If ever a place looked like it would not survive a clean up of New York that was it.

We walked up to Times Square, and the Virgin Megastore where I purchased my first CDs of the trip. Being an avid record collector, and keen to try to spot some undiscovered talent that would become the next big thing, I had originally intended to buy a CD by an unknown American band in every city we visited. That this idea had not come to fruition was clearly illustrated by my two purchases, Billy Joel's Twelve Gardens CD - bought as near to Madison Square Gardens, where it was recorded, as possible - and a Ray Davies EP. You could not get further away from undiscovered artists unless you bought something by Elvis and The Beatles.

That evening, we ate in the hotel where the food was excellent but the service was bizarre, veering between Fawlty Towers and Monty Python in a way that suggested we had wondered into John Cleese's mind circa 1975. A Manuel like waiter sat us down with our menus and we studied the options as quickly as we could before he returned with undue haste to take the order. We made what we thought were good choices, and were promptly told that they weren't.

"You should have the Chef's special, it is much better," the waiter began.

"But we don't want to eat it, we want the Salmon," we responded, before a sense of caution emerged and we added "Is there anything the matter with it."

"No, it's nice but it is not remarkable compared to his special."

"But we want the Salmon."

"It's not so nice."

"What's the matter with it?"

"Nothing, but the special is better. Are you sure you won't try it?"

We were sure. We ordered the Salmon and waited for it, and a bottle of wine, to appear.

The fish appeared first along with the sauce. The wine appeared next. The vegetables remained conspicuous by their absence. Before it reached the stage that a search party could be set up to look for them the Maitre'd appeared and innocently asked, "is everything all right?"

"We're still waiting for vegetables," was our innocent response, and this was when we moved from Fawlty Towers to Monty Python. His horrified reaction suggested he would get all the serving staff to ritually sacrifice themselves by way of a request for forgiveness, and the amount of apologies we received went way beyond anything a ten minute wait for a plate of vegetables could legitimately justify. Thankfully, rather than order the demise of everyone associated with the food preparation, he eventually went for the less dramatic offer of free dessert served by a very apologetic waiter. We gratefully accepted.

After the meal we headed back one last time to The Press. New York had been good, but not as good as I remembered. Perhaps, if you're on a break from London, you shouldn't go to a city that is London multiplied several hundred times over. Sounds obvious now, but then hindsight is a truly wondrous thing.

4 – Boston

July 21. After the crime wave in Washington I was starting to wonder if I was carrying some kind of bad luck charm around with me as, a few days before picking up a car in Boston, an accident in one of the Big Dig tunnels in the city had led to a bridge collapsing killing the passenger and seriously injuring the driver of a car. Over the days since the accident more structural faults had been discovered and the news was now full of Bostonians saying they were going to avoid driving anywhere affected by the dig.

The aim of the Big Dig is to improve the city for pedestrians, getting cars out of the city by developing a network of underground tunnels and roads. It has been several years in the planning, and the delivery of it means that routes change almost weekly as different stretches of road are dug up while work proceeds on tunnels underneath them. This perhaps explains why it took our taxi driver about twenty minutes to cover what should have been a two mile journey from the station. The long taxi journey followed a long train journey. We'd asked to be booked on a fast train at ten, but instead got tickets for a slow train at twelve. The journey should have taken four hours. It was delayed an hour before leaving, and then a further hour as the air conditioning and lighting on the train repeatedly broke down. We got to Boston at six.

We were booked into the Omni Plaza Hotel, the oldest continuously running hotel in Boston, and the place where JFK announced his intention to run for the Presidency. It has a formal air to it as you'd perhaps expect given its history. We got a snack and went off to explore. We spotted theatres, cinemas and restaurants for future reference and then it started raining. The rain was mild compared to Wednesday's storms, which were now being held responsible for a blackout in Queens, but still bad enough to effectively rain the evening off.

We headed into a soulless bar where, after one drink, we decided we'd sooner get wet than stay for another. Dodging the rain by running in and out of doorways, we made it to the Hub, a bar with several TV screens and baseball on each of them. It had a good local feel to it, and was also shockingly cheap. We ate and drank for several hours. I was drinking Coors Light, one of many light beers that have their calorie count - around a hundred a bottle - rather than their alcohol content on their labels. The popularity of diet beers in a country where portion sizes are massive, and low calorie meals almost impossible to find, is baffling. I couldn't help feeling they had missed the point about them helping you lose weight only as part of a calorie controlled diet.

Back in the hotel bar we were served by a bar man with attitude, and an upper lip that was very stiff for an American. He gave me a look of contempt when I ordered an aforesaid light beer, obviously believing the formal air of the hotel had to be maintained by guests drinking appropriately refined drinks. I vowed not to come back, but as it was raining again I didn't let my principles stop me ordering another drink that evening. It's alright to make a statement, but better to do it when you don't have to get wet.

July 22. Most people know at least two things about Boston. The first is that it is where Cheers was set, the second is that the inside of the bar looks nothing like it did on TV. The bar is located on Beacon Hill. Its original name was The Bull and Finch, but it has now been renamed Cheers Beacon Hill. The reason for the addition of Beacon Hill to the name is that the owner of the original bar, possibly frustrated with the number of people leaving complaining it's not like the one on TV, opened a second Cheers Bar at the Faneuil Hall Marketplace. The second bar is billed as a replica of the TV bar, and, as if that wasn't enough incentive to get people to go from one bar to the other, there is also the Cheers trail, which links the two bars and eleven of the sites on the Freedom Trail, the two and a half mile trail of sixteen nationally significant historic sites. All very good, except that, in order to achieve this, the Cheers trail is so circuitous that even at the height of the Big Dig there would be a quicker way to get between the two bars. Still, if you follow it and make it to the end you do get to a bar just like the one off the telly, assuming you ignore the addition of a dining area and outdoor seating section, and also accept that the atmosphere is altered somewhat by loud music which would surely have made Norm leave for

Gary's Old Towne Tavern if it had happened on the show. That aside it could be the same place, if only it was at the bottom of a set of stairs rather than at street level in a market place, of course.

We went to both bars but didn't do the trail. Our route was a longer one, borne largely out of the need to avoid the frequent heavy rain that was becoming a common feature of one of the hottest summers on record. We stopped at two large indoor shopping centres, Boston being one of the few American cities where these haven't been replaced by big-box developments. We brought books and we brought clothes, but we still didn't buy CDs by unknown American bands. The rain held off for most of our time in the shopping centres and started up again a few minutes after we left and reached the open spaces of Copley Square, where another downpour left us sheltering for half an hour before venturing out into the Back Bay area.

Back Bay lives up to its billing as a happening place, with a good selection of bars, restaurants and small independent shops at one end and more expensive restaurants and designer shops at the other. We had a lunch of sausage and chips in a small pub, no prizes for guessing which end of the street it was in. The chef seemed disappointed that we were not stretching his culinary abilities further. The rest of the afternoon was spent nipping into shops and feeling far more relaxed than we would have been doing the same thing in New York. The city was drying out and a good atmosphere was emerging.

In the evening we headed down towards the Harbour past the Faneuil Hall Marketplace, and down to the riverside where we sat out at an almost beach front style bar savouring the atmosphere, before taking a stroll around the harbour and back to Bertucci's in the marketplace for a pizza that was a vast improvement on the one we didn't eat the previous Saturday in Philadelphia. After that we had a drink outside the replica Cheers Bar, and joined several other non-locals in moaning about how they are ripping people off and should have made it smaller. We stopped off at a couple more bars on the way back to the hotel, and at each of them nobody knew our name.

July 23. After a day exploring by ourselves we took the inevitable sightseeing bus trip. One of the first sights we saw was the Make Way for Ducklings statue in the Common, which for those in the know is a piece of Boston heritage, and, for anyone else, are a few sculpted ducklings in a park.

The ducklings stem from a children's picture book called, unsurprisingly, Make Way for Ducklings. The book tells the story of a pair of mallard ducks who decide to raise their family on an island in the lagoon in Boston Public Garden.

In the same way that Boston took the Cheers association to its heart and wallet, it also whole-heartedly embraced Make Way for Ducklings, and where the Mallards settled in the book, a bronze statue of Mrs. Mallard and her eight ducklings was erected in 1987. The statue is a popular destination for children and adults, the book is the official children's book of the Commonwealth of Massachusetts, and since 1978 the city has hosted an annual Duckling Day parade each spring, where children dress as ducklings and retrace the path taken by Mrs. Mallard and her ducklings to get from the Charles River to the Public Garden.

A similar statue was erected in Novodevichy Park in Moscow in 1991. The statue was presented by Barbara Bush to Raisa Gorbachev as a gift to the children of the Soviet Union. The adults of the Soviet Union showed their appreciation by vandalising four of the ducks, cutting the statues off at the legs. This could have been taken as an anti capitalist gesture were it not for the fact that they did this to sell them as scrap metal, the value of the parts presumably being greater than the whole. Luckily for duck lovers, glasnost was restored and the ducks were replaced in September 2000 at a rededication ceremony attended by Mikhail Gorbachev.

After the tour reached the Inner Harbour we headed off to walk the official Freedom Trail, which includes no Cheers Bars, but does include Faneuil Hall which was expanded in 1806 by Charles Bulfinch, after whom The Bull and Finch was presumably named. The trail was the idea of local journalist William Schofield who, in 1951, had the idea of linking the museums, churches, meeting houses, burial grounds, and other markers of the American Revolution, into a pedestrian trail. Whilst most people these days would have just decided to set up their own walking tour and register the trail as their own, Schofield had higher ambitions, which were realised when the trail was officially preserved and dedicated by the citizens of Boston in 1958.

Following the Freedom Trail is comparatively easy. The trail is marked in red along the streets of the city. If you want to know whether you are on the Freedom Trail simply look down and see if there is a red line on the road beneath you. If there is then you are on the trail. That said, somewhere near the Paul Revere House and a street with Italian Restaurants which, surprisingly, isn't known as Little Italy, there is a sudden mass of red lines and a variety of ways to head, and when we reached this point we chose a route which brought us to a sudden dead end and then led back to where we started from in a large circle that passed no Freedom Trail sites. Not sure whether this says something about the pursuit of freedom, or just about our ability to pick the wrong turn from any number of right ones.

Helping us to realise we were heading in a circle, there was a large street parade which continued to unexpectedly appear before us whenever we thought we must have left it behind a long time ago. The parade was a bit like the Notting Hill Carnival on a very small scale, complete with dancers with head-dresses and costumes that defied gravity, and rituals such as children rushing to put dollar notes on the most elaborate costumes. Good as it was, we eventually decided we had seen enough and headed into a cafe hoping it wouldn't miraculously reappear down the next road we took.

It didn't, and we headed towards the harbour where the Freedom Trail seemed to get lost and buried under Big Dig roadworks. With several hours of walking under our belts and most of the freedom trail covered we abandoned our search for it and headed back to the tour bus. Our plans for a stop at Harvard University were thwarted by the announcement that this was the last bus of the day and there is very little of the University that you can walk round on a Sunday anyway. We decided the benefits of getting off the bus were outweighed by the prospect of a long walk back, and decided to admire the fine establishment from the comfort of our seats.

After leaving the bus, a long rambling walk took us back around the Esplanade and assorted leafy parts of the river, before bringing us out along old style shops and houses that mysteriously lead us back to Beacon Hill. Such a long walk called for a drink and the venue of choice had to be the original Cheers Bar, where we took the obligatory photos with Norm, the Indian, and the Cheers sign either side of a pint.

In the evening, this being a Sunday, we went for a Sunday roast at the Beantown Pub round the corner from the hotel. This being America, the roast came with white gravy and a sweet muffin where a Yorkshire pudding would normally be. Good job we weren't feeling nostalgic. After that we went to Dick's Beantown Comedy Vault where it was amateur night. We weren't expecting a high standard of acts, but even the small amount of hope we had seemed misplaced when the woman on the door asked whether we had come to see anyone in particular, and was surprised to discover we had still dragged ourselves along in spite of not knowing anyone who was appearing.

As it was, although it was a bit hit and miss, the standard of the acts was generally high, and we weren't the only people who didn't know any of them. Early on the host quickly revealed that part of the show would be filmed as one act wanted to use his performance for a show reel to get on the Jay Leno show. No one knew which act is was, and no one would have thought it could have been anyone from the group who heckled the compere and most of the early acts. After all, surely a would be star would try to get the audience to like him, or at least not despise him as a self centred wise-ass who had to 'contribute' to the acts of people he saw as lesser lights. Then again, humility and wisdom are not skills you need if you are blessed with colossal talent. Unfortunately, he wasn't. When he finally got his slot, he died on his arse. A slow and lingering death, that could only have been more slower and more lingering if he had completed his allotted ten minute slot rather than realising the game was up, and cutting it short at the point when a routine based on a word play around genes and jeans failed to draw a single laugh even from his friends, who realising they were no longer in the company of a star, and illustrating the fickle nature of celebrity, disassociated themselves from him as swiftly as possible.

Before he could leave the building the compere managed to get in a line good enough to negate the need for any earlier response to the heckles as he said "thanks, I'm sure that will do your chances with Leno the world of good." I think he had a point. I can't remember this budding comics name, but somehow I don't think this means I've missed an opportunity to say I saw the next Robin Williams at the start of his career.

July 25. More sightseeing - Boston has a lot of sights to see. Having seen them at ground level we now saw them from the second highest point in Boston, the Prudential Tower. The highest point in Boston is the Hancock Tower, a 60 storey, 790-foot tall glass building on Clarendon Street, which also ranks as the tallest building in New England. It has an observation tower that was closed after September 11. This is possibly no bad thing given the risks it posed to nearby buildings and pedestrians even when there weren't terrorist alerts.

When it was being built, the retaining walls in the tower's foundation warped, giving way to the clay and mud fill they were supposed to hold back, and damaging utility lines, pavements, and nearby buildings. Once it was built there was a problem with the glass panes used in the building, and as the exterior consists of nothing much besides glass panes this was pretty serious, particularly for passers by as 4' x 11', 500 lb windowpanes detached from the building and crashed to the sidewalk hundreds of feet below.

Eventually all the panes were replaced by a different heat-treated variety at a cost of several millions. Even then a device called a tuned mass damper had to be installed to stop the building swaying in the wind and leaving its upper-floor occupants suffering from motion sickness.

All in all, the Prudential Tower, at a mere 52 storeys and 759 feet seems a more trustworthy building, and you can still get up to the Observation Deck on the 50th floor. As well as the views you also get a history of Boston and early immigration to America. The ease with which you could originally get into the country is in sharp contrast to the process now. Seeking your fortune, escaping from poverty and wanting to make a living in a free country are all noble motives, but clearly outweighed by not having a job or any money to live on while you find one. If only we could go back to the good old days, only without the potato famines and slavery.

Back on ground level we took the Boston Movie Tour, a walking tour starting in the Common and covering a square mile from there. Any hope we had of getting to know real Americans was shattered when we discovered the only other people on the tour were also British, and were here for a wedding. This did however give me renewed hope that I could win the tour quiz, unless they also happened to know anything about obscure American films that had not got UK releases.

First stop on the tour was part of the Common used in The Departed, which at this time was a forthcoming film, rather than an Oscar winner. I went into an early lead guessing that Matt Damon co-wrote Good Will Hunting with Ben Affleck. We left the common and went past scenes from A Civil Action, Legally Blonde, Mystic River, the US version of Fever Pitch and a whole host of films they'd never heard of and were never likely to. I maintained my slender lead as we passed John Kerry's house, which was used in the original of The Thomas Crown Affair.

In spite of it being a movie tour, we also went past Ally MacBeal's office, and down Beacon Street to that famous Boston Bar, "just in case you haven't already seen it" as the tour guide said - yeah, right. Somewhere along the way I realised the biggest difference with Boston TV scenes and Boston film scenes is that in films Boston buildings are used as stand-ins for buildings in other cities, whereas in TV the buildings are in Boston but the rest of the filming is in LA. I also realised I was way ahead in the quiz as we entered the final phase of the tour by the bench on the Common where Matt Damon and Robin Williams sat in Good Will Hunting. My joy in victory was short lived as the prize was a mini Boston clapperboard, and everyone else also got one. And to think of all the effort I'd put in.

At the end of the tour no one tipped the guide, which may be because he ran the company and obligatory tipping only applies when dealing with poorly paid wage slaves and not company owners, or may be because we were all British and sensed our first opportunity to make a silent protest against the tipping culture. At the start of the tour we were told that, as the first all British group they'd had, he might put our photo in their newsletter and on their website. Perhaps the lack of any tip explains why this never happened.

We decided to round off our stay in Boston with a trip to the cinema to see Clerks 2 - not as good as Clerks 1, but a lot better than the reviews made it out to be. Afterwards, we headed off in the direction of the harbour. The only problem was we'd intended to go in the direction of Back Bay. After discovering that the Tapas restaurant we thought we saw on Saturday was actually a sign left behind by a previous owner, in front of one of the few bars that offered no food, we got a taxi and headed over to Marlborough Street for a meal outside at the Armani Restaurant. Not as expensive as the name might suggest, and the best food we'd had in Boston, a nice way to round off the stay before taking to the road the next day.

25 July. Two weeks into what was once going to be a road trip and today was the day I got a car. The longer I'd been here the more nervous I'd got about driving. I knew it should be simple driving on the other side of the road, but I remained convinced that the first thing I'd do after picking up the car was drive out, turn right and crash straight into a line of oncoming traffic.

Added to this was the fear of driving an automatic. I knew theoretically it should be easier to drive an automatic, with no need to keep changing gears and no clutch control required for braking or accelerating, but I also knew that my left foot would instinctively go down on the nearest pedal as I pulled away in traffic, and I would bring the car to a sudden, abrupt, and dangerous, halt.

None of this however worried me as much as the fear of death by gunman. A fear that began that morning when I heard about a gunman in Illinois who had killed four motorists and passengers by shooting them from bridges over the road. Later in the day, as I learned more about the story, I was less worried about being shot, and more intrigued about the driving habits of the average American family, as all the shootings, including a family of four, had happened at around four in the morning. I'd be more likely to die from falling asleep than being shot if I were on the road at that time. Indeed I'd probably survive by virtue of my head slumping into a sleeping position seconds before the bullet pierced the window.

Getting to the Hertz rental office to get the car was not easy. The office was meant to be at the Back Bay station. We took a taxi to it and looked around unsuccessfully for the office before asking the guy at the ticket booth for help. He pointed me to a phone in the corner. I went over to it, picked it up and got a pre-recorded message giving me the next instructions as if it were a spy movie. The phone didn't destruct, but the instructions told me to head back up much of the road we'd just come down. Another taxi driver, who could see our annoyed-looking faces, told us he could take us there but it would be ten dollars because of the traffic. There was no traffic and this was more than the first taxi cost, but it was our only option. We got in and were told to pay up front. Nice!

At the rental office the staff were very helpful, but totally disinterested in how much of the country we were seeing or how it compared to the amount they'd seen. As long as we stayed out of Mexico, and remembered to get an oil change after we'd done three thousand miles, we could go wherever we wanted. They also had little interest in giving other useful instructions, such as how to get the trunk open - as I was in the States I could not refer to it as the boot - and how to move the seat forward, so after a few minutes of trying every button or key combination I could find I went back to ask one of the staff who had until then been content to watch the funny English man try to sort it out himself. With the seats in the right position, and the luggage in the trunk, I was ready to head off and carefully and slowly reversed out of

41

the parking place. Well, in reality I moved the car backwards and forwards for about five minutes, varying the angle of the car and the distance travelled by a few degrees each time, until I was finally in line with the exit in front of me and there were no cars between me and it.

Pulling away, I realised another thing we hadn't been told was how to work the air conditioning. We decided to go with the traditional English method of cooling the car by winding the windows down. This worked, but we couldn't get them to go back up. We drove along to the first convenient place to stop and read through the instruction book, so that we didn't have to spend a hot day in a hot car with windows open and no air conditioning, and then we were finally on our way.

5 – New England

We were heading to Chatham in Cape Cod. The drive went well until the very end where the last direction of 'turn left onto main road avoiding rotary' meant nothing to me, not knowing what a rotary was, or how I was meant to avoid it. As it actually meant 'turn left at the roundabout and don't go all the way round the thing' it was small wonder that I carried straight on until we eventually reached the main Post Office sorting office, and I guessed we'd perhaps gone too far.

The guy in the sorting office looked at my directions and then recited them back to me as if to help me find the way. This may have worked if I'd been on any of the roads listed on the directions, but if that had been the case I wouldn't have had to ask for directions. I decided to take a simpler approach and ask if he had a map of the area. I spotted the right road and he told me it was not as far away as it seemed, but I would have to go further than it looked. Confused, I followed the map and much to my surprise found he was right. The road leading up to the one for our hotel was shorter than it seemed, but the road the hotel was on was longer. Wise old man.

Chatham was reminiscent of a remote place in Cornwall. At one end of town there were a few shops, a couple of cafes, and three or four bars and restaurants. In amongst these was the all day cafe which was closed, and the 'dolly llama' which was a doll shop boasting neither dolls of llamas or Tibetan spiritual leaders in its window. The main beach was down at the other end of town. Quite a long way down in fact. To get to it we passed a number of small inlets that would be okay for sunbathing but offered nothing else. For that reason we carried on following the beach signs and were finally rewarded by discovering a slightly bigger inlet that was okay for sunbathing but offered nothing else. Not even a coffee shop or an ice cream van.

We stayed there for a while until we were too parched to do anything but head back to town in the desperate search for a cold drink. This was our first exposure to small town America, and already the cosmopolitan feel of city life seemed a long way away. Later in the day the 21st century began to seem an equally long way away.

By 8:30 I felt like I'd been caught in a time capsule and been transported back in time to the Wild West. It certainly didn't feel like we were just a few hours out of Boston. After a relatively early drink we had headed to the restaurants. The first restaurant we tried was already closed, the second was no longer serving food. I repeat that the time was 8:30 in the evening. We went to the restaurant in Chatham's main hotel and were greeted by a waitress who sounded as if she was in a perpetual state of surprise and wonder at the world. One of the things that seemed to surprise her was that we were trying to get a meal. One of the things she wondered was whether they would still be able to serve us. Thankfully she was told that we were just in time and we had a meal that ticked all the classic hotel meal boxes by being very large but having nothing that could be described as either wonderful or disgusting or indeed tasteful in any way whatsoever. We sensed asking for dessert may be pushing it a bit too far and headed to the cafe/bar on the edge of town instead.

In western movies anywhere described as being on the edge of town is likely to be a dangerous place where strangers aren't welcome. The Chatham cafe/bar, which had now reverted to bar mode, tried its hardest to fit this description. The bar and most of the clientele looked like they had come straight from a trailer park. Two people at the bar scrutinised us as if contemplating whether to assault us when we left for the evening. Luckily, when the drinks were served I gave the obligatory two-dollar tip and the nearest of the two men pulled a chair out and looked at the other in a way that seemed to say "they're okay, they know our customs, we don't need to kill them."

After the baseball on TV ended and with the time approaching eleven, the bar quickly emptied, and we were clearly stopping the barmaid from leaving. We finished our drinks and left, deciding that if Cape Cod really is the playground of New England's rich and powerful, Chatham isn't part of it.

July 26. Be wary of trusting tour itineraries prepared by people who aren't in the country, let alone the area, you are touring round. That was the lesson for the day as the instructions we were given, which were to take the ferry from Hyannis to Martha's Vineyard, turned out to be complete and utter rubbish, as did the instructions to return the following day on the car ferry to New Bedford.

Neither Hyannis or New Bedford have car ferries coming in or out of Martha's Vineyard. This meant an adjustment to plans and some delays today, while for tomorrow it was the first portent of approaching doom, but more of that later.

Ringing the Hyannis ferry terminal I found out we had to go to Woods Hole in Falmouth, and asked the landlady at the Inn for directions. The first directions she found told her we should take Route 28 along the coast. She promptly dismissed this telling us to steer away from it to avoid delays. So sure was she in this belief that she then spent the next twenty minutes trying to get us alternative directions. I was not convinced by these and eventually decided that staying any longer was self defeating if we wanted to save time. We took Route 28, it was relatively traffic free, and passed through a whole new side of America. Somewhat annoyingly, places such as Dennis, Yarmouth and Hyannis all seemed to offer so much more than Chatham and were also nearer to the ferry port. In between them was a dazzling and bizarre array of motels boasting crazy golf courses alongside free internet and cable TV on their advertising boards. It all seemed a world away from Chatham, whilst still being the same world away from Boston.

We reached Falmouth, another lively looking place, at about one and found out how to get tickets to the Island. The ferry company issue timed tickets and standby tickets. Timed tickets for the day had all gone, so we bought standby tickets for the outbound journey and timed tickets for 6:30 in the evening for the return. We were told we would be able to get in the standby queue earlier, but needed the timed tickets to make sure we definitely got back - another early but unrecognised indicator of doom.

We waited as two ferries went out with full car loads, then, as the third ferry filled up and we wondered whether we'd miss that one as well, we were called on to take the last space. This turned out to be a mixed blessing. On the blessing side of the equation we didn't have to wait for the next ferry. On the curse side I had to try to reverse into a narrow space bordered by a car on one side and the Atlantic Ocean on the other. In the absence of any crash barrier or chains, the boat may just as well have been a raft for all the protection it offered against a watery end. Notwithstanding this I still tried gainfully to reverse, looking over my shoulder and wishing this was an English car so that I could at least see how close to the edge I was. I decided that hitting a car was better than hitting the ocean and, in a protracted slow motion move, was getting close to doing this when either out of sympathy, desperation or sheer irritation one of the crew offered to reverse for me. I duly accepted and he managed to get the car into place in one swift clean manoeuvre. I cared not what this said about me as they put a small rope across the front of the boat - no ferry doors here - and headed off across the ocean.

Our immediate impression of Martha's Vineyard was good, it had a remote hideaway feel. The impression was quickly shattered when we reached the Island Inn, our home for the evening in Oak Bluffs. While the Inn in Chatham was not a traditional tavern style place, it was a nice collection of quaint houses with some charm. The Island Inn did not have such appeal. It was a large field with an admissions hut and a collection of little chalets that looked like public toilets from the outside, and 1970s style Butlins rooms from the inside. The Island Trailer Park would have been a more accurate names. I wanted to grow a moustache and declare my name was Earl just to fit in. We explored the grounds and found a launderette and restaurant. The former looked run down, the latter was closed. We decided to get back to town. Any town.

Thankfully there was a bus service from outside the Inn which ran around the main towns and sites until midnight. We hopped on the first bus we could get and went to Edgartown, a quaint little town with a few cafes and shops, a little town hall, and a bank. Edgartown is also the place where you can get the ferry to Chappaquiddick, where Edward Kennedy made a wrong turn onto an unlit road with a wooden bridge over a pond. He failed to spot the bridge and ended up in the pond alongside Mary Jo Kopechne. Kopechne died, Kennedy survived but fled the scene. We contemplated crossing to the Island to see the bridge, but, like Kennedy, we gave it a miss. We looked around the town and had a late lunch, which restored our sense of calm and equilibrium, then moved on to Vineyard Haven which, completely at odds with its name, is a dry town, with little to recommend it. We got back on the bus and headed into Oak Bluffs, the liveliest of the three towns, and a place that has a feeling of exclusiveness which is only shattered by a dodgy bar and the fact that it can't be that exclusive if it has the Island Inn a couple of miles down the road.

We spotted the Oak Bluffs Inn, a traditional style Inn slap bang in the centre of town, and cursed our luck. At the seaside style shops I bought a shirt and some shorts to get into the holiday mood as we wandered round the harbour before stopping at the Zapotec Restaurant, a Mexican which was serving an absolutely fantastic Tuna dish as special of the day. After the meal we went to the Sand Bar, which made up for not being on the beach by having a specially created beach of its own round the outside tables.

Once we were too drunk to notice the wondrous décor and surrounds of the Island Inn we got a bus back to it, the last one of the evening. I would like to say it didn't seem too bad by then, but it did, and the only consolation was that we no longer cared.

July 27. We checked out of the Island Inn early in the morning. At check out a lady getting into another car remarked "wow, you've come a long way, what did you think of our Island?" I wondered how she could tell we were from England without us even uttering a word.

I replied "the Island is beautiful," partly because it is, and partly because an answer of "it's okay but the campsite's shit" would not have gone down too well.

She looked puzzled and then said, "you're not from Nevada then?" A penny dropped somewhere and I realised what she meant when she said we'd come a long way. Our car had Nevada plates, therefore we were from Nevada.

I explained "we're from England, we've hired the car, we picked it up in Boston and we're travelling round America." She then became the second person to note that we would see more of her country than she had by the time we left.

We got back to the ferry port at about eight thirty. We missed the entry and drove past the small terminal building before deciding to park elsewhere and get breakfast. The monumental mistake this was had nothing to do with the revolting ham, egg and cheese bagels and the coffee that was still too hot by the time the last part of it headed for the bin. The mistake was getting so near to the standby queue and not parking there for fear that we would not have enough time to eat before being called on to a ferry. At eight thirty in the morning you probably do have enough time to get a breakfast without risking losing your place. By quarter past nine you have enough time to get breakfast, dinner and possibly an evening meal.

Along with other would be travellers we watched a near hourly cycle of a large ferry followed quickly by a smaller ferry coming in and going out. Each time a ferry came we thought this would be ours, and each time the hope was shattered as ten minutes before loading commenced, the timed ticket cars arrived and suddenly there was space for no more than two standby cars at most.

They were a chatty bunch down there however. Twice more I was asked "you've come a long way, what did you think of our Island?" and twice more the English accent led to the observation that "you're not from Nevada then?" Twice more I explained we were from England, had hired the car in Boston and were travelling round America, and twice more I heard that we would see more of the country than the person I was talking to had done. When the opportunity came to go round this conversational merry-go-round once more, I smiled, puffed my chest out and said in my best fake Nevada accent "it's mighty fine mam, we sure loved our stay here." There is a limit to how many times you can have the same conversation.

Other conversations revealed how willing Americans are to open up to complete strangers. None more so than the lady whose frustration at the delay in getting a ferry masked a far greater and more primitive frustration that was not being helped by the queues. She was heading up to Boston to meet a guy she'd met on the Internet. They'd Internet dated a few times and were now finally meeting. She candidly told us she'd been waiting months for sex, but in spite of this had reached the point where if she didn't get on the boat soon she'd give in and wouldn't care if she never had sex again. That, more than anything tells you how frustrating it is to wait in the queue at Martha's Vineyard ferry terminal.

Luckily for her, she managed to squeeze on to the quarter past one ferry and off to her date with a man she'd never seen in the flesh, but presumably would before the evening was out. We went to a riverside cafe for lunch as we were once again told we could leave our car for an hour before the next ferries came in.

At about quarter past two we were finally called on, and got off the ferry around three. We then began the journey to Providence, a longer journey than we had thought it would be, and starting later than we had thought it would do. Inevitably, we met up with rush-hour traffic somewhere along the way, delaying our arrival still further. From such a poor start, the chances of Providence becoming a highlight of the trip were always going to be small, and in that respect it lived up to all we

48

could reasonably expect.

We reached our hotel around half six, the arrival delayed a little longer as the directions to the hotel failed to point out that it was on a one-way street and we would be heading past it from the wrong end.

Our chance of catching up for lost time was dealt a killer blow early on by the hotel concierge. Whether he thought we looked refined - a positive interpretation - boring - a negative interpretation - or just too old to go anywhere happening - an accurate interpretation, I couldn't say, but for one of these reasons, or out of some other entirely unknown motive, his directions and guidance to somewhere good to eat steered us away from the downcity area where the hotel was and across the bridge to the other side of the city. The empty side.

The Old Statehouse was undoubtedly impressive and the surrounding parks scenic. Had we got there in the daytime they could have been features of the stay. But we didn't, and a Statehouse and a park are not great places for an evening. The road leading towards them was a fairly anonymous road of big shops and chain restaurants where you took your life into your hands every time you tried to cross. Coming off this were assorted other roads with occasional restaurants that catered for clientele that wanted a sedate but costly experience and had no interest in discovering anything original or genuine in the city. After looking in at a couple of places we decided enough was enough and cut our losses and headed to the downcity area. Most US cities have a downtown, Providence has a downcity, perhaps they don't realise you don't have to be a town to have a downtown. In contrast with the other downtowns we'd seen till then Providence's was run down. The only bars and restaurants that were open were small back street ones that had hopefully long since seen better days. I say hopefully as I would hate to think this was as good as it had ever got.

The streets were largely empty and the few people that were out didn't create a feeling of safety. We found one half decent bar which was far too bright, particularly in contrast to the surrounding area, and had the obligatory TV sets showing the obligatory baseball matches. We walked past the Providence Performing Arts Center, located on an unwelcoming street, where in a few weeks time we could see someone formerly of Chicago - the group not the place - playing, should we be fool enough to come back. For the second time we cut our losses and headed elsewhere, although we were running out of elsewheres to head to.

We went towards the river and found Ri Ra Irish Pub and Restaurant where something that resembled an evening seemed to be happening. We got a meal billed as traditional Irish American - Corned Beef Hash for me and Sausage and Mash for Liz - and then took in an Irish band in the saloon half of the pub. The evening had gone up from the low position it could not have sunk from, but then, when we headed to McFaddens restaurant and saloon, it dipped again. McFaddens was another riverside bar, only this time it was largely devoid of people. CDs played at a level that would have rendered them unlistenable had there been anything resembling a crowd in there. If Providence had a lot to see we had missed most of it. If we had seen all it had to offer getting there late was no bad thing.

July 28. I started the day by reading through the Providence Phoenix, a free paper I had picked up in McFaddens. Looking through it I worked out we should have gone to Little Italy the previous night. We didn't go to it, because we didn't know it existed. We didn't know it existed because the concierge didn't mention it to us. The concierge didn't mention it to us because…and that is where the trail of clues breaks down.

Taking it from a different line of enquiry, we asked the concierge for areas with restaurants. Little Italy has more restaurants than anywhere else in the city, and by the looks of it more restaurants than the rest of the city combined. The concierge didn't tell us about it. And there the trail breaks down again, leaving responsibility for any failure to discover what Providence has to offer resting, for reasons unknown, entirely with the concierge.

All I can think of, in his defence, is that to get to Little Italy it looks like you have to cross Interstate 95 and then carry on walking a few blocks that don't appear to offer anything of note or anything at all, before you get there. That may be the reason we weren't told about it. Either way we decided not to test this theory, and instead made an early exit. We were heading north to Portland, Maine and irrespective of whether it would turn out to offer anything more than Providence had we were determined to get there early enough to find out.

Portland was a stopping point on our way to Canada. You may wonder why we were going to Canada, given that our plan was to see the United States, and Canada, of course, is not one of them. Taking ten days out of our journey to see another country may not have been the most productive use of our time, but we figured that we couldn't not go. Canada is to the US what Scotland is to England, a small country north of the border with an apparently different outlook on life. A rival with a disparaging attitude towards its nearest neighbour, who in turn looks on it fondly but slightly contemptuously, like the simple child in a family of geniuses. Is it just because of its size and status that Canadians are so different from Americans, or did those differences always exist, and were they the reason why the US got so big and Canada stayed so, comparatively, small in the first place. I wasn't sure if we would find the answers to any of this, or indeed if we would even notice that much of a difference, but we wanted to try. Also we had a vague idea that by going to Canada and then re-entering the States we would start the clock ticking again on our ninety days, and that in itself was reason enough to head there.

We arrived at the Eastland Hotel around lunchtime. Determined not to let concierges lead us down wrong roads into deserted wastelands, I studied the cartoon style map of the city and the Welcome to Portland book in the room and worked out a route round the city.

We headed through the Arts District, down Temple and Union Street to the Old Port. Portland is one of the few working waterfronts left in the United States, the largest tonnage seaport and the second largest fishing port in New England. This all sounds very impressive, but in practical terms a working waterfront means parts of the Harbour are less than scenic and you wouldn't really want to stroll down the whole length of it. To capture the real feel of the Old Port area you have to go down the roads behind Commercial Street, a mix of narrow and not so narrow cobbled streets filled with cafes, restaurants and bars alongside one-off shops which, courtesy of more downpours, we ended up spending a lot of the afternoon in.

The charm of the area still came across in spite of the rain, which was why we persisted with dashes inside shops and a drink in Rosie's Restaurant and Pub rather than just heading back to the hotel to keep dry. Alongside the designer, and not so designer, clothes shops an unexplained slew of dog based shops loomed up as if to confirm this was a quaint New England town. Agatha and Louise's offered decorative items and gifts for dog lovers of all ages, and boasted a phone number of 879-PAWS, while Bark'n'Roll - self-service dog wash, biscuit bakery, unique dog food and accessories - had the equally dog-tastic phone number of 780-WOOF. Fetch - natural foods, treats, toys and gear for cats and dogs - for some reason didn't have a doggy themed phone number.

With the rain showing no sign of ending we finally admitted defeat some time around five and returned back to the hotel. The entertainment round up programmes had not yet started so we checked out the weather forecasts. I like to think we would have checked out the weather forecasts anyway, but maybe the still unfolding stories of Christie Brinkley's unfaithful husband would have distracted us. The weather forecast offered the kind of precision and clarity that celebrity news shows can only dream about. A forecaster told us that the rain would continue to be heavy until 7:30. Taking his word for it we headed up to the twelfth floor bar to look out over the wet city. Rain and lightning continued unabated until, exactly as predicted, they stopped at 7:30.

Not believing anyone could be this accurate we waited a while longer before deciding we could head back out without risking a further drenching. We went back into the Old Port area and back to Rosie's for a chilli bowl. The waitress from earlier in the day looked at us as if to say "did you ever leave here?"

While the daytime had a feel of a Saturday about it, which, seeing as how it was a Friday, was a sign that the absence of routine quickly leads to a lack of awareness of the calendar, the evening in the old port had far more of a Friday feel, with the bars full to bursting and music coming out of most of them. The arts district was a lot quieter with a better-dressed crowd, and consequently far less to recommend it. Nonetheless the office of the Community Television Network on Congress Street provided the first indication we'd had of the survival of the small town American spirit in the face of the corporate behemoths, with windows berating the ownership of national and local media and calling for the public to seize back control as part of Portland's resistance to mass owned TV networks.

The Community Television Network schedule meanwhile offered such delights as 'Webbs Mills Church Service', 'the Cornell Drum Show' - featuring local musician Cornell Welsh - and 'Nostros - we the people' a Spanish video magazine. From this we concluded that the public maybe shouldn't try and seize back too much control.

Community TV aside, Portland was a great little place. Had we not been going to Canada I doubt we would ever have gone there, so it was very much a chance find, and as places to stumble upon go it was one of the best. It was also one of the driest that night as the news reported large parts of Maine were without power as a result of the storms. All in all I was pleased we had stayed there.

July 29. In Boston we saw Clerks 2. In the Subway restaurant in Portland we saw what could have been the auditions for Clerks 3.

For anyone who hasn't seen the movies, Clerks 1 and 2 tell the story of Dante and Randall. In Clerks 1 they work in a video store and in Clerks 2, made ten years later, they work in a fast food drive-in. The career progression tells you all you need to know about the two central characters. They are not people you would aspire to as role models, unless you work in Subway in Portland.

Of the two staff in there the first could recite the items they didn't have with consummate ease, not caring that they had ended up with so little food so early in the day, while the other confessed he would not be able to prepare our meal as he'd only been there six months and couldn't prepare food.

Just as I was wondering what vigorous training programme Subways staff must be subjected to, he elaborated on this by telling us it wasn't that he hadn't been taught any food preparation, just that he was never normally in this early so hadn't been shown the breakfast menu - spreading a croissant with butter and adding ham and cheese before placing it in an oven being an altogether different proposition than spreading a baguette with butter and adding ham and cheese before placing it in an oven.

Not that food preparation came easy to his colleague, who told us he could only do one order at a time as they only had one oven. We guessed that the oven couldn't be very wide if it couldn't hold two identical items for two identical amounts of time. To complete the gathering of geniuses there was also a customer who demonstrated a startling lack of knowledge of the range of sauces in an average diner. He gave the answer "hot sauce" to the question of "what sauce would you like?" and after the staff tried to narrow this down by giving a list of sauce names, not one of which was hot, he replied "Can I have hot sauce?"

The list was read through once more, this time excluding anything that would not be classed as hot or spicy. "None of them I just want hot sauce" was the response. At which point our food was handed over to us and we sat down while they attempted to find which sauce truly deserved the name hot.

After a last stroll round the streets to take photos of things that were far to wet to take photos of the day before, we packed our bags and prepared for the drive into Canada, and on to Quebec. Taking our directions from the '1993 Collins Road Atlas: USA Canada and Mexico' that I'd picked up at the house of a friend of a friend after spotting it poking invitingly out of a book cabinet, I estimated we faced a four hour drive. The porter gave a different view which was "you'll be driving all day, it'll take about eight hours," and with that we headed off into the unknown, wondering which of us would be proved right about the length of the journey.

Part 2

From Canada to Chicago

6 – Quebec

The journey began on Route 95. This was the first road where we had to pay a toll and so inevitably it was in a poorer condition than every other road we'd been on so far. From there, we joined the 201 and that was where we stayed for the next few hours.

The 201 is a very long stretch of road. It starts at a place called Waterville in Maine and runs to the Canadian border. Large parts of it are single track, and assorted small towns with reduced speed limits makes it slow going until the towns are replaced by countryside, mountains, lakes and ponds, which have uninspiring names like Little Big Wood Pond, the Long Pond and, most insultingly of all, Pleasant Pond. We passed so much that could be classed as outstanding natural beauty, and the scale of our journey became clear. We were seemingly, or actually, hundreds of miles from the nearest recognisable city and thousands of miles from home. It seemed like we had covered a distance greater than all of the UK, probably because we had, and yet in terms of the overall length we'd be travelling it was comparatively nothing.

The scenery gradually became less impressive, and we had begun to wonder just how far it was to the border, when, all of a sudden, the Canadian customs loomed up in front of us and we had the answer.

The car in front seemed to have been singled out for special attention by the customs officers, but we escaped with just a few questions and, once we answered them, we were across the border and into Canada. The feeling of suddenly being a lot nearer to Quebec lasted as long as it took to realise that in reality we were about ten feet closer than we were before crossing the border and still had a long way to go.

Once in Canada the 201 becomes Provincial Route 173 and runs through to Quebec City. It isn't only the name of the road that changes. The condition does as well, deteriorating rapidly. We bounced along the road looking for somewhere to stop for food and found a cafe and service station where other changes signalled that we were out of the US and into a part of the commonwealth. Distances switched from miles to kilometres, volumes from gallons to litres, and, as we were in the French part of Canada, menus were in French and English and French was the first language of our waiter. The main indicator that we had left the US wasn't any of this however, it was that the price of gas suddenly increased exponentially.

We arrived at the Hotel Manoir Victoria at half six, the driving having taken six hours, meaning the porter's guess on travel times had been equally as inaccurate as ours.

Positioned in the heart of Old Quebec the hotel couldn't have been in a better location, and so, after a brief rest we left to savour the delights of the city. The Upper Town part of Old Quebec is as close to a classic European city that you can get outside of Europe. If you think of the best, most traditional parts of Edinburgh, Bath and York, then remember that this is the French part of Canada, and add in a few market places and squares, you can begin to get a feel for the flavour and atmosphere of the place.

As with most European cities on a Saturday at the end of July, large paved areas were filled with the obligatory street entertainers, as jugglers, fire-eaters and singers drew in attentive crowds who rushed away the moment the performance ended and the question of paying was mentioned.

Adding to the continental Europe feel, the main streets leading up to the Chateau were filled with families on holiday taking slow walks and browsing in gift shops, while everyone that wasn't with parents sat outside at one of the many bars listening to someone with a guitar playing sing along classics they'd never heard of.

While this could have been the universally accepted definition of cloying and twee, it surprisingly wasn't. That's not to say the snails pace walking, and the inability to get round pedestrians whose routes are blocked by other pedestrians heading at the same slow pace in the opposite direction didn't get to us eventually however, and we headed away from the main square and down some side streets where, after a fair bit of menu browsing, we settled on La Caravelle, a small and perfectly acceptable Italian restaurant that offered nothing special food in surroundings that deserved something better.

We ended the evening downstairs in an Irish bar back in the main square where traditional Irish music was sung in French by Canadians with bad Irish accents. That's how cosmopolitan Quebec is.

July 30. The Hotel Manoir Victoria refers to itself as a European style hotel. On the upside, this means that the entrance and lobby have an old style feel of opulence and grandeur that suggest a history they possibly don't possess. On the downside, it also means that the width of the bedrooms are only marginally greater than the width of the beds and side tables, and their length is short enough for even a whisper to be heard at the opposite end. That said, in contrast to hotels in Paris, they are veritable mansions.

The hotel also claims to be the oldest hotel in Quebec, although as claims go this is a bit like saying you have a hundred year old broom that has only had the handle and brush changed twenty times each.

In its original incarnation not only was it over the other side of the road, it also had a different name, which arguably means it was a totally different hotel. It became the Hotel Victoria in 1895, and only moved to its current site in 1904 two years after a fire destroyed the original hotel.

While that may make you think it's still been there a long time, the story doesn't end there.

The hotel expanded to much of its current ground size after 1927 when a hotel on a neighbouring road burnt down and the owners of the Victoria bought the vacated site. The new, larger, hotel was largely burnt down in 1942, then re-modelled at the start of the fifties.

Between 1978 and 1988 it was closed for business. The new owners acquired further land by taking over the next door building, and the building last increased upwards as recently as 2004.

From all of this you can draw two conclusions. One is that the hotel you stand in really isn't the oldest hotel in Quebec. The second, from the number of times it has burnt down in whole or in part, is that arsonists in Quebec view it as a trophy every time they have a box of matches and a spare half-hour. It turns out that a lot of Canadian buildings seem prone to bursting into flames, whether prompted to or not, as we were to find out over the next few days.

The Château Frontenac, the historic hotel that provides the focal point of the old town landscape, has a better claim to the oldest hotel title than the Manoir Victoria on the grounds that it opened in 1893, two years before the Victoria got its name and eleven years before it got its site, and it hasn't closed or been burnt down since. From it, we took the Old Quebec Funicular Railway down to the Lower Town, passing on the opportunity to walk down the Escalier steps on the basis that Escalier apparently translates as neck-breaker, which didn't do too much to sell the route.

The lower town has the port, as indeed it should, given how silly it would be to put a port in the upper town. This offers great views across the Saint Lawrence River, a vast expanse of water that you can sit and stare out at for ages. However, even on a day when we were largely walking, sitting, and staring, that would have been a waste of time so we headed round the quaint cobbled streets of downtown with - as the brochures would say - their eclectic mix of shops and cafes, before heading towards La Citadelle of Québec.

Like the Manoir Victoria, La Citadelle has a long history of fire damage and rebuilding, but as it was a military garrison, and the most important fortification built in Canada under British rule, this probably isn't surprising. It is in the shape of a four-pointed polygon, with each point forming a bastion, and covers thirty-seven acres. It was designed according to a defence system developed by a French military engineer. The construction of the outer walls began in 1820 and took thirty years to finish. The Quebec Conferences of 1943 and 1944, in which Winston Churchill and Franklin Roosevelt discussed strategy for World War II, were held there. All of which made it inevitable that we wouldn't be allowed to wonder around it aimlessly, and would have to take a guided tour if we wanted to go inside.

As we were in the mood for walking round aimlessly, and not in the mood for taking guided tours, we contented ourselves with wandering around the vast grounds that surrond it, and idled away more of the day by doing so. Noting that Quebec is the only fortified city north of Mexico whose walls still exist, we then decided to see what was on the other side of them.

A different type of city emerges beyond Porte St-Louis and Porte St-Jean, the main gates through the walls from the old town. The contrast with the old town is immense, but still not as immense as the contrast with anything else in North America. If the old town is Grand Place area Brussels, the new town is the Champs Elysses, with wide tree lined boulevards and large modern cafes and restaurants along the Grande Allee. Lunch was spaghetti at Aux Vieux Canons, a name that said Quebec on a street that said France.

In the evening we tried to find the same part of the city by the same route but, after heading through a different Porte, we emerged in what seemed an altogether different area, as if the Portes were some kind of transporter that took you to a different location every time you went through them. We walked along the remaining city walls and past more Porte's than we could remember seeing until I became convinced that the road ahead was the one we should take. Liz, unconvinced, decided to wait. When I came back I feigned an air of false confidence, which matched her feigned look of lack of surprise that I was right, and we headed off confidently to the Voodoo Lounge for a Thai meal outside on a Sunday evening. A leisurely walk back and a couple of drinks in a quieter than Saturday old town rounded off the perfect lazy Sunday.

Our only disappointments with Quebec were not being here long enough to see the Montmorency falls across from Ile d'orleans – one and a half times as high as Niagara but a lot narrower, which probably explains why they aren't such a tourist draw – and finding out that the five day New France Festival began a couple of days after we left. Another bit of bad timing, and not the last we would have on the trip.

7 – Montreal

July 31. A driving day. Nothing as long as the drive to Quebec had been, and not as long as some of the later drives would be, but a driving day nonetheless. We'd been advised to avoid what appeared to be the charming Canadian Autoroute 40 which ran alongside the St Lawrence River – at least according to our map - and take the Trans-Canada Highway 20 instead. This gives you a quicker journey, but one which lacks any great character. Given that we were in no particular hurry, I can only assume that the advice to go that way was symptomatic of modern day impatience, facilitated and supported by the rise of the Interstate, and that stopping and smelling the roses is now seen as an unproductive use of time rather than a pleasant distraction.

Once we were on the open road I put the radio on. As I still hadn't sussed out how to get to beyond the radio's five pre-set frequencies, we had come across a wide, and not necessarily good, range of music so far. Crossing states in a car programmed elsewhere means that, even if you do get a good station to begin with, you soon discover that one state's 92.6 FM classic indie music is another state's 92.6 FM old time country and western station, with a gap of thirty or so miles in between with nothing other than white noise. Nonetheless we had still driven long enough and stumbled on enough chart stations to get an idea of what was big in the US and Canada, from which I concluded that my chances of discovering unheard of bands were slim at best. Most of what we heard was the same as I was listening to before we came away, or in some cases - Natasha Bedingfield's Unwritten - about a year before. The three songs we couldn't avoid were Rihanna with SOS, Shakira with Hips Don't Lie and Gnarls Barkley with Crazy. All we were missing was Chris Moyles, and that's a sentence I never thought I'd find myself writing.

The one band I hadn't heard of that were getting frequent plays were Blue October, with their single Hate Me Today. It is possibly the most whinging, self pitying song you are ever likely to hear, consisting of an impassioned plea by a former drug addict for his ex-girlfriend or mother to hate him today, and hate him tomorrow. I can't help thinking it would be easy to do this. Even if the rest of Britain hadn't discovered them, I wasn't going to take them home with me.

We were staying at the Delta Hotel on Montreal's Avenue President Kennedy. The Hotel failed to get off to a good start with a concierge worthy of particular mention for his devotion to bad service.

Parking outside what appeared to be the main entrance, largely because it was very near the check-in desk, we went in and paid for the valet parking. The concierge duly informed us that he could not provide valet parking unless we drove the car round to the other entrance. The other entrance was a massive forty feet away, and right next to the entrance to the car park, which begged the question of what were we paying him for. Having moved the car to a mere ten feet from the entrance, I looked over to him and he looked back and didn't move. I was clearly meant to guess the exact point at which the entrance he wanted me to park at started. I drove to within a foot of the ramp for the car park and he still feigned complete disinterest. I gave up and decided to take the short journey up the ramp myself, a sense of achievement only slightly overshadowed by hitting an air vent at the front of the parking space. But at least I wouldn't have to pay an extra five dollars a night for the privilege of having him drive it those few short feet.

It was perhaps fitting that my first impression of the hotel was bad, as my second, third and forth impressions weren't that good either. The hotel was very big and very impersonal. The room lacked anything that could be described as welcoming, looking like the sort of place where countless business executives would stay and regret the fact that their hectic meeting schedule meant they saw little of the city apart from their functional room. Even the addition of a balcony didn't give it any charm, largely as it was little more than a block of concrete with a rail round it. It looked out over nothing of note and had an appearance that suggested they had forgotten it was there.

But you don't come to a city to stay in a hotel room, and rooms do not define the city, so we left the room and explored the downtown that began pretty much where the hotel ended. It had the same level of heart and soul as the room, so in this case the room pretty much did define the city. We walked down St Catherine's Street, the main shopping street, and a place with a severe lack of character. I was half way round the world on a street I wouldn't go to if it was half a mile down the road. So far Montreal was a place to avoid, but I was of course basing this on one hotel and one street. Snap judgements are often right. The evening didn't improve matters much. We picked one of the two or three pubs we had seen earlier in the day in the hope of finding a welcoming pub with a good crowd. What we found was a half empty pub, where, as I sat with my girlfriend believing we looked very much like a couple, a man at the bar asked us whether we were here for the Games, the games being the 1st World Outgames, a gay and lesbian olympics that was taking place in Pride Week in Montreal. This raised so many questions. Do I really look so effeminate that even as I sat with a woman people assumed I was gay? Did Liz look like a lesbian? And why were the Outgames the only event so far that had coincided with our stay in a city. This isn't to say I had anything against the games, just that the New France Festival would have figured higher in my list of things to see.

As to the man who asked the question, the number of times he emphasised how he would be leaving after this drink to get home to his wife spoke volumes, although it didn't look like there was anyone in the bar that would provide an opportunity for his true sexuality to emerge in any event.

Our exit from the pub was timed to perfection with the short but severe storms that ushered in the second half of the evening. Forked lightning lit up the sky, constantly hitting the same spot as if the Gods had found a particularly bad sinner to strike repeatedly. We decided not to wander any further and so went to Les Trois Brasseurs on St Catherine's Street. In line with everything else so far, the meal sacrificed taste for functionality. After we finished the meal the rain was slowing. We had a walk around to look for other signs of life, and made the discovery that there were none. The city seemed to be closing up at ten o'clock. We went back to the hotel bar, which being a hotel bar didn't close at ten. Instead it closed at eleven, at which point it was made clear that we had to go.

I wanted to like Montreal, but somehow it just didn't seem to want me to.

August 1. When you are away for longer than you've ever been away before it is perhaps inevitable that at some point you think you could quite happily go home. I'd thought that the night before. Traditional frames of reference had been replaced and new ones hadn't yet appeared. It didn't help that I was in a place I didn't like. Somehow it didn't feel natural to carry on, but in the absence of anything else to do, and because it is the natural reaction to such an existentialist crisis, we left the hotel, put on a smile, and took a city sightseeing bus.

The tour guide was a French Canadian who was very proud of the city's French origins, and completely oblivious to the fact that all of us on the bus were aware of these seeing as how all the street and building names are in French, and French is the first language on all menus. His tour speech sounded like an 'allo, allo' style parody. In between telling us about the regular visits from French Presidents, he corrected us silly English people who pronounced the city's name as it is written, telling us it is actually Mon-rey-al, with the T being silent. Every subsequent mention of Mon-rey-al saw the 'al' getting increasingly guttural until you could almost hear the flem building up ready to fly the very next time he pronounced the name in a way no one else did all the time we were here.

The tour didn't do a vast amount to change my view of Montreal as a place with a chip on its shoulder, and no apparent reason for having it. We saw what the guide proudly proclaimed as "our Empire State building – only smaller at 22 storeys," which made me wonder whether they had perhaps missed the essential defining feature of the Empire State building. We also saw many other Mon-rey-al equivalents of American and English buildings, so many in fact that I thought the place really should try and have some original buildings of its own. Then I saw the hideous yet unique Congress building and promptly changed my mind.

While the Congress building is ugly it paled in comparison to the architectural wonder that is Habitat 67. Habitat 67 is a housing complex designed for the 1967 World Exhibition by the architect Moshe Safdie. Billed as an avant garde design that would promote a new way of living, our tour guide proudly informed us that all the rooms in this vast building were cube shaped, that groups of cubes together formed apartments, and groups of cubed apartments defined the shape of the building itself. What he failed to note however was that each cube is a hideous concrete box and that stuck together they form an even more appalling concrete eyesore that would long since have been demolished as slums had they been in London or Manchester. In Canada they had never even been damaged by fire, a sure sign of their lack of architectural worth.

Walking around the city after the tour it was noticeable that for a city with a Gay Pride week and the Village - a large gay neighbourhood in the centre of the city - Montreal does not come across as a very gay friendly city. It does however have a thriving straight sex scene with a surprisingly large numbers of 'sexi dance' 'dance contact venues' 'peep shows' and good old fashioned sex shops sitting inconspicuously in major streets next door to cinemas and every day department stores.

Indeed, while the sex industry hasn't been driven underground, a lot of the main shopping facilities have. As to why they have done this when there is so much unlovely space above ground is anyone's guess, but done it they have, and the Underground City is a thirty kilometre subterranean network of shopping malls, hotels, movie theatres, concert halls and restaurants, all connected by what is described in the guides as 'Montreal's clean fast and convenient metro trains (our "tube").' The addition of the bracketed words seem wholly unnecessary and a further example of a city that is trying to mimic other large cities rather than being itself.

In truth, Montreal is not as bad as I've made it out to be, and in typical style we did manage to completely miss the Boulevard Saint-Laurent which apparently would have given us a different impression of the city. For us the Old Port area was the best part, in the way that old port areas usually are. The best sights are there, the best museums and art galleries are there, and the best places for lunch are also there, notably the Cafe outside the Chateau Ramesay Museum which has a great setting and great food. The area around Place Jacques-Cartier and Rue Saint-Paul got the tour guide recommendation for places where the real Mon-rey-alians eat and drink, and it was there that we headed back to in the evening. As recommendations from irritating people go it was one of the best of them, certainly at the start of the evening when it was far livelier and had more character than anywhere in downtown.

We ate in Galliano's Pasta Bar and then ventured into a nearby bar and restaurant for a drink. We sat outside upstairs on a balcony looking out across streets that were alive and lively. The balcony had a loose cover over the top of it, and behind this there was a larger canopy cover. A few minutes after getting our drinks, the rain started. Then the wind started blowing the trees opposite. Then the rain got heavier and the wind got stronger and the rain came in in spite of the covering, which itself started to look susceptible to the wind. We moved back under the canopy surveying the now slightly emptier street. The wind got stronger. The loose cover was taken down before it blew down. We moved further back to the furthest point where we could still claim to be outside. Then there was a flash of lightning, the wind attacked the canopy and the canopy no longer looked secure. The front half of it started to fold and buckle under the pressure. The street was empty, and the trees were joined by the lampposts in a vigorous swaying dance. We stayed upstairs but moved into a section with a proper roof. As the front of the bar was still open to the elements, when the rain and wind got harder, we, and everyone else, moved downstairs.

With a captive audience unable and unwilling to venture out into the night there was only one thing a good bar owner could do. Rub their hands and celebrate the windfall in profits. Sadly, the owner was not in and his staff weren't that enterprising. At ten o'clock they told us that their shifts finished shortly so it was last orders and we all had to drink up and leave. Only one of them seemed to realise that leaving wasn't a good option for them either and served one more drink for anyone who wanted one - which was everyone - but after that it was goodnight and out into the now less fierce rain.

On the Place Jacques-Cartier the weather had also taken its toll. Most of the bars had closed up early and the few that were open were practically deserted. We found one that was still serving, and rounded off an evening that had promised more than it eventually delivered. We walked past the edges of The Village, which also seemed strangely quiet, and headed up St Catherines Street where the sexi dancers had no doubt earned more money and done more sexi dances than they would on a dry night. Back at the hotel the bar looked closed, and our stay in Mon-rey-al came to an end.

Not a place I'd return to in a hurry.

8 – Ottawa

August 2. The journey to Ottawa was a long and fraught one. All went okay till we got off the 417 and couldn't decide whether we needed to turn right or go straight on. We went with the second option. Wrong choice. We realised our mistake after a few miles, which unfortunately was just after we missed the best opportunity to rejoin the 417. We found a road to turn round in, and then for the first time, I did the favourite British driver abroad trick and pulled onto the wrong side of the road. As a side road at least there were no cars on it, although I like to think that if there had been I would have realised what the right side of the road was in the first place.

We headed back and joined Bronson Avenue, a long road leading towards our hotel. Once again we went the wrong way, but this time we carried on oblivious thinking surely it couldn't be this far to the city centre.

Being lost became only a minor worry when the car started bleeping for no apparent reason. Once a minute a couple of little bleeps came from somewhere near the dashboard with no clues as to why. I pressed a few harmless looking buttons that locked and unlocked doors and switched lights on and off, but the bleeps continued.

With no sign of the city centre we pulled into the University Medical Centre car park to get directions and find out what was causing the bleeping. I looked through the manual and checked what all the warning lights and bleeps in the car's repertoire could mean. None of them applied, and the bleeping mysteriously continued when I turned the engine off.

In contrast to identifying the cause of the bleeping, getting directions was easy. Following them was harder. Distracted by the bleeping, I couldn't remember whether I needed to go left or right or straight on at an island in order to reach a bridge I may have already crossed. We pulled in again and got more directions. We were nearly where we should have been, but the bleeping continued.

On the positive side, the car hadn't blown up. On the negative side, it could only be a matter of time till it did. Suddenly it occurred to me that the only thing I hadn't tried to switch off or adjust was the air conditioning. I turned it off and waited. The bleeping stopped - Hallelujah! We left the air conditioning off and got on to Bronson Avenue. We were on the right road, going in the right direction, but getting a bit hot. I tentatively pressed the button to turn the air conditioning back on. No bleeping. Sorted. Cool in more ways than one.

We arrived at the Delta Hotel on Queen Street having taken two hours to do what should have been a ten minute drive. After checking in I turned on my phone. It lit up and then turned itself off. I switched it back on. It turned itself back off. I put the plug in, just in case it needed charging. It lit up, it stayed lit up, it announced it was charging and it gave a little bleep to confirm it. The same bleep we'd heard earlier. The bleep of a phone telling me it had very little charge left, the length of time it had bleeped for suggesting that it liked to exaggerate the imminence of its demise. I resisted the temptation to hurl it against a wall.

While the Delta Montreal epitomised everything there is to dislike about chain hotels, the Delta Ottawa was friendliness and customer care personified. As if to make me feel wanted and loved by all, the hotel hairdresser offered to stay open just that little bit longer when I asked for a haircut. The hairdresser was a man who combined the hair and craggy face of Gordon Ramsay with the size and posture of Anthony Worral Thompson. If he comes to the UK his future in celebrity chef parodies is guaranteed. Thirty minutes and thirty dollars later I was heading back to the room, chatting to a cleaner who had worked there for twenty years and loved it so much she never wanted to work anywhere else. All that was needed to complete the picture was some motherhood and apple pie, but we were in the wrong country for that.

With the afternoon all but over, we headed towards Parliament Hill. Parliament Hill is a national landmark. The buildings and monuments that line it are almost as impressive as the views out from it to the Ottawa River. Unlike the grounds round the Houses of Parliament or the White House, Parliament Hill is a public park, the public are actively encouraged to visit it, and they do this in droves.

Venturing inside, meanwhile, is seen almost as a civic duty that everyone has to fulfil at least once in their lives. From late June through to Labour Day free tours run round the Centre Block until eight at night. Having expected our sightseeing ambitions to have been dealt a fatal blow by our late arrival, I felt a smile return to my face and my love of humanity grow when I discovered this. Actually that's a slight exaggeration, but I was pleased that the tour was still running.

The Parliament Buildings have of course been the victims of fire. The only part of the Centre Block to survive a fire on February 3, 1916 was the Library, which with over half a million books was probably the building most likely to burn. The Victoria Tower, which had a Big Ben style clock, crashed down to earth shortly after midnight, staying up, as if out of a sense of duty, until it had chimed the midnight hour. Its bell is now one of the monuments on the Hill. The tower was replaced by the Peace Tower, dedicated to Canadian soldiers who died in World War 1. At three hundred foot tall it was once the tallest building in Ottawa. It held the title until some time shortly after a height limit on other buildings was removed.

After the tour we planned to see more of the city and return for the Sound and Light Show, which promised music, lights and giant projections on the Parliament Building from half past nine. Rain, again, stopped play. As we crossed over from Parliament Hill towards the tourist information office an immense downpour started. We sheltered in a bar until it eased off and then headed up towards ByWard Market, home to a vast array of restaurants, one of which was Truckers, which was a vast array of restaurants in itself. The Truckers menu read like the result of a competition where people had to write down as many dishes from around the world as they could in ten minutes. Being unable to decide what we wanted it was the ideal place for us.

Newcomers to Truckers are given a tour of the menu, with all the dishes on display in their own designated sections. We were guided past an Italian section, Chinese section, burger section, and dessert section to name but a few. We were told the simple pricing structure. For $15.95 you can have all you can eat, travelling the food globe without any limit on your frequent flyer miles. This may make it sound like a low end of the market place, and it is fair to say that it isn't the most refined restaurant you will ever eat in, but what it lacked in high end style it made up for in atmosphere. Also, and more importantly, with the rain starting again, we knew there was no question of being asked to leave.

We sat, staying dry and getting fatter, as the rain became torrential and cars drove through roadside lakes delivering a double whammy to any pedestrians already getting soaked from above. It was clear that thunder and lightning were going to be the only sound and light show at the Parliament Buildings that evening.

As the rain slowed we ventured out in the hope of having an evening uninterrupted by rain. We managed one stop, a Scottish Pub just on the edges of ByWard Market. After we left there, confident that the rain had slowed enough, we found we'd been lulled into a false sense of security as it came back with more ferocity than ever. At the first road crossing it was inches deep. At the second you could have rolled your trousers up and paddled in it. We had two choices, the short paddle across, or the longer drier walk round. Either would have been good if we'd decided straight away. Instead, we debated the merits of each option, and our eventual choice made no odds, we still got soaked.

Eventually we got a taxi back to the Hotel and changed out of our wet clothes before going down to the bar for a night-cap. Unlike the Montreal Delta the bar was still open and still welcoming after eleven. We stayed for a couple of drinks while debating whether a day could be classed as crap just because it started with getting lost and ended with rain. We disagreed on this. Metaphorically speaking, Liz's glass was half empty, mine was half full. Not that it really mattered as, either way, the bar was still closed.

August 3. We had breakfast in the hotel and agreed it was a shame we weren't staying longer in Ottawa. This was both a sign that Ottawa appeared to be a far better place to stay than Montreal, and also a result of the rain having ceased and there being a city we could have discovered in warm and dry weather. Sadly we couldn't stay, we were booked in to Toronto that evening and left sometime that morning.

The drive to Toronto had little of note other than the alarming state of Canadian music as revealed by a countdown of the top ten albums. This revealed that while the USA worshipped at the altar of Hip Hop and Bling, their Northern cousins rejoiced in ring tones and B-ding ding ding with Crazy Frog having the number one and the number ten album. Perhaps I should have expected it from the country where the Princess Diana tribute version of Candle in the Wind was number one for a year, even longer than Bryan Adams was number one in the UK with the Robin Hood theme. Bryan Adams, in case you don't know, is Canadian.

9 – Toronto

We reached the city at the heart of the rush hour. The expressway into the city is a seven-lane road which was proving the claim that traffic expands to fill the number of lanes provided. All of the lanes were slow moving and, with exits for toll roads on one side and city centre turn-offs on the other, it was hard for anyone to work out what lane they needed to be in, let alone actually get into it. The turn off we were looking for was Yonge Street off Route 2. We reached it sooner than we'd expected, when the appearance of the skyline suggested we still had further to go. Those are probably the two best reasons I can give for missing it. We concentrated our efforts on finding a way back that did not involve leaving the slow moving seven lane southbound highway to join the equally slow moving seven lane northbound highway. We took the next turn, where instinct and a brief look at the map confirmed this was a road into the city that led onto Yonge Street.

Finding Yonge Street isn't too much of a challenge as long as you are heading west or east and haven't gone past it. It is the longest road running from north to south in all of Canada, so if you carry on going you will eventually reach it. Nonetheless, at one point Liz declared that we were heading in the wrong direction. I looked at the map to double check and decided it was the map, rather than the car, that needed turning round. We found Yonge Street somewhere near its start and headed to the Westin Hotel somewhere near its end. The hotel had the most impressive entrance of any hotel this side of Vegas. At a length of five cars and a width of four, and with a roof lit with thousands of white light bulbs, it is probably safe to say it plays as big a part in climate change as a string of factories in India.

Toronto looks and feels how you would imagine San Francisco to look and feel if you haven't been there. It has a large harbour and a skyline dominated by skyscrapers. The first weekend in August sees the start of the Carimba festival, a yearly Caribbean festival which sounded so good that it was inevitable it would start shortly after we left. The only hint of the festival we got was the large numbers of Caribbean tourists checking in at the Westin, all looking like they were expecting some not to be missed entertainment which we would not be there for.

In a rare mode of advanced planning we booked on a tour round the city and a boat trip round the Toronto Islands for the next day. We also booked an evening table at the CN Tower, allegedly the world's tallest building at a height of 553.33 metres, probably the only one of the three things that there was any need to book in advance. After that we spotted the Steamwhistle Brewery, and the forth and final piece of Friday's sightseeing jigsaw fell into place.

With the next day planned we went back to the lakeside to finish this one off. As the Lake was Lake Ontario it looked and felt more like a river than a lake. Full of good restaurants and bars, we settled in for the evening, leaving the city for another time. At the Boathouse Bar and Grill we got a good seat by the window. Being away from the busier parts of the restaurant meant there was a more intimate feel to go with the view. After asking for a couple of minutes to decide what to drink, we escaped the attention of everyone, including the staff. Twenty minutes later I finally caught the eye of a waitress to get our order taken. Food and wine eventually arrived and we enjoyed an unhurried meal drinking wine at our own pace without anyone periodically coming round to pour it or ask if we wanted dessert. The enjoyment was of course offset by having no one come over after we finished the wine and never once being offered a dessert menu, but there is always a balance to be struck in these things.

Just before the urge to see if we could leave without paying became too strong, we went to the till, paid up and left. A light rain started so we went inside a nearby bar where a Scottish woman was telling stories that required a heavy pinch of salt to accompany them to a couple of Brits more interested in her than her stories. For once, the rain stopped rather than increased so we sat outside at a second bar lit by harbour lights and overlooking the lake. What more could you want?

August 4. Our morning tour guide gave us the history of Toronto from the perspective of a German who married a Canadian and settled there forty years ago. The city has changed radically over the last thirty years with the building of the CN Tower and a string of high rise buildings and apartments that now dot the skyline. The building programme has also helped to move the city outwards to such an extent that Front Street, which, as the name suggests, was once the furthest forward street in the city, now has four or five other streets between it and the lake.

The building programme goes on, with the aid of Chinese and Japanese investment, which means existing city centre apartments remain reasonably affordable, but also means that some areas are separated from the rest of the city by expressways and contain nothing other than apartments. Amongst the non-apartment skyscrapers are two that show Canadians are good at making money out of building designs. The Scotia Bank has nineteen corners on each floor, as the company responsible for building it worked out that corner offices rent for more money than non-corner offices, and asked the architects to build as many corners into the design as they could manage. As a result, the rents flood in to the redstone building. Meanwhile, the exterior of the Royal Canadian Bank is made entirely out of gold. It cost a fortune to build but paid for itself courtesy of caution and good fortune. The caution was worrying about rising prices and buying more gold than was needed in case they had miscalculated the dimensions. The good fortune was the original estimate being correct and the price of gold rising as feared. The gold left at the end of the project was sold for more than the cost of the entire building. A lesson for today's planners, although gold probably wouldn't be the material of choice for most people.

As night follows days, the boat trip followed the bus trip, and took us over to the Toronto Islands, a chain of small islands that provide a shallow natural harbour for the city. At one point most of the Islands had apartments, but then the local government changed their mind over using the islands for accommodation, and tried to get everyone to move back to the mainland. Most residents left willingly. Only Algonquin and Ward's Islands resisted and thus began a twenty-five year court battle at the end of which about seven hundred residents won the right to a ninety-nine year lease. A grand victory for the people in some ways, but not in others as residents have to spend at least two hundred days a year living on the island or they forfeit the lease. On top of this, Toronto council won't grant residents access to boarding spaces on the mainland, so they have to get the public ferry whenever they want to visit the mainland. A late night out isn't an option either, the last ferry to and from the mainland leaves far too early.

Further souring the taste of victory, in the winter the waters freeze up and the short ten minute ferry stops running leaving you with no choice but to get a ferry with ice cutters which heads into the other side of the city and takes about ninety minutes each way. In spite of this most of the residents have remained and there are long waiting lists of potential buyers for apartments that will never be sold. Stubborn people these islanders.

After the boat it was off to the Steamwhistle Brewing Company. The brewery is located in the John St. Roundhouse, which was originally a steam locomotive repair facility. Open since the end of the last century the company was born of frustration at the take-over and subsequent closure of Upper Canada Brewing, one of Canada's largest microbreweries. This coupled with the replacement of distinctive tasting beers by mass produced varieties, and, more importantly, their own redundancy, led to three former brewery workers deciding to open their own brewery in 1998. Their aim was not just to make beer, but to make a pilsner that Canadians could be proud of. A humble, yet noble, aim, reflected in the name Steam Whistle, which they took from the sounds of steam rushing from factory whistles in the 1950s when life was simple and the whistle signalled the end of a days work and the time for a drink.

The company is owned by its employers. The guided tours are given by people who are part owners of the brewery and community supporters known affectionately as The Good Beer Folks. They talk with real enthusiasm about the establishment of the company and its profile in Canada. The tour is worth doing for the story of the company, and for the chance to pull the Steamwhistle, which I of course did. The other thing to add is that the beer itself is good, with a fresh natural taste that made it my beer of choice in Canada. Steamwhistle has a website, but unless you live in Canada you can't buy the beer, so my love affair with the company started and ended here.

In the evening we went to the CN Tower. Originally developed as a telecommunications tower, it now serves no purpose other than to be the world's tallest building. It has three observation towers, and a glass floor at 342 metres. The highest observation level is at 447 metres, which means the last hundred metres are there just to show off and make it harder for any new buildings to be bigger.

The restaurant is called the 360 because it revolves through 360 degrees, rather than because it is 360 metres up from the ground. It isn't far off however, at around 350 metres. The centre of the restaurant does not spin so if you leave your table for any reason it won't be in the same position when you come back.

The restaurant is pricey - around a hundred dollars for a main course, dessert and bottle of wine - but then what else would you expect when food and views combine to such great effect. The restaurant is a very romantic place, particularly if you're lucky enough to get a table on the outer rim, which we were. Over the course of an excellent two hour meal we completed about two circuits of the city. The feeling you get as you look out over the city from such a great height is incomparable. The feeling we got later as we looked down from the glass floor was also incomparable for different reasons. The glass section is only a small part of the floor, and many people are too nervous to cross it. I was too curious not to. Watching the people walking underneath, the contrast with the vastness of the view from the restaurant could not be greater, and yet they complement each other by making you realise that in the grand scheme of things no matter how big you, or the world around you, may seem there is always a bigger world to look out on. Before I got too philosophical about this I went for a Steamwhistle to end the day in a more grounded manner.

10 – Niagara Falls

August 5. Had breakfast at a riverfront cafe feeling sad to be leaving and missing the Carimba festival. It was a holiday weekend and, once we left Toronto, traffic quickly slowed to a crawl. It continued as a crawl for some time until we crossed a bridge and doubled back to Niagara.

We made it to the Sheraton on the Falls without ever taking a wrong turn. Getting the very last bit of the route right was a big relief as a wrong turn would have taken us to the Rainbow Bridge and back to America with the prospect of negotiating passport control twice in a few minutes in order to get back.

Contrary to its name and its press blurb, the hotel is not directly on the falls, no hotel is. Nor is it directly opposite the falls, again no hotel is. That said, it probably does have the best views of any hotel by virtue of its position, and by being considerably taller than the nearby Brock Plaza Hotel. The size of the hotel is only an important factor if you are towards the top of it. A strange quirk of fate borne of incompetence meant we were.

The room we'd been allocated wasn't ready when we arrived, and still wasn't ready after we'd been for a walk and lunch. I complained and the assistant manager overheard, intervened and put us in another room. The original room was on the third floor. The new one was on the eighteenth. The view of the falls was out of a side window, but we were not talking a 'try really hard and you can just about see it' side window. The window covered all of one wall, and the view took in all three of the falls in a sweeping panorama.

From a trivia and general ignorance point of view it was only then that I learned there is no Niagara Fall. The Niagara Falls is a collective name for three falls on the Niagara River. The biggest is the Horseshoe Falls, the only one even partly on Canadian ground. After that there is the American Falls and the Bridal Veil Falls, the smallest of the three and such a short distance from the American Falls you suspect they either have been, or one day will be, united.

As to Niagara as a whole, the place combines the best of nature with the worst of mankind, and could in itself destroy any impression that Canada is simply America but with taste and restraint applied. Up the road from the hotel was the Hard Rock Cafe, further along was Planet Hollywood, round the corner was Ripleys Believe it or Not – which I wouldn't have believed - a Guinness World Records Museum, and a Madame Tussauds. For dining there was McDonalds, Burger King and Wendy's all nearby. It was as if someone thought an area of outstanding natural beauty was not enough to draw people in, and decided to recreate Blackpool around it.

We walked along the front, dodging the hordes to look out over the falls, before getting tickets for the Journey Behind the Falls, where we descended more than a thousand feet and travelled through tunnels to look at the Horseshoe Falls from below and behind.

We were given pac-a-macs to keep the water off us, and lead down a long corridor for a view behind the falls through an average size window without glass. I peered through and saw nothing but white. It took a while to work out that this was water. Not being able to see the top, bottom or edges of the fall made it a strange, out of context, and out of focus, view. The below the falls view was far better as we were led on to a ledge where we looked up and got soaked by spray even though we were at least a hundred feet away from the falls. This was the first of three falls experiences we did. It was good, but if I could only have done two, this wouldn't have been one of them.

Finding somewhere to eat was difficult, due to a mixture of too many people and too few decent restaurants. We ended up in the Beef Baron Restaurant. The name says it all. It was a slightly run down Steakhouse with grand pretensions. The food, when it arrived, didn't disappoint us. It tasted every bit as uninspiring as we expected.

We rounded the evening off in a nearby bar listening to a band doing passable cover versions of minor hits, marvelling at how a place could be so beautiful and so ugly at the same time. A unique achievement, and one that should never be attempted.

August 6. An early debate about what we were going to do began with Liz deciding she didn't want to do anything given that she hated the place so much. After a bit of to-ing and fro-ing - better known as arguing - we agreed to get something to eat, and take it from there.

After breakfast we decided to cross over to the American side of the falls. The Rainbow Bridge has Canadian and American passport controls at either end. In the middle of the bridge there is a sign marking where Canada ends and the USA begins. The bridge offers great views across the falls as well as the opportunity to stand with one foot in one country and one in another.

Much to our surprise, the US side of the falls were quieter, more scenic, and far less developed than the Canadian side, the beauty of the falls enhanced rather than compromised by the surrounding landscape. This was what we'd imagined the Canadian side to be like, particularly when it was recommended we stay there. It was like someone had flipped the countries around just to confuse people trying to cross the border and leave the US. As I soaked in the new relaxed atmosphere I wondered whether the people who told me not to stay on the US side really had any idea who I was.

Of course, the reason for the unspoilt beauty and lack of development is probably because it is the oldest State Park in America, and therefore largely protected from new developments. The non protected bits host the obligatory Hard Rock Cafe and a string of hotels in different stages of development suggesting that laws are getting relaxed and making you hope for a change of policy before they relax into the park itself.

We walked through the park, crossing over to Goat Island and looking out over the top of the American Falls, before taking the Cave of the Winds trip, the second falls experience, and the one which comes top of any list you can draw up. After queuing for who knows how long we went into a lift, having been given another pac-a-mac, walked through a bit of a cave, and came out towards the bottom of the Bridal Veil Falls. There were three stopping points, each closer to the falls than the last one. The first gave a full view from a distance. The second was up some wooden steps to a platform within thirty feet of the falls and around two-thirds of the way up. The third, optional, stop was up a few more steps to another platform about five feet from the falls. The view and the experience were beyond fantastic. Water cascaded down in front of me with tremendous force and speed. It was truly exhilarating to feel nature so close up. I felt insignificant standing watching something that was there long before I came and will be there long after I've gone.

Anyone would.

After this everything else could have been an anticlimax, but wasn't. We carried on through the park, passing the white water rapids that feed into the falls, and came out at the top of the Horseshoe Falls where we watched as the water was drawn to the edge and began its rapid descent to the rocks below. The panoramic views in the pictures are only half the story of the falls. You have to see what happens to create that view to truly and fully experience it.

Of course for some people even this isn't enough and the complete falls experience includes going over the top in a barrel or some other contraption that you would put money on breaking into a thousand pieces when it hits the rocks below. There have been fifteen people who have done this, ten have been successful. Given the rather rudimentary barrels they've used this is even more surprising a statistic than you'd imagine. Sadly success does not always seem enough, and of the ten who did survive a few were foolish enough to think this meant they could do it a second or third time. All who tried it more than once met their end on their final attempt.

Roger Woodward managed to go down without the questionable protection of a barrel and still survived. The absence of the barrel was by default rather than design. His father could not steer the boat he was in clear of the falls. His father died, but both Roger and his sister, who was also in the boat, were saved. Roger, who was seven at the time, went down the falls after leaving the boat but was rescued when the crew of the Maid of The Mist spotted him and threw him a life ring. His sister, Deanne, remarkably didn't even go down the falls and was rescued on a small ledge twenty feet away from the start of the falls. The ledge remains but is now treated like any other ledge near a mass of water, and gets coins thrown into it for no apparent reason. Oddly enough, no one ever tries to get the money out, no matter how desperate they are for cash.

After a few hours we headed back over the Rainbow Bridge to Canada. We went for a meal at the Secret Garden, a small outside restaurant near to the Rainbow Bridge. The name Secret Garden suggests a hidden treasure that few people know about, and despite its position - a few steps, some trees and a garden away from the main street - the name is apt as it is relatively undiscovered. This suited us, but perhaps the owners would prefer it if they had to call it the Very Well Discovered Garden with Large Queues for Meals. The waiter told us about fireworks over the falls planned for later, we'd seen nothing about this and would probably have ended up in a bar wondering where everyone was if we hadn't been to that restaurant.

With an hour to spare we went to a 4D falls movie. The forth dimension consisted of seats that shook, gusts of wind, things that tickled the back of our legs, and occasional jets of water from all directions. Rather than create the felling of heading down the falls, it conjured up the feeling of a student parody at a fringe festival. I was surprised there wasn't someone at the front with a bucket of water, or a small person under my chair tickling my legs. It's definitely fair to say that the forth dimension didn't add much to the other three.

The firework display took place between the falls rather than on them, and as such was not all it was cracked up to be. The all colours of the rainbow lighting near the falls throughout the evening was more impressive, and we watched this and warmed more to the rest of Niagara, mainly as it was now a lot emptier than the night before. After a drink outside at the Hard Rock Cafe – chosen due to a lack of other bars – we walked up some of the streets of arcades, believe it or not's, haunted houses, and waxwork museums. The level of tack was still annoying, but now it was a side-show rather than a distraction from the main feature, and the next day the turnaround was complete as we booked a third night.

August 7. Having decided to stay another day, we went on the Maid of the Mist, the boat that takes you into the eye of the Horseshoe Falls, but stops before you get close enough to be hit by anyone coming down them in a barrel. The crowds getting on to the boats, wearing the obligatory pac-a-macs, prompted a nearby Chinese woman to ask her husband "why are they all wearing those blue coats, are they convicts?" We could almost see how she got that impression. The queues for the boats were far shorter than they had been at the weekend. We got the last couple of places, which would normally mean a lousy or non existent view, but, with seats round the edges only, the boats seemed designed to make every view a good one.

And then we became good old-fashioned holiday makers. We headed up to the Imax theatre for the 3D falls movie - more convincing that the 4D version, but far too pretentious for its own good and still lacking anything to make you feel you're hurtling down the falls – and then moved on to the 'Over the Falls' exhibition, to learn more about the previous barrel voyages, see some of the vessels that survived the drop and pose for the inevitable wacky photos pretending to be sitting scared inside them.

Heading down from there, we found an excellent tapas cafe called Café Tu Tu Tango. Downstairs they had local art on display, while upstairs we chose to dine out alfresco on a roof looking out across Canada. The food came as it was done so you got it at its freshest, no point asking or expecting it all to be brought at the same time, they wouldn't do it. The drinks were chosen from a good range of beers and cocktails and all in all, it was the best non-tourist location in Niagara. Not that there was much competition.

In the afternoon we played Galaxy Golf, a luminous crazy golf game played in the dark, with extra-added light from cartoon figures of the Simpsons. As an added bonus for crazy golf aficionados everyone who completes Galaxy Golf gets a discount voucher for Dinosaur Golf. Sadly we didn't have time to put our voucher to good use, but its fair to say our objection to the aesthetic destruction of the area could now be seen as hypocritical.

Continuing the abandonment of our loosely held principles, in the evening we went to Planet Hollywood for a surprisingly good meal that was shockingly large even by Canadian and US standards. Another drink and a further hour in an amusement arcade was followed by a visit to the Guinness World Records Museum to round off our stay in Niagara.

The thing with Guinness World Record Museums, and world records as a whole, is that they mix spectacular genuine achievements – biggest selling recording artist, longest shot put ever – with the sort of thing where the idea says more about the record holder than the achievement ever could. People deciding to stand on one leg for longer than anyone else, or walk backwards for several miles, must have both an immense ambition to be famous and a lack of anything that could be recognised as a normal skill. That said, they still have an imagination. If you have neither skill, nor talent, nor imagination, the only way to get a world record is to eat a lot of something. To reduce the likely competition, the something you eat should also be revolting. Looking round the museum I discovered with a sense of national pride that most such record holders come from England.

The winner for eating your way into the record books is Peter Donahoe from Northampton who achieved at least six record breaking attempts between 1978 and 1984. Whether he was pushed by a desire to gain ever more gastronomic titles, or by a form of paranoia that made him think there would be too much competition for him to be sure of retaining the pickled egg eating title, I have no idea. Whatever drove him, he continued to gather records and also spread his attempts around the UK, picking up one title in Birmingham and two in Kilmarnock. Maybe his talent, like his stomach, was too immense to be confined to Northampton only.

One record Peter doesn't hold is the record for filleting and eating kippers. That honour goes to Reg Morris from my hometown of Walsall. Reg is immortalised in the museum in Niagara, and probably a few other places, for the twenty-seven kippers he filleted and ate in sixteen minutes and fifty six seconds in 1998. I saluted a genuine Walsall hero that evening, and hoped that one day someone in Niagara might know Walsall for some other reason.

11 - A Strange Town on the Road to Nowhere

August 8. Originally we intended to drive through Canada and re-enter America as near to Chicago as possible. Several things worked against that idea, well just one actually – none of the possible routes really worked. The first and shortest route would bring us back into the States at Detroit, which I'd been told was not worth seeing. The second route, re-entering at Port Huron, would mean a drive cross-country and as the point of staying on the Canadian side was to drive along the Great Lakes that was quickly ruled out. The third route took us to Sault Ste Marie, and brought us to Chicago via Milwaukee. After an initial drive north it would have been a lakeside route for much of the way. Sault Ste Marie had been recommended as a must see place, and Milwaukee would have given me the chance to be the Fonz for a day. The problem was that it wasn't really a route, it was more a major diversion. There is no logical route from Niagara to Chicago that goes via Sault Ste Marie. Once we realised this, we decided to cross back to America at Peace Bridge, head south through Fort Erie and cover a few states in rapid succession. Fonzie's hometown was off the agenda.

The passport check back into the States was quicker than it had been as a foot passenger on Sunday, when the border guard sounded like she thought every one trying to enter the country had a sinister reason for doing so. We hoped that the guard today would give us a fresh stamp to show us as new arrivals, but it didn't happen, and our original 90 day visa free period was still running. Enjoyable as our Canadian jaunt had been, we'd learned little about the country's views of the US. The most incisive comment we'd heard was on a radio show where the talk was of Canada's dismal showing in some sporting event. The one crumb of comfort the presenter could take was that "at least we beat the yanks."

The England/Scotland comparisons seemed particularly relevant at that time.

In truth, rather than finding out why Canada was different from the US we had simply discovered that countries are different from themselves as well as from each other. Montreal was different from Quebec, Ottawa was different from Toronto, and Niagara was different from any recognisable place other than seaside resorts. Maybe the country was more relaxed and the people more at ease with themselves, but that may just be what we had wanted to believe. All in all, as this is the level of social insight I attained, it is probably just as well that I have never claimed to be a social anthropologist.

Once in the States we picked up Interstate 190 followed by Interstate 90, both of which were as bland as they sound. Consequently shortly after we crossed the New York State line into Pennsylvania, we turned off for State Highway 5. This may not sound any less bland than Interstate 90, but State Highways are older roads largely constructed in a time when the quality of the journey was as important as the final destination. As a result they take the path less travelled, through, rather than past, small towns. State Highway 5 also takes you along Lake Erie, as a result of which we had the romantic notion of chancing upon somewhere, deciding it looked good and staying for the night. Maybe we were just in the wrong part of the country, but it never really happened like that.

The first place we stopped at was Erie, billed as the largest town in the Lake Erie area. The others must be incredibly small. Erie centres around a small square with streets coming off it, and a harbour a couple of miles away. Apart from a quaint restaurant the harbour has little to attract passing travellers. We had lunch at the restaurant, ordering sandwiches with a variety of meats and salads on a variety of breads. They were delivered with all the right ingredients in all the wrong combinations. We proceeded to take them apart and rearrange their contents to something more closely approximating our order while debating whether to try and find a place to stay for the night.

It wasn't a long debate. The main town seemed nice enough, but we wanted to stay on the lake, rather than in a town taunted by an empty harbour two miles down the road. We crossed into Ohio and headed towards Conneaut, the next town large enough to warrant having its name printed in bold in the '1993 Collins Road Atlas: USA Canada and Mexico.'

The outskirts of Conneaut suggested the inskirts of Conneaut would not be thriving. We passed a large factory miles away from anywhere with nothing advertising what it actually did. In addition to burgers and fries, the small cafe opposite it offered exotic dancers. I imagined a busload of exotic dancers travelling out daily so that they didn't have to take jobs in the historical railroad museum, one of only two places of interest marked on the map for Conneaut. The other is the information centre, where you can find out where the historic railroad museum is. A question mark is the symbol used to identify information centres on maps. It seemed somehow more apt than ever in Conneaut.

After Conneaut we went through Ashtabula, which sounded like an abbreviation of a long word that should eventually end with 'bibbedy, bobbedy boo' and then on to Geneva on the Lake. This sounded promising, surely any place that actively proclaimed itself to be on the lake would be good to stop for the evening. But Geneva on the Lake was no ordinary lakeside resort.

The entire town had the air of the seaside town that they forgot to close down. The funfair was completely empty only a day after a bank holiday north of the border and at the height of the summer season. A small amusement arcade and cafeteria advertised itself as offering 'Las Vegas entertainment.' Inside on the left two women sat playing cards while on the right there were a few fruit machines with no players. It was so not Las Vegas that we wondered how they ever came up with the comparison, until a look at the clientele suggested they'd probably never been further than Geneva on the Lake and thought that this was what Vegas was all about.

There were a string of motels in and around the place. From the outside most of them did nothing for the image of small town America. From the inside they did less. We stopped at one and went into the main office. No one was about and all seemed empty until, a few minutes later, a strange looking man came over from a nearby garage and asked if we were looking for a room. As I couldn't think of anything else I might have been doing in a motel, I said yes even though he looked as if he would give Norman Bates a run for his money in the 'least desirable motel owner ever' awards. I was relieved when he said he would get the owner. The relief was short-lived. He was even stranger looking. He could have been his brother or his father, but was probably both.

He offered to show us one of his available rooms. For some strange reason we accepted. He lead us down a corridor to a room and said, "I think is empty," the word think said in a way that belied both a lack of certainty and a lack of business. He opened the door to a room that looked like a student bedsit from the eighties, and noticed, as we did, that the corner of the bedsheet was pulled back. He turned and repeated his belief that this was an empty room. Just as we thought he would admit he was wrong, he opened the door fully, then closed it quickly realising the room was not as empty as he thought. He told us he'd get the key for another room. In time honoured tradition we made our excuses and left.

The next inn we tried was a little better, largely as the room we were shown wasn't occupied. It looked a little cleaner, maybe an early nineties style rented studio flat. It also had a balcony that looked out on to the lake, giving you a two-foot by five-foot place where you could stand and stare at a vast expanse of blue water. Not wanting to drive much further I was nearly tempted to stay, until a look from the couple in the next door room that shared the balcony, suggesting they did not want anyone else invading the vast space, made us think again.

We got back in the car and passed a sign for a caravan/mobile home park that also said 'motel' and 'vacancies' and pointed down a road. We missed the entry first time round. This was perhaps meant to be a message, but we foolishly ignored it, turned round and drove back. The entry didn't show any immediate signs of having a motel at the end of it, but we continued until we reached a man in front of a car with a particularly ferocious looking dog. We decided not to get out and ask him whether the building a short way behind him was the motel. Something said we wouldn't be staying there even if it was.

We parked on the main road and had a walk to see if there was anywhere else worth checking out, there wasn't. We got back into the car, not wanting to continue driving but bowing to the inevitability of a long drive to who knows where, and then, to our surprise, half a mile later we saw The Lodge at Geneva on the Lake.

The Lodge would look fairly impressive anywhere, but at this time and in this location it stood out like a beacon. Set in part of the Geneva State Park Beach and Marina, somewhere we didn't know existed, it had green grass, a beach and the opportunity for a long walk along the lake. My immediate reaction was to wonder what it was doing here. When we saw the words Conference Centre, I had a sinking feeling that that would be all it was and wondered whether anyone had ever faked being part of a conference to stay there. I would have done, but it wasn't necessary and, for not much more money than the motels we'd looked at, we got a room.

We sat outside looking out at the lake. We read a bit, walked along the lake towards a boat house which didn't have a bar for non-members, and then walked back into town, believing that without the stress of looking for a place to stay we might see it a different light. I was so hopeful I decided to buy a camera film in the hotel shop. The only problem was they didn't sell them. When I attempted to buy one in the town I discovered a strange fact about Geneva on the Lake. They don't appear to have heard of cameras. At the first shop they were polite enough to just say, "no sorry we don't." At the next place the mere concept of camera film seemed somehow new and unheard of. It took three attempts before I gave up trying to explain what one was. Maybe they just found the thought of anyone wanting to mark a visit there with a photo too incredulous to believe, or maybe they just didn't expect anyone to visit in the first place. Both could be reasonable assumptions.

A few of the bars in town looked interesting, and, because it seemed like the sort of place where you should, we were tempted to have a big steak at one of the restaurants, but in the end we decided to eat at the Conference centre and headed back in case they were about to shut.

On a nearby group of tables a local business, or at least a business from somewhere in Northern Ohio, were having a meal to celebrate twenty-five years of existence. The food was interspersed with the usual presentations of awards and anecdotes before the inevitable closing speech on how well they treat their customers and how that is key to their success and must continue. I wondered what they had been doing for twenty-five years, it obviously wasn't anything to do with cameras. No photos were taken by any of the group all the time we were there.

August 9. Before breakfast I ran along Lake Erie, looking out at the lake which stretched as far as the eye can see and breathing in air so fresh you'd never believe it could exist.

Heading out from the Lodge we passed through the town of Geneva - the bit of it that is not on the lake. In complete contrast to the motels and funfairs it looked like any normal town with restaurants, banks and shops. They probably even sold camera film.

The plan today was to drive across Ohio. On the radio we heard KT Tunstall's Black Horse and the Cherry Tree, which had been a minor hit in the UK more than a year earlier. It begins with a count in followed by a 'woo, hoo' refrain and a guitar strum before the song kicks in proper with what is normally described as a 'gutsy' vocal. It was a song I'd never heard before, but by the time we left would hear more than any other song ever, and would know off by heart.

We took the coast route, seeing places with hotels that we wouldn't want to stay at, and places without hotels that we would want to stay at. We planned to spend the evening in Toledo, a place chosen for no reason other than the opening line of Kenny Rodgers Lucille, which refers to a bar in Toledo, across from the depot. Not much to go on, and not something that suggests a wild happening place, but nonetheless we chose it.

Toledo's local rock station was running ads for its club night, which boasted a two-girl wet T-shirt dance competition. The hottest raunchiest two-girl couple would win a hundred dollar prize, and just in case any potential entrants didn't realise it, the DJ kindly pointed out that you didn't have to "play for the other side to take part, straight women can do it too," before adding that "the only thing you need to enter is to want to have fun and to love getting down." Presumably you also had to be willing to snog a friend and rub your breasts against hers through a wet top while hundreds of men got over excited, but he didn't mention that.

We turned off towards what should have been the harbour, past a sign saying 'Welcome to Birmingham, an ethnic neighbourhood' in an area that didn't seem to have a neighbourhood at all, and then reached a ship yard followed by an industrial area, before concluding that this probably was the harbour. A few more misplaced attempts to find a town made us wonder whether there was a town to find at all, or whether there was just a bar in Toledo across from the depot, where presumably they had a two girl wet T shirt dance competition to give a new meaning to the words 'you picked a fine time to leave me Lucille.'

We neither went to the club or to Toledo in the end. We took US Highway 20. Apart from a few motels and some restaurants towards the start we passed nowhere that was quaint enough to stop at, and very little to stop at at all. The road linked with Interstate 90 as we crossed into Indiana. We joined it, pulled off at the first turning and checked into the Holiday Inn Express.

There is very little I can say about the hotel. It was a shopping mall hotel. One of a few as you leave the Interstate, and the easiest one to reach, being on the north side of the relatively small mall. You can't get

89

an evening meal there and there is no lift. We only found out the latter of these facts after we'd been given the keys for a second floor room. For food we were told that the pizza place on the southern side was the best place to eat. This being a shopping mall there was no way to walk from the north side to the south side without hurling yourself into the path of moving traffic so we drove the less than quarter of a mile to reach it.

After a mini shopping expedition we went to Bubbas Pizza. It turned out that the reason it was the best place to eat was because it was also the only place to eat. It looked like something you'd find on a small road somewhere off a London high street rather than in a modern shopping mall. If you ate in, you would be more likely to soak up vinegar and cooking fat than ambience. We ordered pizzas and drinks to go and then headed back to the hotel. Up to now Liz had been sending a postcard to her sister from every location we visited. This was the first and only time she didn't. Not unsurprisingly there were no shops selling postcards to show your friends what a delightful bustling shopping mall this was. Even Bubbas Pizza offered no souvenir reminders of your time at the counter. We went to bed early ready for the last stretch of the journey to Chicago.

August 10. Today was the day when the plot to blow up four planes from Heathrow to America was foiled. Watching the TV in the self service breakfast bar, we heard that Heathrow was in chaos, there were delays and cancellations both there and at other airports, and vastly increased security checks everywhere. There was something about the way the reporters repeatedly said, "British Police claimed to have broken up a terrorist cell," with the emphasis on "claimed to," that suggested they weren't overly convinced about this. They also repeatedly emphasised that these were British born terrorists, as if we could rest easy in the fact that they hadn't come from America. They still added that they were Muslims however, just in case we would otherwise forget we were in a war on terror.

To us, it was a far away story, much as it would be to anyone miles away from the nearest big city at a mall hotel just off Interstate 90. We had a bigger threat to face when a severe weather warning interrupted the mornings entertainment on WK whatever FM.

Severe weather warnings are always proceeded by a noise that sounds as if the radio has just lost the signal. They never come

90

unannounced. They also always come during the middle of records, never at the end, and are read by someone other than the radio presenter. All of this is done to add an extra gravitas to the report and make sure you can't mistake the warning for jovial DJ banter. Unlike independent radio stations in the UK, where everything is as light hearted as possible, the weather here is a serious business. You would never hear a DJ saying, "that was Gnarls Barkely with Crazy and, hey, we've got some crazy weather to tell you about."

Warnings of severe storms, high speed winds and possible tornadoes somewhere in Indiana were the subject of todays weather warning. Unfortunately the geographical locations and timings they gave out, something about the upper quartile of the north west moving through the lower quartile between eleven and twelve, meant we couldn't actually work out whether it applied to us or not. We did the only thing we could do and decided to copy everyone else. If they didn't heed the warnings and get to a place of safety, then the storms weren't going to be round here and we could stay on these roads.

As tornado avoidance strategies go, this one is only any good if you are the only person trying it. If there are endless others who can't understand the weather warning and decide to take their lead from the cars in front, you get a whole interstate full of people heading blindly into the eye of a storm, all trusting each other's equally ill informed judgement. Consequently, we caught the storm a short while before we reached Gary, which was a place as opposed to a man standing outside cursing his luck at getting wet.

The sky turned dark and the rain came down with a force that was unexpected even after the storms we'd seen before. Not far from the last exit we'd confidently drove past, and miles away from the next, massive forks of lightning suddenly lit the sky, and trees shook. We were in the place the storm was most likely to happen at the time they'd predicted it was most likely to occur. The greatest relief of the morning came when the road took a turn and we realised we'd just been skirting the edge and it was now heading south while we went east. We got through Gary and crossed into Illinois, heading on to Route 41 and into Chicago.

12 - Chicago

On Lake Shore Drive as we tried to reach the W Hotel we were once again caught out by the size of the road – three lanes each way – and the fact that we were on the wrong side of it for the hotel. When we passed the North-western University Campus and the Academy of Science we knew we had gone to far, and turned round and headed back. We adopted the principle that turning left whenever you have a chance will get you back to the road you should be on and facing the direction you should be facing. Surprisingly it worked and we checked into the hotel at half past twelve. The valet seemed surprised we were there that early. The receptionist reacted with the same surprise and then asked us how the flight and the airport was, at which point I realised they assumed we'd flown in today, and were amazed at the lack of delay in our flight, and the fact that we'd got here at all, while Heathrow and everywhere else was in chaos. The palpable sense of disappointment when I said we'd been here a month made me wish I'd said we'd been on the last flight out before it all happened, just to give them something to tell the other guests later.

The W Hotel is in a good position overlooking a beach that I never knew Chicago had. In spite of the closeness of the beach to the hotel, getting to it was a complicated affair as the two are separated by the six lanes of Lake Shore Drive, so a walk up the road, through the subway, and back down the road, was needed to reach sand some thirty feet in front of us.

We didn't head to the beach that day. Instead we went to Michigan Avenue, a five-minute walk from our hotel, and formerly where the lake ended. Chicago is a city of skyscrapers and, in much the same way as Toronto, the outward and upward expansion of the city has been relentless. Aided in part by the 1916 great fire of Chicago, the starting of which, contrary to popular opinion, had absolutely nothing to do with

Mrs O'Leary and her cow, the city expanded out with skyscrapers built everywhere there was a vacant space. As part of the land refill and building programme the original Chicago beach disappeared and Michigan Avenue ceased to be where the lake came to. Some years after the beach went, the people of Chicago decided to get it back and shipped in sand to replace the sand that had been washed out to Lake Michigan. They have to do this every year, but at least they have their beach back.

The top half of Michigan Avenue is more commonly known as the Magnificent Mile, mainly because it is the premier shopping district in the city rather than for the grandeur of the buildings. With consummate ease when we reached Michigan Avenue we promptly headed in the opposite direction from the Magnificent Mile and onto where it becomes plain old North and South Michigan Avenue.

Walking down the north part we stopped at the Chicago Cultural center, a block long building stretching from Randolph Street to Washington Street. The building is a maze, with entrances on various roads, access to and from the east and west side only possible on certain floors, and a tourist information centre and bakery cafe dissecting the first floor of the building, which in Britain is what we'd call the ground floor. Built as the first permanent home for the Chicago Public Library, and originally known as the People's Palace, it still offers a mixture of exhibitions and concerts. We went to the 'Landmark Chicago Gallery,' with photographs and artefacts from the city's history, which gave us a good feel for the history of the city and the history of Route 66, or the Illinois bits at least, which started just a few blocks away. The original starting point, Jackson Boulevard, is now a one way street. As it runs in the opposite direction from Route 66, and small things like no entry signs won't stop devoted road warriors, it is probably just as well that the plaque marking the start of the road is on nearby Adams Street, even though, in spite of numerous changes, Route 66 never actually started there.

Opposite the Cultural Center is Millennium Park, a twenty-four and a half-acre addition to Grant Park, the largest park in Chicago. Until 1997 the land was controlled by the Illinois Central Railroad and was covered with railroad tracks and parking lots. Mayor Richard M. Daley, son of a previous Mayor, vilified and worshipped in equal measure by the city's residents, decided that the area should be turned into a new public space. What Mayor Daley wants normally happens. A short while after

9/11 he led a late night removal of a city airfield with no prior consultation on the grounds that it was a good thing and he was cutting through red tape by doing it. In 2000 however, even Mayor Daley couldn't beat the odds, and given the history of buildings with Millennium in their name, it was perhaps inevitable that the park wasn't actually completed and opened until a couple of years after the turn of the century.

Calling Millennium Park a park is an uncharacteristic underselling of the finished product as the vast amount of features added by architects, artists, planners and landscape designers make it so much more than a normal park. Walk a short distance and you reach the Jay Pritzker Pavilion designed by Frank Gehry. The pavilion is an outdoor concert venue, but the stage is completely dwarfed by the exterior, which stands at one hundred and twenty feet at its highest point, and has a billowing head-dress of stainless steel ribbons framing the stage opening, and connecting vast series of steel pipes that support the sound and lighting equipment. It is more impressive than the average park bandstand.

Walk a bit further and you reach Cloud Gate, the work of British artist Anish Kapoor. It is a one hundred and ten ton elliptical stainless steel structure, sixty-six feet wide and thirty-three feet high, with a twelve foot arch in the middle. It looks like a large drop of liquid mercury with a mirror like surface that produces bent and refracted reflections of the city at every turn. No one with a camera will pass it without taking a picture of them reflected in front of strange bending skyscrapers.

Further on still there is The Crown Fountain, designed by Spanish artist Jaume Plensa, and consisting of two fifty-foot high glass block towers, which project video images of Chicago citizens while water comes from outlets in the screens across their faces. There are a thousand faces randomly shown for about four or five minutes each, mesmerising anyone standing watching it. Contrasting the brilliantly realised architectural design with the great foul up that is the seemingly simple Princess Di memorial fountain in Hyde Park you really feel proud to be English.

In the evening we went to the Szechwan restaurant just down from the Magnificent Mile. Up to this point we had slavishly followed the guidebooks and tipped about fifteen per cent for each meal. The Szechwan restaurant was where this tradition came to an end. It wasn't that the meal was bad, quite the opposite, but there is fast service and

94

there is taking the food away before the last mouthful leaves the plate and enters your mouth. This distinction did not seem to be recognised at the Szechwan restaurant. This wasn't because they were keen to get guests on to the next course, they just seemed to want to get home and get all the inconvenient people, known as paying customers, out of the way. Just after nine, we finished our main course and the waitress took away the plates with undue haste. The bottle of wine suffered a similar fate as soon as she poured the last of it into glasses just about big enough to hold it. No question of whether we'd like another glass or a dessert, being asked if we could open our mouths just a little bit wider to get that last drop in just a little bit quicker would have been less surprising.

With the waitress exuding such warmth I left the tip section on the promptly delivered, not yet requested, bill blank. She decided now was the time to engage in jovial banter, which was the terse statement "you haven't given a tip." No question of why or whether there was anything we weren't happy with.

I joined in with my own one line answer of "I know," before getting the follow up question of "will you give tip?" and giving the follow up answer of "no, I won't." I took my card and we left the restaurant while a genuinely puzzled looking waitress scowled behind us.

A trip to a good Irish bar – one of many in the city – followed before we returned to the Hotel and the 33rd floor bar. The views out to the lake on one side and to the still-awake skyscraper office blocks and apartments on the other were magnificent, but few people seemed to be taking notice of anything outside the bar. This was probably because the bar was shrouded in near darkness and couples getting intimate with each other occupied most of the two-seater sofas. There was something quite fascinatingly voyeuristic watching this and wondering how many of them had left someone else at home. I could have done it all night, except that had any of them looked up they might have thought I was a private detective and the evening could have got a little unpleasant. With that in mind, I didn't.

August 11. We went on the sightseeing buses. We had two guides over the course of the day. The first was Clarence, who was self styled as "your big mouth tour guide" but did very little to earn that name delivering a largely factual tour with little by way of anecdote except where there was some connection to his family. Consequently we found out where his cousin got married and where his first child was born but learned little in the way of city scandal. In contrast to Clarence the second guide was the most hyperactive tour guide known to man. Standing on the top of the open top bus looking down to see how many people were getting on, he jumped down, turned around and did everything except pick a bale of cotton, to start his repertoire.

His stories also had an entirely different nature from Clarence's and were often preceded by the tour company policy that they can tell whatever anecdotes they like as long as they are true. So for that reason I have to believe that he did used to be a valet for Oprah Winfrey and I also have to believe that her valets showed their gratitude for her staff management skills by farting in her car every time they picked it up or dropped it off.

Whilst this was a good story, my favourite was one that was not a personal anecdote but an explanation of the reason why they started cementing gaps in the various bridges over the Chicago River. The bridges had always had slats on them and tourist boats had gone back and forth underneath them without any trouble until the day in August 2004 when the Dave Matthews Band came to town and their driver dumped about eight hundred pounds of liquid waste out of their tour bus just as they went over the Kinzie Street Bridge, and just as a sightseeing boat went underneath it. For Dave Matthews Band followers on that boat, this was the moment when the shit well and truly hit the fan. As expensive dumps go, the contents of the toilet take some beating. The band ended up donating fifty thousand dollars to the Friends of the Chicago River, fifty thousand dollars to the Chicago Park District, and paying two hundred thousand dollars to settle the civil lawsuit that followed. Now they probably avoid cities with bridges as much as boats in cities with bridges avoid them.

Their effluence would have floated southwards towards St Louis and the Missouri River, although this would not always have been the case. The river used to flow in a north-easterly direction, creating poor quality water for the people of Chicago. Their way of tackling this was to invest a lot of time, effort and money to get the river to flow in the other direction. Consequently Chicago's crap heads towards St Louis. Courtesy of the Busch brewery – the owners and makers of Budweiser – in St Louis, the shitty water now makes the journey back to Chicago.

On the Magnificent Mile, near to the Chicago River, we found the obligatory street performers and watched as a six foot man slowly wound his way in and out of a two foot square box. I always wonder how anyone discovers they have the ability to do this sort of thing. What was he attempting to do the first time he managed it, and at what point did he realise he could make an act out of it? Maybe he found out by accident, in which case it was appropriate that he was performing near to the Wrigley Building, home of Wrigley spearmint gum. Chewing Gum became Mr Wrigley's main product by accident. He started out selling washing powder door to door, and gave sticks of gum to people who bought from him. Realising that the gum was more popular than the washing powder, and also cheaper to make, he changed his business plan and the rest is history.

Mr Wrigley, or his gum company, were also responsible for another iconic invention – the barcode. Wrigley's was the first product to have a barcode. History does not record whether any shops had a scanner to read it with at the time.

In the evening we went to the Navy Pier. We grabbed something to eat at Capis Italian Kitchen at the entrance to the pier. The food was displayed and served in a style reminiscent of a school canteen or old English service station. It tasted of something but no one could be quite sure what.

Navy Pier is the place that really shows the diversity there is in Chicago. A smart city with shopping, financial, theatre, and ethnic districts and an unashamedly classic beach holiday style pier. The main pier is divided into an upper and lower section. The upper section has fairground rides as well as a Pepsi music stage that no one who works for Pepsi has probably ever been to. The lower section has the family pavilion, a covered shopping mall with cafes and restaurants, and an Imax 3-D theater. For the best entertainment, food and drink, however, you have to walk down the uncovered side of the lower section, past small stages where local entertainers perform and karaoke sessions take place, and on till you reach the beer garden and live bands stage, where you can sit and hear old style feel good soul and R'n'B until the late hours of the evening if not quite the early hours of the morning.

Before going there we decided to conquer the seas and take a ride on the Seadog, a speedboat complete with navigator and tour guide who barked enthusiastically to all when she welcomed us on and off the boat, a trick she no doubt first tried at an interview to show how much she got what the seadog company were all about. In the daytime the Seadogs - there are two of them - offer a relatively sedate architectural river tour through the river locks, in the evening they travel slowly out from the lakefront until they reach the point where the speed limits end and the dog begins to bark, rapidly increasing speed to fifty miles an hour, heading to the North Pier and back, and then off again in the other direction. With musical accompaniment provided by Gnarls Barkley's Crazy - what else - and jokes about the rich residents of the city and the driver, you could forget you were in a major city until you look over at the skyscrapers a short walk away from where you are bombing around on a lake.

Thirty minutes later we were back on dry land, or to be more precise, dry wood over a wet lake, and off to the end of the pier for a band and a beer before the trek back up a road, through a subway, and along another road to get back to a hotel a stones throw away from the pier.

August 12. Last night I had the strangest dream. I dreamt that I was back at work. I had been away from work for about a month, and now I was back and feeling like I had never been away and the trip had never happened. I got very pissed off with this and contemplated how it could all seem so far away just a short time after returning. Then, still in the dream, I was thinking that I couldn't even remember the flight back anymore. As I thought about this, I realised that the reason I couldn't remember the flight back was that I hadn't flown back. Then I realised that if I hadn't flown back I must still be in America. Then I realised that if I was still in America, anything that involved me being in England must be a dream. Then I woke myself up to escape from the dream. Then I was back in America and I was happy.

None of this, of course, is of any relevance to the events of August 12. The proper travelling and exploring for the day began after the dream, which is good as otherwise I would have been sleepwalking, with a visit to the John Handcock Center and the Handcock Observatory.

You can't get to the top couple of floors of the Handcock Tower as Jerry Springer owns the lease on them. His nearest neighbour is Oprah Winfrey who is owner of the upper floor of a neighbouring tower block. I can't imagine them waving to each other across the Chicago night sky somehow.

The observatory is on the floor below Jerry. It combines displays on the history of Chicago, and the emigrants who came to the city, with great views out, and the opportunity to pose for hilarious photos looking like you are outside washing windows, or suspended on a piece of scaffolding eating your sandwiches. People spend at least as long taking photos as they do reading the historic stuff.

More hilarious photo opportunities came outside the Museum of Contemporary Art on East Chicago Avenue. Not everyone sees the full comic potential of the building, one review described it as 'far from the dazzler some might have expected from a contemporary art museum,' and went on to describe it as having 'a subdued almost sombre presence.' There is some truth in this as a description of the building, but the reviewer must surely have failed to notice the sculpture of a jack-knifed car pulling a caravan just outside the entrance. This may be because it is usually obscured by the likes of myself and countless other tourists interacting with art by taking photos scratching our heads, looking puzzled and pretending to try to push one or other vehicle back down.

In between the Hancock Observatory and the Museum of Contemporary Art we took the Ethnic Chicago bus tour. The tour went through Chinatown, which in typical Chinatown style consisted of restaurants, some Chinese shops, supermarkets and a Gateway arch. The uniformity of Chinatowns the world over makes you wonder why they still get included on sightseeing tours as unique attractions. Maybe tour planners don't travel too much themselves. After Chinatown the tour headed on to Little Italy. Wherever you have a Chinatown in the States it seems you also have a Little Italy, while for no apparent reason, other than naming conventions, you never see an Italytown or a Little China.

Most of the old restaurants in Little Italy are gone. A few new Italian restaurants dot the streets, but they do so alongside new Irish Bars, and look like they've been assembled from a flat pack box with 'ACME authentic style building' written on the side. The lack of the old buildings and, perhaps more importantly, the lack of the old Italians make it hard to justify retaining the Little Italy name.

Much the same could be said about the Jewish part of town, which doesn't even have a sweet homely name to retain. The establishment and disintegration of the Jewish area is in part a tale of two mayors. Mayor Daley senior took the view that voluntarily segregated neighbourhoods gave each minority group their share of the city spoils, and building and maintaining communities would help him stay in power. Mayor Daley junior, on the other hand, places less importance on maintaining traditional communities, and more on expanding city-style living as far as possible. As a result, his investment and rebuilding programmes have led to most of the old owners of properties selling up and moving away, with the houses and restaurants they vacated being demolished and replaced by rebuilding programmes in various states of completion. There is now almost nothing in the Jewish area that indicates its Jewish ancestry unless you really know where to look.

To find a district that has kept its identity you have to head to Greek Town, which retains a strong Greek feel, even if the biggest landmark in the area is now the Harpo Studio, owned by Oprah Winfrey. While yesterday's guide was clearly not a fan of Oprah, today's respectfully referred to her as "Miss Oprah," and "a good person," although, it has to be said, she seemed to believe every body was a good person no matter what scandal they may have been associated with. She was a very spiritual person, encouraging us to pray for various people who had suffered some form of family crisis as we passed their houses. That is to say they had recently suffered a family crisis and she encouraged us to pray as we passed their houses, and not that the crisis was triggered by us passing their houses, although, if they had their windows open, hearing her recount their tales may have upset them a bit.

After the tour my quest to buy a CD by an unknown artist came to an end in Virgin records where I bought Drowaton by Starlight Mints, after an hour long search of the listening posts for new artists. From the first dozen or so CDs the best was The Pipettes who, on closer inspection, turned out to be from Brighton. Either side of them came a vast amount of impassioned hardcore emo rock that made me want to slap the lead singers and tell them to get over themselves. Against that backdrop Starlight Mints had sounded fresh and vibrant and inspiring with an album of quirky music that sounded like early 10cc transported thirty years and several thousand miles away. Believe it or not this is a compliment. Apart from the intriguing distinction of being available to order online from Tesco, the album and the band made no impression on Britain.

In the evening we headed over to the River North area. We went to Fado an Irish bar and restaurant. For ex-pat Englishmen or soccer fanatics the place is ideal. It shows every live UK and Irish soccer match it possibly can. Next door to Fado is Chicago Blue, which, as the name suggests, is a blues bar. In the early evening it opens out on to the street. This lulls you into a false sense of security as you imagine you will be able to drop by and listen to good old-fashioned blues anytime of the evening. By the time we left Fado, that illusion was shattered. There were doormen in place and doors and windows alongside them. Add to that a cover charge and a packed venue and it became inevitable that we'd chalk this one up as a place to return to. As with any place we chalked up as one to return to, it was inevitable that on the day we chose to go back it would be closed.

After we left the Rock Bottom Micro Brewery, a couple of blocks away from the hotel, we somehow managed to get lost trying to figure out what should be a simple way back. Never has getting lost been such a worthwhile experience. I don't know exactly what route we took, although I do know we would never be able to find it again. We found ourselves in an old style well-off neighbourhood with endless streets of traditional houses and a couple of small parks. A complete contrast to anything else in central Chicago, I'm guessing no one ever finds it other than by accident. If they did they would probably turn it into apartment blocks or restaurants as quick as they could say, "my, this is quaint."

Quaint as it was, we needed to get back, and our search for a place from which we could plot a route to the Magnificent Mile lead us to further discoveries, first down Delaware Street, a place we'd failed to find on a map earlier when we were trying to find a cinema, and then to where State Street meets Rush Street and the collision produces a triangle of restaurants and bars. Suddenly Sunday night was lined up. With a sense of triumph from adversity we stopped at a small late night bar near the hotel where the barmaid demandingly enquired "where's my tip?" before I could even look at the coins she'd given me and return some to her. Only the desire for another drink led to us staying there longer. Only the fear she struck into my heart when I ordered the next drink led to her getting another tip.

August 13. Another lazy Sunday, much of it spent on the beach. As with Navy Pier, the beach adds another dimension to Chicago and on a Sunday it should to be the place to be, but in spite of relaxing sunbathers and energetic skaters, roller bladers and joggers, it doesn't get overcrowded, so maybe it isn't. A stroll along the beach was about as energetic as Sunday daytime got. Perfect.

In the evening, as planned, we went down Delaware Street and back to the cinema. American city centre cinemas, much like English ones, are a dying breed. The only rarer breed of cinema are ones that have not one but two films that could be classed as non-blockbuster. This cinema was both, which probably explains why it had been hard to find. The choice of films were The Night Listener, one of the few recent Robin Williams films where he doesn't play a wacky larger than life relentlessly optimistic American which a cheesy smile, and Woody Allen's Scoop, the second of his three English movies and part financed by that most English of institutions, the BBC. We plumped for The Night Listener, figuring that a low budget movie with Robin Williams was unlikely to ever make UK cinemas, whereas a Woody Allen film made in England and backed by the state owned TV Company was bound to get a release. When we returned to the UK The Night Listener was just finishing at the cinemas. A few months later it was announced that no one had took on UK distribution for Scoop and it was unlikely it would ever be shown in England.

After the movie we had a meal at Tavern on Rush, a place we'd booked earlier after they'd told us they could squeeze us into a table. In spite of, or maybe because of, it being pricey the Tavern was a disappointment. It was the sort of place where people without much to shout about go out for the night and shout about it. Tonight the shouting was provided by a group of Australian businessmen trying and failing to impress the waitress by extolling the virtues of the leader of their group. From the conversation, if conversation is a suitable description for loud excessive bollocks talked by pissed blokes, we'd have guessed the man had to be some kind of famous superstar, perhaps Russell Crowe, a man whose name usually springs to mind alongside the words loud, pissed and Australian. When we turned around however we found nothing more than a short squat bald man of indeterminate age who looked like a bathroom salesman. Good to see you don't have to be famous or gorgeous to be hero worshipped by your friends. Sad to see that being a drunken loud idiot in a group of drunken loud idiots does seem to be a pre-requisite.

As for the food in Tavern on Rush, like the customers, it was loud with nothing much to say. Liz got a Feta Cheese Salad that lacked several key ingredients, the most notable of which was Feta Cheese. I had something only slightly more impressive, which without any ingredients missing had nothing else to remember it by.

Last stop for the evening was a small bar where we found a small table, and were then asked whether other spaces around the table were free. Shortly after confirming they were, we were joined by the entourage of a hip hop act playing a few dates in the city. I say joined, but surrounded would be a better phrase. There would have been too many of them for a large table, even without us sat on the end of it. The number of people was only outweighed by the volume of food, as they went through the bars fantastic looking late night menu – a menu that made us wish that Tavern on Rush hadn't managed to squeeze us in after all. Before the temptation to steal their food got too strong we left and went back to the hotel.

August 14. Last day in Chicago. Last day of breakfast at one of the many Corner Bakery's – a chain of cafes all cited on corners, that will presumably continue to expand until there are no more corners left – and last day of having to contend with the most frightening set of car users anywhere. In Chicago, it seems walking is for tourists, and Chicago drivers don't like tourists.

To round off our stay we headed down to The Art Institute of Chicago. If the Museum of Contemporary Art is the jumpy upstart, then the Art Institute is the fine upstanding father. Outside the Art Institute there is nothing as modern or wacky as a sculpture of an upturned car and caravan, instead there are two distinctive bronze lions which draw in the tourists who, being told it brings you luck if you touch their tails, touch their tails and take photos doing so.

Inside, there are three linked buildings and exhibitions from pretty much every period and continent imaginable. The great thing about the exhibitions are the quality of the collections, even the Renaissance paintings are worth looking at irrespective of how many old masters you've seen before. The furniture exhibitions are less self indulgent and far more interesting than the names suggest, and every gallery draws you in. All of this comes at a mere seven dollars, except on Tuesday's when it's free. For all these reasons and more, it's a must see place.

After the Art Institute, we moved on to The Loop. The Loop is part of Chicago's downtown area. It gets its name from the elevated subway system that runs round it before spreading out to the outlying areas of the city. It is home to the city's commercial, Governmental and cultural buildings, which means it's only worth a visit in the daytime when the workers are there. Luckily for us it was the daytime. On a Saturday you can get a free Loop tour train taking in the areas main sights. Unluckily for us it was a Monday. We didn't fancy our chances of randomly picking a train and finding it was going round the loop, and not heading for the outskirts of nowhere, so we walked round the area before heading back to Millennium Park for the rest of the afternoon.

In the evening we returned to River North for a good, and incredibly large Argentinean meal at Su Casa, and for our second attempt at going to Chicago Blue, which resulted in our second visit to Fado when we found out it was closed. And with that our stay in Chicago came to an end. Chicago was a place I could easily imagine returning to live and work. Friendlier and more relaxed than New York, but still a big city with a thriving and lively centre. It was the last place we'd have a chance to say that about for some time.

Part 3

Route 66 and beyond

13 - Springfield

August 15. When we first realised we would have to scale back on our ambitions of seeing the whole of the States we decided to travel Route 66. We planned to start at the beginning and finish at the end, and for that to be the whole journey. This came from a belief that Route 66 is the Mother Road and takes you from east to west, so it must be the road to travel if you want to see all the country has to offer. It turned out, on closer inspection, that Route 66 only starts in the east if by east you mean somewhere inland about seven-hundred miles from the nearest point on the east coast, and that much of America is not merely not on Route 66 but also nowhere near it. The birthplace of the nation is not on Route 66, the birthplace of Elvis is not on Route 66. The home of the president is way off to the east of the road, the home of Country and Western music is way off to the south. Any journey round America that missed all of these as well as the likes of New York, Boston, San Francisco, and Dallas would not really be the journey we wanted to make.

Not that Route 66 is full of dull places, but for each great place there are also endless empty miles of roads dotted only with run down old towns with no known claims to fame and no one left to tell you their unknown claims. Consequently our plans changed and it was only now, more than a month in to the trip, that we were heading on to Route 66. Well, sort of on to it, as another thing we didn't realise was that it doesn't actually exist anymore, at least not officially.

I doubt we are the only people who have gone to America expecting it still to be intact. Surely a road that was immortalised in song and rooted in American culture would be treated as a living landmark, as much, if not more, of a draw for tourists than the places it passes through. Think again. Route 66 was gradually bypassed or swallowed up by Interstates and State Highways, and was officially decommissioned in 1984. By the time of the '1993 Collins Road Atlas: USA Canada and Mexico' the only references to it were a few thin lines, several states apart, with the number 66 appearing above them.

We knew where the original road started, and had taken a photo of it the day before to mark the start of the journey, but we didn't know where it went next. Rather than heading round the back streets of Chicago looking for it, we took Interstate 55 in the general direction of the old road. The traffic was heavy and slow moving. Not far out of the city we became aware of a two lane highway running parallel to us. This was Route 66 and it was having the last laugh on the Interstate. While we crawled along the crowded six lane super highway, traffic on the practically deserted neighbouring road zipped past unawares.

After a short distance in miles, but a long distance in time, we saw a sign for an original Route 66 diner. We didn't need any further encouragement. We left the Interstate and joined the Mother Road.

The diner was outside the small town of Dwight. It welcomed the world-weary modern day traveller with old-fashioned signs and an old fashioned gas station with old-fashioned pumps. It gave us a first glimpse at what travelling must have been like before the rise of the motel chains and roadside Macdonald's. Even though it was not long since breakfast I couldn't pass up the chance of having something to eat and drink. A part of me was expecting to find that the joys of the old road and the old diners were something eulogised only by those who had never been there, but this wasn't the case. I had a burger that tasted as if it was prepared on the premises by someone who wanted to make sure their customers were set up for a long journey, rather than prepared somewhere else by someone who didn't know how to drive or where the food would be eaten. I may be exaggerating slightly, but it was good quality basic food in a good quality basic diner. It tasted like nostalgia, whilst still being within its sell by date.

Leaving the diner we crossed the road to look at a map of the local area. Unlike the national road planners, the Illinois Route 66 Heritage Project has been active in preserving what is left of the four-hundred miles of road that run through the state, keeping alive towns and villages that may otherwise have long since ceased to be. The map told us exactly where Route 66 ran, and from then on were helped on our way by signs proclaiming 'Historic Route 66.'

Every time we approached anything resembling a major junction another 'Historic Route 66' sign appeared, guiding us on through places such as Dwight, Odell and Pontiac, all offering a glimpse of small town America that seems almost apocryphal nowadays. The towns usually consisted of a gas station, a diner and some small locally run shops with streets spinning off around them. The Interstate was never too far away, often running parallel to it and occasionally subsuming it, before letting it veer off towards places such as Normal - a town for people who don't want to stand out – and Shirley and Maclean, neighbouring towns with which the actress of the same name has no connection whatsoever.

Although there was nothing in any of these towns that made us want to stop and have a long look at, it was still fascinating to see places that were so close to, and yet so far away from, Chicago. You wouldn't get this on a drive along the Interstate where towns are nothing more than words on signs alongside billboards telling you which garages and chain motels are at the next exit. Most Americans have probably forgotten there is a world off the interstate, which may explain why we were given directions back to the I-55 when we reached Springfield and asked a passer by for directions to the nearest hotel. Helpful as he was, he could not understand our disappointment that there might not be anywhere to stay where you can go out at night without a car, and eat at restaurants that don't seat eighty and have branches at most major junctions.

We parked in the car park of the tourist information centre, already closed even though it was only five o'clock, and decided to head off on foot to the town centre. As if laughing at our naivety, our passer by gave us directions to the main streets and told us we might find a hotel but we shouldn't hold out too much hope.

Just when it was starting to seem like he had a point, we spotted a large Hilton type H on a distant building. The H for Hilton is as distinctive as the M for Macdonald's to a tourist. Hardly a small town American hotel, but better than nothing if it was in the centre. We headed towards it, as if guided by a beacon, and just over the road from it saw the 'President Abraham Lincoln Hotel and Conference Centre.'

Why any hotel anywhere in America would think they had to add 'President' to the name in order for people to realise which Abraham Lincoln they referred to is beyond me. In Springfield it was an even bigger mystery. The town is a shrine to the man. With minimal effort it could be officially designated as a Lincoln theme park, such is his dominance over the cultural and tourist attractions in town.

The reason why he is celebrated so much is that Springfield is where

Lincoln lived, practised law and sat in the House of Representatives. Astonishingly enough, for a place so small, Springfield is also the State capital of Illinois. This would be unusual in the UK, but in the US it is fairly common for the biggest city not to be the state capital, just as Washington is the capital of the whole place in spite of having a population that would fit several times over in New York.

Contrary to what the name may suggest, the President Abraham Lincoln Hotel and Conference Centre, is not a big hotel. The small town feel of the hotel is in keeping with the small town feel of the city. The centre has four hotels, a few small independently owned shops, and some restaurants and bars dotted around the main square and the roads coming off it. You can walk around the city without ever having to worry about getting lost and ending up miles away from your hotel in an area you'd rather avoid.

It isn't just the size that gives Springfield a small town feel. There are the little touches such as the way the shops all open up at about half eight or nine in the morning and close by half past five in the afternoon. Ten o'clock starts and late night openings have no place in Springfield culture apart from a couple of nightclubs which open at eleven, after the bars close, and shut at three in the morning. Even this adds to the old fashioned feel, restoring a long forgotten distinction between the hours and functions of pubs and nightclubs.

Our evening started in the hotel bar, the Globe Tavern, where a fairly distinguished looking man insisted on buying our drinks after hearing our accents. He told us that several years previously he had been in Gloucester, and the locals had shown such kind and good hospitality to him and his wife that he had always said he would repay them by buying drinks for any British tourists he saw in his home town. We had provided the first opportunity for him to make good on that promise, so overseas visitors were clearly a rarity.

After the drink we went out to discover Springfield and to get something to eat. Robbies looked like it could be good, but a sign outside said 'sorry, closed early - gone to races', so we stopped at Maldaners on the corner of Monroe and 6th where it was still warm enough to sit outside and watch a ghost tour pass the bottom of the road telling tales of Lincoln related hauntings. The food was excellent with real care taken in the preparation of it. Maybe it's because it's a state capital, but Maldaners proved that there is still a market for great restaurants to flourish in small cities. After the meal we headed into a couple of bars and shook hands with a Democrat candidate canvassing in the streets ahead of the forthcoming elections. He stayed chatting to us even after he found out we couldn't vote for him in this, or any, election. He would have got my vote if I'd had one to give.

At the end of the evening we returned to the hotel passing Robbie's along the way. It was still closed, but the site of a disconsolate figure sat at a far table with his head in his hands indicated that Robbie had not had a good night at the races, and would not be able to close for business on another night.

August 16. There is a lot to see and do in a day in Springfield, as long as you want to see and do things to do with Abraham Lincoln. There is the Old State Capital building, Lincoln's old offices, Lincoln's old home and other bits of Lincoln memorabilia at every turn. If you don't want to see things to do with Lincoln, there is the Dana-Thomas House, and that's about it. Designed by Frank Lloyd Wright in 1902, it is classed as the most luxurious, best preserved and most fully furnished of his houses. Whether it lives up to this epithet I can't say. As someone who doesn't know who Frank Lloyd Wright was, and doesn't have a great enthusiasm for turn of the century houses, it wasn't much of a draw in comparison with places associated with a great historical figure.

Springfield was not Lincoln's hometown, he moved to it in his twenties to practice law. The main law office where he worked, and where he wrote his first inaugural speech, was the starting point for our Lincoln pilgrimage.

The exterior of the offices is original, but the interiors aren't which means the items in there are 'from the period' only. Some of the furniture may have been there in Lincoln's day, but you wouldn't really put your money on it. The case notes, and other bits of Lincoln's writing, are genuine, however, and the guided tour was worth doing as much for the insight into Lincoln himself as for the hard history it contained. Our guide told us that Lincoln suffered greatly from melancholy and was prone to severe depression. The treatment he received for this included potions with Mercury - the use of which was believed to turn men with hats mad - and opium. One emerging theory about Lincoln is that his genius derived in part from this drug taking. His delivery of great oratory, in spite of having little or nothing in the way of notes, and with frequent departures from what pre-scripted parts he did have, supports this potentially controversial theory. External evidence of rock stars producing their best work when stoned, and bland AOR when they go straight, provides extra support.

After the Law Offices we went on a tour round the Old State Capitol. The tour was divided into two parts - the courts and the state offices. In the courts we got a knowledgeable guide and a detailed history of the 19th century justice system and Lincoln's time there. In the state offices we got a guide who had just arrived for the day, knew very little and mumbled into a carpet.

From there we left Lincoln behind for a while and went to the New State House. The continued use of new in its title can only be because the Old State House continues to exist, seeing as how it's been the seat of Government for almost 140 years now. Even New Labour took less time to shed the new tag. The New State House is larger than the Old State House, the need for a bigger building being the reason it was built. There was a tour going round, but not wanting to do another guided tour for fear of mumbling guides and State House overdose, we decided to do a quick self-guided walk instead. We headed upstairs and were walking past the Governor's Office before a tour guide spotted us and told us we could only be there if we joined her tour. We joined the tour, went past the Governor's Office, then sloped off and wondered down another corridor and some stairs where we probably weren't meant to be on our own. It seems that national security is not as strongly protected in the Illinois seat of Government as it is in Washington.

After lunch at Robbies, where a large number of customers were covering his racing losses, we went back to Lincoln land with a trip to the only house he ever owned. The house has stood continuously, it is not a reconstruction, and it also retains some of the original furniture. More impressively the interior has been restored to exactly how it was in Lincoln's day with other antique or replica furniture added where the original no longer exists. They have done this by using three drawings from a feature on 'our new president and his home' that ran in an 1861 edition of Frank Leslies Illustrated Newspaper, proof that Hello magazine is not an original concept.

Realising that we were standing where one of the greatest ever presidents lived gave me a real feeling of standing on a piece of history. More than the law offices or the state capital, the house gives you a feeling of what life was like for Lincoln. It opened up my interest in the rest of his life and what it could have been if he'd lived. On the day he left for Washington his parting words to Billy Herndon, his partner at the law offices were allegedly "If I come back we'll start up again like I've never been away." The use of if rather than when is seen by some as meaning he was anticipating the possibility of his assassination, but equally could mean he was imagining some other potential future or a long run as president. The saddest part of the statement is that no one ever got to find out what he meant.

As for Mary Todd Lincoln, after living the happy life of a socialite in Springfield the move to Washington saw the second of her children die, her husband assassinated and her own mental health slowly disintegrate. The death of a third child aided her decline and the one surviving child, Robert, got her sectioned, leaving her to die pretty much alone and insane. Being married to a key figure in a nations development ought to be some kind of guarantee for a fulfilling and good life, but you can't help feel she would have come to a better end if she had married someone less ambitious.

But enough of Lincoln and depression. After all America is the land of hope, optimism and freedom, and what better symbol of these is there than the State Fair. State Fairs are traditional in most, if not all, American states. The Illinois fair runs for ten days and was in its 154th year. It began as a showcase of Illinois agriculture and has slowly turned into a summer festival with a full range of entertainment and a long list of corporate sponsors. The agricultural theme, however, remains, and while Foreigner and Blood Sweat and Tears headlined the grandstand stage on veterans day, the Sale of Champions and the auctioning of the Land of Lincoln grand champion steer were equally likely to get the crowds.

Between the two extremes there are fairground rides and entertainers. We stopped at the Happy Hollow to catch one of three appearances of Peers Mutville's Comix Dog Show. Peers looked like the classic seventies children's entertainer, with big comic hair and large trousers held up by braces. He had about half a dozen performing dogs in his show, and carefully cultivated his animal friendly image until it was shattered by a St Bernard who only had a couple of stunts to perform and, understandably given that he's a dog, tried to build up his part by joining in other tricks, much to the annoyance of Peers who tried and failed to look as if he found this endearing. Unsure about the ethics of the show and the credentials of the dog-meister himself we didn't tip at the end.

After that I contributed to a major piece of University research, which may sound unlikely at a State Fair, but if I add that the research took place somewhere at the back of the ethnic food area - which included Ireland and Australia but not England or Scotland - it may start to make sense. The University of Illinois were carrying out the 'Roadside Conversations' project as part of the celebration of 50 years of the Interstate. I should have objected to this as a Route 66 traveller but I didn't, mainly as it was the Route 66 posters outside the tent that led me to it, suggesting the researchers weren't too sure what they were celebrating either.

The project consisted of a van, driven through the state and other parts of Interstate 80, rigged up with recording equipment to film people's recollections of journeys on the highway system. Passers by were invited to record a story with the aim of building up a shared journey that turned personal recollections into a collective public record. Needless to say the chance to get my own small piece of immortality somewhere on a website was too much to resist. Sadly, as usually happens at such times, I was unable to think of anything even remotely interesting to say.

As the camera started rolling, or, to be more precise, the digitial recording button was pressed, I began to talk. My contribution was a vague and painful description of how we were travelling around America and where we were going. There was no evocative description of the beauty of the open road, or the feeling of complete freedom you can get from driving along it, just some mumbling in an English Midlands accent either side of a whole host of cheerful sounding optimistic Americans. On the positive side, one year later the website set up to host this permanent history of American travel, and my small part in it, was no longer available. So much for immortality.

After a visit to the Harness Racing event, where instead of having a skinny rider on their back, horses got a not so skinny rider trailing behind them in a harness, we left the fair, missing attractions such as the Milk a Cow Tent, the Alpine Goat Show, and the Piglets on Parate Birthing Centre, which means I still have no idea what Parate is.

Back at the hotel, a large number of police cars were around the entrance to the car park. They were here from all across the state to help police the fair. The risk of the Land of Lincoln Grand Champion Steer being the subject of a kidnap attempt clearly called for a large police presence. Agriculture is big business here. At the reception a man booking a room explained he couldn't confirm whether he would extend his stay by a day or two, as his wife was expecting a calf. I assumed there was also a cow involved in this somewhere, and hoped Illinois people weren't so keen on agriculture for there not to be.

In the evening we took the ghost tour, which wasn't really a ghost tour in the traditional sense of the phrase. There were no people robbing graves or killing people for body parts, and, as you may have guessed, most of the tour centred around Lincoln who apparently can haunt bits of Springfield - watch out for footsteps behind you if you go near his house at night - at the same time as he re-appears in the White House where he either comforts or worries new presidents, depending on how they take to a long dead president trying to help them.

Ghost tour over, we went for a meal at Augie's Front Burner on 5th Street. Less imaginative in menu than Mallanders but still an excellent meal and a place that seemed to be frequented by people who worked in the State Senate offices and delighted in repeating overheard tales of scandal in the Government. If I had heard of any of the people they were talking about I would have been even more fascinated than I was.

After the meal we went to a couple of nearby pubs where local bands showed why they would never be national bands and girlfriends competed with pinball machines for their boyfriend's attention. It felt like anytown anywhere, which, in a place where the presence of one of the two best known presidents is everywhere, is no mean achievement. We went back to the hotel and the stay in Springfield was almost at an end. Two days here and not one mention of Homer Simpson. D'oh.

August 17. Crammed in a trip to Recycled Records before leaving the hotel. Recycled Records is possibly the best second hand record shop ever, and a real find for anyone who still collects LP's from the fifties onwards. Taking the 'Stairway to Heaven' at the back of the store I entered into a vinyl wonderland where the fastidiousness and attention to detail of the most expensive specialist shop was combined with the 'we stock anything' selection policy of the average charity stall. With credibility being no barrier to inclusion, music, films, stage shows and comedies of all descriptions were in stock, but were displayed within categories and in alphabetical order with no chance of that obscure blues album being next to the obligatory copies of Leo Sayer's Endless Flight and Dean Friedman's Well Well said the Rocking Chair.

Assorted albums grabbed my attention, but a fear of records getting broken on journeys in and out of cars and planes prevented me spending anything.

I did get a copy of The Sangamon Star a pisstake of a local free paper for Sangamon County, which was actually amusing rather than the collection of self-reverential in-jokes that such papers usually are. Thirteen editions of the Sangamon Star were published between 2005 and February 2007 when it became an on-line only publication, a move that did not seem to meet with a great deal of success. The website was disabled later that year, and all traces of the paper had gone - there's one in the eye for anyone who believes the growth of the internet makes the decline of traditional newspapers inevitable.

Back in the concourse at the President Lincoln, a smart looking woman was having a non too smart phone conversation to AT and T, one of the big cell phone providers, berating them for the failure of their services and for what she had to do to get them to correct it. The woman on the other end of the line was taking the tirade well, but audibly explaining why she couldn't do anything other than the procedure she'd outlined. The volume of her voice seemed more like a response to the volume at the other end rather than a sign of aggression, but finally she cracked and responded to the threat of changing service provider, with the words "Lady, I couldn't give a rats ass if you stay with AT and T." This sounded out across the concourse as the call came to an abrupt end and the smart looking woman probably started to wish the call centre was based in another country where being rude to a customer was an unknown concept.

14 – St Louis

We packed our bags and headed for St Louis, stopping for a late breakfast at the Cozy Dog Drive In on 6th Street. The Cozy Dog Drive In has been a landmark on Route 66 since 1949. It is known as the place where the corn dog was born, and neither the fact that the corn dog is basically sausage in batter on a stick, or that it was actually invented in Amarillo in 1945 by Ed Waldmire, the old owner of the Cozy Dog, are allowed to get in the way of this.

On our way to St Louis we passed through more places that the Interstate had bypassed more than two decades before.

One such place was Farmersville where the bright old 1930s sign still stood, proudly proclaiming 'Farmersville, a great place to live and raise a family.' The paucity of houses in the town, and the 2000 census showing a population of 768, suggested that the marketing of the town hadn't really worked. Further along from Farmersville was a reminder of the importance of religion in small American towns with a sign on the roadside consisting of the word Jesus in big letters set against a bright striped background. With no churches or housing nearby it was anyone's guess who or what, other than Jesus himself, the sign was promoting, or who it was promoting it to.

A short way past this sign another misconception about Route 66 was shattered. As well as assuming the road would officially exist, I also imagined that its route would never have changed. Wrong again. Even before the Interstate arrived Route 66 had changed several times to meet changing demands as new areas and industries developed, and others declined, their demise often accelerated by the re-routing of the road. In Illinois there are stretches of road that were part of the route from 1926-1930, from 1930-1940, from 1940-1977 when Interstate 55 arrived, or from some or all of these periods. All Route 66 eras are marked on the guide maps and there are signposts along the way that will take you on to anything that was ever part of the road. In general, the longer the road remained part of Route 66 the straighter it is and the more closely it aligns with Interstate 55, while, at the opposite end of the scale, the earlier it ceased to be part of Route 66 the more likely it is to turn into a dirt track and come to an abrupt end in a field with no signs of life around it. This is great for the road enthusiast with no particular place to go and a motorbike to go there, but not so good for the person with a Ford Fusion and a desire to get to St Louis in the shortest time possible.

The appeal of travelling down a legendary road can soon disappear when you find yourself somewhere with no signs to towns, and no towns without signs. With some way to go before the Illinois state line, we headed on to what was probably part of the 1930-1940 stretch of road and drove through a country road with hills and forests and little else, including road signs. Eventually we drove into the small town of Worden - population 897. We passed a few shops and pulled off into a street of fairly nice semi-detached houses, where we saw a scene that should only exist in old films.

A police car was parked on the roadside and the policeman was talking to a young boy and his father as they stood on the street outside their house. Next to the child a small sign advertised home made lemonade. Rather than arresting them for trading without a licence, the policeman chatted happily in the bright sunshine before buying a bottle for himself. Jimmy Stewart would have come over all emotional had he been alive to see this. I felt confident and happy to approach them and ask for directions to St Louis, certain that no one would ask to see my licence, search my car, or do anything else that did not have the express aim of helping a weary traveller.

I asked the way to St Louis, pronouncing it St Louie, on the basis of the song. The policeman looked at me in a kindly way, as if I was a misguided tourist guessing at pronunciations, before telling me the way to St Louis with a non-silent S at the end. I thanked him kindly and, in my desire to get back in the car before I forgot the directions, forgot to buy a bottle of lemonade.

The directions led us back to where Interstate 55 and later day Route 66 became one. As we approached St Louis the array of versions of Route 66 seemed to grow exponentially. Looking at a map trying to work out which one to take was like trying to follow one of those maze puzzles on the back of cereal boxes asking whether Snap, Crackle or

Pop's route gets you to the centre. It didn't helped that sometime in the sixties Route 66 bypassed St Louis. It also didn't help that, while Illinois is very good at promoting its own bits of Route 66, its maps offer not the slightest hint of where any version of the road goes once it crosses the state line for Missouri. This says a lot about Illinois' attitude towards its neighbouring state.

We picked a route into the city that was only slightly longer than the ideal route, taking in a nice but brief bit of scenery as we crossed the state border, and made our way to the Omni St Louis. The concierge offered to park the car. We accepted expecting to see him drive the car into a multi storey car park with small lanes and hairpin turns at each level. We went up to our room and looked out to see the car parked in an open air car park next door to the hotel. I decided I should investigate further before I hand over keys and six dollars in future.

Incurring more unnecessary, if not extravagant, expenditure I checked a bag of socks and underwear in for dry cleaning on the grounds that my supplies were running low, my wash bag was getting bigger, and unlike Liz I could not muster the required enthusiasm or stoicism required for hand washing. After this we headed into the hotel bar where the bartender gave us coffee and a diet coke for free for no other reason than we were his only customers. I was starting to feel a sense of unease about St Louis in general, and our decision to book two nights here in particular. We'd made the decision off the back of a leaflet which made it sound like a fairly sizeable city with lots to see. Looking back on it, the leaflet may be one of the few examples of good marketing there is in St Louis.

We went into the city for a brief bit of sightseeing, heading to the Gateway Arch, a six-hundred and thirty-foot high reinforced steel arch that looks like it is waiting to be sprayed gold and have another arch added to it so that the worlds largest Macdonald's can be built underneath it. It was erected in 1965 as a monument to St Louis' role as the gateway to the American West. Even the least geographically astute will realise that America could not have realised how far west it would spread if it once thought St Louis was the gateway to it.

The arch was the main sight we saw on the leaflets advertising the city. We had thought this was because it was an incredibly impressive structure, but it turns out that there is another equally valid reason, which is that there are precious few other sights in St Louis. The building of the arch was meant to signal the start of the city's renaissance. Buildings in the area around it were cleared so that it could dominate the skyline. The end result, with the arch isolated from the rest of the city, seems somehow symbolic of how misplaced the hope of a renaissance was.

The run down nature of the city became more apparent later in the evening when we headed downtown to the area around the recently opened Busch baseball stadium. The concierge at the Omni who, like all of the staff there, was incredibly helpful and knowledgeable about the city, recommended the area if we wanted good Southern or Mexican food and some good music. Both of these sounded like good ideas, so we went with his suggestion. He even offered to get his driver to run us down to it. We declined, in favour of that forgotten American past time of walking, but as it turned out, the offer was probably less out of a belief that no one wanted to walk, and more out of a knowledge of what the walk would entail.

After a few large roads with scattered bars and restaurants we drifted into streets full of empty office blocks with no signs of life, and ended up walking past deserted parking lots and empty streets which the average tourist would think twice about passing alone. Finally we reached a small stretch of three bars just past the stadium. Had there been a game that evening the streets may have been fuller, but as it was the bars seemed like they lived on in proud defiance of the destruction of much else around them, illustrating a lot that is positive about the spirit of the people, and a lot that is negative about the fortunes of the city of St Louis.

Much the same could be said about the first bar we went into. Later that night they were due to have a band on, but as we sat outside in the hot evening sun, eating Jambalaya and drinking beer, the entertainment was provided by a drunk guy who'd fallen over and hit his head while someone tried to prevent him getting in.

We headed off to the bar on the other side of the road, probably only about two minutes walk away, but still long enough for us to be approached by an alleged war veteran who started a very amiable conversation about the cost of hotdogs at baseball games and how he'd got a free ticket for tonight's game, a tale not hindered by the fact that there wasn't one. He went on to ask us where we were from and tell us how much he loved the UK, a line not hindered by the fact he had probably never been to the UK, before telling us he was a vet and down on his luck, and asking if we had any change to spare. He may or may not have been telling the truth about this.

After that, and still before we had managed to get across the road, an extremely drunk woman came out of the bar ahead, declaring that she was glad it had been closed down, even though it was clearly still open. In a busier city all of this may have seemed part and parcel of a normal night out, but here it seemed to be part and parcel of a run down city, albeit one that was trying to get back up again.

When we finally made it over the road we entered a bar that had relocated en masse to its garden and had music on. The headline act was a lady called Kim Massey. Her band played a couple of songs before Kim entered the stage. She was an old style R'n'B singer in every sense of the word, more than several stone overweight and in her late forties at least, she sat on a chair and controlled everything as only a large old R'n'B singer can. Her band revered her as if they were playing for a legend, which they probably were. Her set was a mixture of good original material and standards that sounded like they came a bit too easy, and hence were delivered without much conviction. Thankfully there was more good stuff than standards and we stayed for most of the set before taking the lonely walk back to the hotel where the empty bar made it all too easy to pass on a nightcap.

August 18. After a late breakfast we went back to the Gateway Arch. The main draw of the arch as a tourist attraction is the chance to ride to the top of it. To do this you take the shuttle that runs up one side of the giant metal frame and down the other. In between the up and down part is a short walk along the centre of the arch, from where you can look out over not very much from a very great height.

We got tickets for the shuttle and stood in the queue. The shuttle pulled in and the protective shutters in front of it lifted. At that point we got to see the inside of the vehicle that would take us up some three-hundred or more feet and realised that this was not a traditional airport shuttle ride. The shuttle consisted of several small pods, about three feet high and five feet wide, but still intended for five people. There were no views out of it on either side. Liz immediately decided she could not face going in it. I had my doubts, but the opportunity to see something from a great height got the better of me, and I joined a pod with three girls, one of whom declared she was claustrophobic immediately as the pod door closed. Luckily we were at the top before the realisation that she was in a place far smaller, and more closed, than anything she had described a fear of could sink in.

At the top of the arch I looked through the small windows on either side, taking in the view and looking for photo opportunities. On one side of the river the baseball stadium was an obvious one, and there was also the St Louis skyline, which revealed that the dozen or so skyscrapers in promotional material were the sum total of tall buildings, rather than a representative sample. Looking out across the river to East St Louis, however, there was nothing to spoil a long shot across the landscape and nothing in the landscape worth taking a long shot of.

Nixon and Kennedy visited East St Louis during presidential campaigns and talked about how the population would top a hundred-thousand in ten years. The reality was that a decline set in, population slumped and the decline has continued ever since. I doubt the people of St Louis care too much as East St Louis is in Illinois and Illinois prevented St Louis maintaining its early economic dominance by preventing any bridges being built to link the two states until their own transport infrastructure was in place. By this time the strategic significance of St Louis for goods transit had been lost forever. Add the diverting of dirty water from Chicago to St Louis and you get the feeling that Illinois is not the nicest of neighbours you could have.

Back at the bottom of the arch I found Liz and we looked round shops, museums and displays about the arch, the history of St Louis and the westward expansion of America. There was also a lot of fascinating and honest environmental information on display, provided by a Parks Agency who clearly took a different view on environmental issues than the administration of the day did. The displays were excellent and well worth a visit, although I wouldn't recommend going to St Louis just to see them.

After the arch we headed to the river. The riverfront is a missed opportunity. While you can walk down to it and get a boat tour, there are no restaurants, no bars and no shops. The area hasn't been developed beyond the boat trip offices, and the large and obvious market created by people visiting the arch remains bafflingly uncatered for.

We went for a sightseeing boat tour on the Tom Sawyer. The tour was carefully and thoughtfully planned, with the aim of overcoming the obvious limiting factor that there were not many sights to see. The narrative was more about what there once was than what there is now,

122

with the building of the city, French occupation of Louisville and the sale of land to America via Spain amongst the main topics. To provide light amusement and distraction, they also sounded the ships horn at full volume to scare away pigeons under one of the bridges, as they showed us parts of the derelict riverside for a second time.

Walking round the rest of the city we saw more tourist and sight-seeing opportunities that had gone missing. First off there was the Old Courthouse where Dred Scott asked for freedom for himself and his wife Harriott. The trial that began here concluded with a final decision by the Supreme Court of Missouri which rendered the Missouri compromise between pro-slavery and anti-slavery factions worthless. It was a pivotal point in the events that led up to the American Civil War. The decisions on Scott's status as a citizen in any state, his entitlement to protection in law, and the relationship between the constitution and state law still resonate today with parallels drawn between this case and the Roe v Wade case in 1973 that overturned many state and federal laws restricting abortion. This building should have a key place in American history, and yet in spite of this, unless you go inside the Courthouse to see the excellent display and the original courtroom where the case was held, you would be hard pressed to find anything telling you what happened there.

Similarly, outside of a small plaque in front of the newspaper offices where he worked, there is nothing to commemorate the fact that Mark Twain lived in the city and drew inspiration from it for his writing. Surely this was worth a museum or two? If this had been Springfield, half the city would be a tribute to Twain by now.

Added to the failure to make the most of what it has historically, St Louis was also the first city we'd seen where the effect of big-box out of town developments was apparent for all to see.

In her book 'Big-Box Swindle' Stacy Mitchell wrote that 'the wreckage of this predatory model is everywhere on the landscape,' 'countless empty store fronts downtown, more than 100 dark (shopping) malls that are sitting completely vacant, and thousands of empty strip shopping centres.' Mitchell could have been in St Louis when she wrote this.

For the most part the city was deserted and lifeless, the out of town malls sucking the life out of the centre. The largest number of people we saw were beggars and alleged war veterans. The city centre shopping mall was practically closed down. Low end food shops and clothes stores with permanent sales were all that weren't boarded up or awaiting something else to move in. The largest department store 'The Famous Barr Shop' was also closing down. Racks of clothes were empty with no more sale stock to go on them. We couldn't even get a drink, as the staff in the coffee shop didn't have a kettle or the keys to the fridge.

We walked down to Lascelles Landing, a small restaurant area further along the river that was developed in 1977. It had some good restaurants, bars and a comedy club. It looked like a lively area, but again it was isolated within the city, rather than coming off some busy shopping or business street.

Back at the hotel. I tried to collect my dry cleaning. Twenty-four hour service was promised, but by eight they were not back and the hotel manager informed me he couldn't contact the company that took them as they only worked Monday to Friday. I asked if they had an emergency contact number. He replied that they didn't, as they'd never had any emergencies to speak of. I felt both proud and pissed off to be the first. He told me if I could give him an address where we would be three days hence, he would send them to me once he got them back. Working out when we were likely to have a definite address at least three days hence, I calculated that my socks and pants would be hanging around for about five weeks before an emotional reunion in Los Angeles. I was no longer sure that dry cleaning had been a good idea after all.

Thankfully when we got back from Mosaic, a fusion restaurant near the hotel, where the food was excellent but there was nowhere nearby to go afterwards, I found I had been reunited with clean undergarments after the driver found them in his van when he was locking it up for the night. I could relax and have a drink in the bar, where we were still the only customers but no longer getting stuff for free.

And that was St Louis. A city that gets shit fed into its river; that had a monument erected to celebrate its place in American history at roughly the same time as it got bypassed by America's national road; and which got its name checked in a song but only after they changed the pronunciation to make it fit with the rest of the lyrics. The hotel magazine on the city said that downtown was declared all but dead nine years ago, but more than 3.3 billion dollars had been invested in it since 2000. It was hard to see too much evidence of this, although there were some signs of redevelopment, and more importantly there seemed to be a spirit of hope and determination, along with a friendliness borne of years of being ground down, amongst the people we met. The barman told me he was moving back to the city, which could have been a sign that the regeneration was starting, but his move from the suburbs was due in part to his dog dying, which put a different slant on it.

Because of the people, I want to believe that city is on the way back up, even if it is hard to do. I don't regret going there, even though two days was probably one too many, and I'd like to come back in ten years time and find a city I barely recognise, full of people and with a sense of fulfilled optimism. Stranger things can happen, I'm just not sure what they would be.

15 - Nashville

August 19. In the first days of driving with the radio on we heard a song called Last Kiss. To a sixties rock/country style tune it told the story of a guy who took his girlfriend out on a date, lost control of the car, and came round to find she was dead. Knowing that he misses her so much he decides he has to be good so that he can go to heaven and see his baby again when he dies. Sounds depressing, and indeed it is, in spite of a rocking sing along chorus. That said, in comparison to the average Country and Western song, it is probably one of the most optimistic pieces of music you will ever hear.

That was the conclusion I reached on a Saturday morning listening to Mount Vernon radio on the way into Nashville. From half an hour's music and chat I decided that everything they say about country music is true. If you play a country song backwards you get a tale about a man who is cured of a disease, meets a beautiful woman, marries her, and suddenly gains a lot of money. Play it the right way round and you understand why so many legends of country die early, bankrupt and the victims of alcohol or spousal abuse.

On Mount Vernon radio morbidity is a way of life. The song that epitomised this was Brookes and Dunn's Believe, a song about old man Wrigley who lost his wife and his baby while at war in the navy and had now died himself. The hope and optimism in the song, and believe it or not, there is hope and optimism, stem from the singers belief that if anyone deserved to die it was old man Wrigley, not because he was an evil miserable old git, but because he had spent all his life being lonely and unable to accept they were dead, insisting "you can't tell me that all this ends in a slow ride in a hearse." Now he's dead, he can meet them again and be happy. As a song about redemption and the existence of an afterlife, it remains a piece of music that would make many people want to slash their wrists, exit this life, and find out if the lyrics are true, just that little bit quicker than would otherwise be the case.

Not that the chat in between tracks was any more uplifting. As with most stations Mount Vernon radio has some fairly long spoken exchanges between DJ's, but rather than chatting about the weather or playing spoof games, the talkie sections consist of obituaries and memorials for "people from our town who have sadly passed away." Mount Vernon radio made me glad my quest to buy a CD by an unknown artist had come to an end, and I has something else to listen to in the car.

We reached the Nashville Sheraton early in the afternoon. The lobby and reception area reeked of extravagance and opulence, but when we got out the lift on the 14th floor, we emerged to décor that was more reminiscent of cheap student accommodation. Clearly the hotel takes the view that first impressions count, and second impressions don't need to be worried about. The approach had paid off as the hotel was full, thanks mainly to the Jesters of Tennessee, who were having their annual shindig in the Racoon Lounge on the 28th floor.

The 28th floor is normally home to the Pinnacle Restaurant, a magnificent restaurant with great views over the city for all guests to enjoy, but the Jesters had not only closed it off to the public, they had also turned it into something more reminiscent of the aftermath of a barbecue in a trailer park.

We found out about the desecration when we gatecrashed their party. We did this completely by accident as we failed to realise there was a reason why the lift had refused to go past the 24th floor. We remained in it when a small group of people, wearing racoon hats that made them look like Howard Cunningham, big Al, and the other grand Pooh-Bahs from Happy Days, got in and did whatever they needed to do to take it, them and us to the top floor.

Apparently the Jesters were Masons, which probably explained the absence of any women, the funny looks Liz received when we were in the Jesters enclosure, and a comment from one of them that they didn't normally have women at these do's unless they were serving food. We found this out courtesy of an overheard conversation in a lift, when a jester in a wheelchair got wheeled out on the wrong floor.

"Can't you check the floors before you push me out?" he asked.

"Well you only had another floor to go," his fellow jester responded.

"And what did you think I was going to do - walk? This is not what I expect from Masons."

And so, their true identity was revealed. I have to say, this was a better way to find out than having someone produce a gun and tell us never to tell of the debauchery and stained table clothes we had been witness to.

After our foray with the Jesters we headed out onto the Nashville streets. The places to go in downtown Nashville on a weekend are 2nd Avenue, Printers Row and Broadway. The 2nd Avenue area in particular is the heart of Nashville. It is where the country music bars start. While some of the bars and clubs have cover charges the majority don't. They all have tip jars, and bands make most of their money from collections at the end of sets, or mid-set collections if they guess that the audience are likely to leave once the jar comes out.

If you don't want to go into a bar you can just stand on the street and listen to the street musicians who are there any time of day whether it's busy or not. Black guys playing sax, white guys playing country music. Some of them are probably only a few steps away from being homeless but still hoping to get a break and make it big in music. Nashville seems to draw in musicians the way Los Angeles draws in actors. People come with dreams, a few of them make it, some find alternative employment and carry on hoping, and others fall by the wayside and end up homeless, and yet they all carry on singing country music, sometimes out of tune, and almost always finding something romantic in their own personal tragedy. Even if you are not a Country and Western fan, it's hard not to get caught up in the atmosphere.

Hard, but not impossible. Liz hated the area, to her the large numbers of people in bars listening to music in the late afternoon were weekend tourists and the atmosphere was anything but genuine. To me the visitors were as much a part of the authentic atmosphere as the locals, and there were probably a lot more locals than she believed. We agreed to disagree and went back to the hotel to freshen up before returning in the evening.

The hotel bar offered fairly sanitised uninspiring surroundings, which, along with the increasingly large and loud presence of the Jesters, didn't do much for Liz's views of Nashville. I didn't help matters by saying that the Jesters were part of the overall holiday experience, seeing bits of life that you couldn't see at home, and getting something other than annoyance from even the most annoying of things. By the end of the sentence I was one of the most annoying of things.

Looking for somewhere to eat was a fraught experience. This was perhaps inevitable. On our first journey onto the Nashville streets, Liz had deemed southern food to be a load of fried rubbish that clogged arteries and put pounds, or stones, on with no great taste to even partly compensate for it. In the evening, out of desperation, I suggested the Hard Rock Cafe, where the uniformity of menus across the country would at least guard against it being classed as southern fried crap. Sadly it also meant it was ruled out as part of a chain, and why go to America for a place you could eat at in London. Knowing I couldn't win I went for the next place we saw, the Big River Grille, a microbrewery and restaurant. I had some Mexican type dish with rice which was good, Liz had some fish dish with rice which she said was fried in far too much oil, in spite of looking dry to the outside observer that I was by this stage. I quietly worked my way through the beer tray with tasters of six different micro brews, aimed officially at people who weren't sure which one to order and unofficially at people who just wanted to drink a lot of beer quickly. The summer beers were best, but I knew somehow that I would not be staying for another drink.

After the meal Liz decided she wanted to go back to the hotel and not go out again that evening. I decided I was staying out and not going back to the hotel that evening. I took her back - however much we were getting on each others nerves I wasn't going to leave her to walk the empty streets of Nashville - then went back to 2nd Street and Broadway to sit in bars and listen to music. As living a cliché goes, being the man in Nashville who had a row with his lady and spent the evening propping up a bar listening to that good old honky tonk music, is as good as it gets.

I walked down Printer's Row where, alongside a blues bar and a country bar, there was a strip joint with a guy standing outside encouraging people to come in to see naked ladies but to get their beer next door as Tennessee law does not allow alcohol to be sold anywhere where there's naked dancing. Presumably this is to mitigate the risk of a bunch of rednecks carrying out unspeakable acts of depravity after seeing naked flesh. As to why Tennessee law also outlaws bingo clubs, meaning that you have to drive seventy-eight miles to Kentucky if you want one, I have no idea. I also have no idea why anyone would want to travel seventy-eight miles for a game of bingo.

I carried on past the strip club, along 2nd Street then into Broadway, taking the long way to see all the bars. The whole area was alive with music and music history. I settled on a bar called Laylas where there was a Hillbilly Country band playing with a line-up that included a guy who allegedly played with Ozzy Osborne and was in David Bowie's ill fated Tin Machine in the late eighties. A bar in Nashville may rate as a higher career achievement for him. The lead singer sang, as they do, and played keyboards with the kind of enthusiasm and extravagance that defined Jerry Lee Lewis in the fifties, bringing to country music the type of approach the Pogues brought to Irish music. They were excellent. I stayed till the end of the set, while others decided that the imminent appearance of a tip jar was their cue to leave.

From there I went back along 2nd Street, and stopped off at a bar where a pub singer covered Red Red Wine, Sweet Caroline, Nothing Ever Happens, and other non-country crowd pleasers in front of an audience of non-country music fans who seemed pleased to have escaped the twangy guitars. As I wasn't so pleased, I had a quick drink and headed back via Printer's Row.

When I got back to the room Liz was half asleep but still asked where I'd been in a tone somewhere between annoyance and general enquiry. I answered in a tone somewhere between chatty and what's it to you and then pretended to fall asleep quickly rather than risk an extended conversation and finding out what the tone really was.

August 20. I thought I should try a traditional southern breakfast so had eggs served with Grits. I had no idea what Grits were, but knew they appeared to be a staple part of breakfast here and in other parts of the south. Having tried them, I have no idea why anyone would want to eat them. They are vile. They look like melted cheese on a bowl of semolina pudding and they taste as if you should stir them a bit longer to form a paste to spread on your wall and stick something to. I left most of them and made do with the eggs which looked like they were the entire weekly output of a particularly active hen.

After breakfast we headed down to the city and stopped on the riverside at Fort Nashborough. Fort Nashborough looks like an original fort, but, as I'm sure you'll have guessed from the words looks like, isn't. It's a small, but good, recreation, on the site of the original, designed to give you a feel for what the fort was like and how it served the state. As is the case throughout the city the fort has plaques with details of Nashville's history and key figures. One theme that unites most of the famous, pre-country music, historical Nashvillians, is that they achieved their fame either by killing Native American Indians, taking land off Native American Indians, or repelling attacks by Native American Indians. I am sure any Native American Indians doing a tour of Nashville feel particularly welcomed when they see this.

Outside of 2nd Avenue, Printers Row and Broadway, downtown Nashville is pretty much empty on a weekend. Nashville is one of the ten richest cities in America but the downtown area does its best to disguise it. The big-box monster claimed another victim as shopping malls and residents headed out of the city centre, leaving behind a business area made up of bars and shops that close at weekends and beggars with no one to beg from. Our tour guide that day summed up the cumulative effect of this when he said "New York's 5th avenue has Macys and Victoria's Secret, ours has Walgreen's and Dollar City."

Sentimentality and history are also not allowed to stand in the way of the out of town behemoths. One of the things Nashville is famous for is the Grand Old Opry, the longest running radio show in the world, broadcast from the equally well known Ryman Auditorium. Or at least it was. The exodus from downtown means that while the Ryman Auditorium is still in the centre, the Grand Old Opry is now ten miles out of the city at Opryland, part of a massive out of town shopping complex, entertainment centre, and hotel. In spite of the Opry being one of the things that defines Nashville, the basic sightseeing tour we took did not go there, there being nothing else of interest to see at Opryland. This says something about the consequences of relocating with a complete disregard for history and tradition.

Tootsies, a honky tonk bar famed for the big name stars that played there before and after becoming famous, used to be a popular place for performers to relax following an appearance at the Opry. Epitomising everything you imagine about the country and western lifestyle, one night in the 1960s the then unknown Willie Nelson attempted suicide by lying down in the street in front of the bar and waiting to be run over by an automobile. I doubt this would happen in the reception of the local Opryland Marriott. If it did, whoever it was would either be moved or ignored, and would only risk death if the valet-parking guy was particularly short sighted.

Grand Old Opry aside, we saw a fair bit as we left downtown and headed into the wider reaches of the city. There is a lot of impressive architecture in and around Nashville, including the Parthenon, the scene of the political rally in Robert Altman's 1975 film Nashville, and a very impressive gallery/museum originally built for the American centenary fair. It was demolished as planned after it, but rebuilt following protests from the people of Nashville, who for some unexplained reason didn't seem to protest before it was demolished. We headed past what we were told were homes of the famous. Anyone from outside Nashville, or not versed in Country and Western history may take issue with the definition of famous, however. Unless you are an Okee from Muskogee or know the name of everyone who has sang the song proclaiming that they are, you could drive past a collection of random houses, make up an imaginary commentary and learn just as much about anyone you know as you would do on this part of the tour.

The houses were all near Music Row. Music Row is within walking distance of Broadway but, owing to the number of major roads with hardly any way of getting across them, you can't actually do the walk. It is home to the old or current headquarters of Sony, Warner, RCA and MCA Universal, as well as long forgotten, but influential, labels such as Curb records. It is also where you'll find RCA Studio B, home to the fabled Nashville Sound pioneered by Chet Atkins, the studio's manager, where the likes of Orbison, the Everly Brothers, Jim Reeves, Johnny Cash and Elvis recorded large parts of their output in the sixties. Country legends such as Waylon Jennings and Willie Nelson also recorded there, and Dolly Parton crashed into the wall of the car park on the way to her first recording session - you can still see where the wall was repaired.

The bottom end of Music Row has smart looking restaurants and shops and also, in the city known as the Protestant Vatican because of the amount of churches it has, a statue of eight naked ladies. The statue is controversial, not merely because of the nudity, but because no one knows what it means, which adds to the feeling that it was put there solely to offend.

Back on 2nd Street, we spent too long looking at the Charlie Daniels Museum. Charlie Daniels is not to be confused with Jack Daniels. Jack Daniel's fans should take the trip to the Jack Daniels Nashville Distillery and the town of Lynchburg, which boasts 361 residents and 27 bars, a bar to resident ratio that is second to none. Charlie Daniels fans don't need to make a long journey to see his museum. Non Charlie Daniels fans may end up feeling that the short walk is still too long.

Daniels is a country music legend, but to most of the world is known only as the guy who sang 'The Devil went down to Georgia' in the early eighties. You may expect his museum to cover a wide range of country music history and stars. Sadly you'd be mistaken, the museum is not called the Charlie Daniels Museum because he's the founder and owner. It's called the Charlie Daniels Museum because it's about him and no one else. If you aren't a big fan of his, and possibly even if you are, you emerge thinking 'yeah sure you've done a lot, but your ego must be bigger than your fame to build such a tribute to yourself.' Then you go into the shop and have a photo taken with a cowboy hat on just because it's Nashville and this is the first chance you've had to do it.

Far better is the Country Music Hall of Fame. The museum is packed with artefacts and items belonging to stars I had hardly heard of till that morning, but I still found it fascinating. The history of country music on display is excellent, taking you through blue grass, honky tonk, hillbilly, rockabilly, and country rock with all the attendant dodgy hairstyles and sequinned shirts associated with the genres.

At the end of the museum there is the hall of fame, a room full of plaques commemorating the living and, more often, dead stars of country. It seems as if most of the people who've made it into the hall died before entering it, or shortly afterwards. You can't even be sure about the ones still shown as living - Sam Phillips of Sun Records has achieved an immortality he couldn't obtain in life as several years after his death the date of his demise is still to be added to his plaque.

In the evening we ate at Demos' Steak and Spaghetti House, a small eclectic restaurant located in a quiet area away from the music bars, which served everything its owners could think of, in every combination that occurred to them. Not that they had thought of an overwhelming amount, but what they had thought of was put together in an intriguing child like style. We had chilli with spaghetti which, while nothing special, at least couldn't be referred to as southern fried shit in batter.

After that we went to Legends where a good touring band played traditional country music. A variety of friends and guests were invited to perform, including two of the barmaids who proved that everyone in Nashville is a country singer, the first in particular slipping effortlessly into a Country and Western style voice that suggested she was waiting on tables until her big break came along. As she was an excellent singer I hope the wait won't be too long. Tip jars came round for each guest, we paid each time, then went back to the hotel while we still had some change left. We didn't go to another music bar. There was only so long that Liz's new found tolerance of country music would last.

August 21. Started the day with a Grit-free breakfast and then headed back to the Country Music Hall of Fame to get tickets to RCA Studio B. This is the only way you can get inside Studio B. Once inside you feel you are in music history. It's not just the artists who recorded in the long since inactive studio that create this feeling, it's also the way they recorded. The band would all be in the same room and the songs were recorded in one take. No separate recording of guitar pieces or overlaying of vocals later in the day, it was all straight to tape, and probably only the eight-track variety at that. With three or four recording sessions a day more than thirty-five thousand songs were recorded in around ten years in Studio B.

A lot of the original recording equipment and instruments are still on display, so you can play a few notes on the piano used in so many sixties classics. My random striking of keys is unlikely to go down in history as the greatest tune ever played there, but it will always have a special place in my own personal history.

Each session lasted about three hours with the set list chosen beforehand so there would be no messing around deciding what songs to record and no classics emerging out of a group of musicians having a jamming session. The production line efficiency was possible because most of the artists sang cover versions, and the same production team and session musicians were used every time. The compliance of the artists was probably a given in an environment where most of them knew they could easily have been replaced if they objected to singing ten songs in half an hour.

The only artist they couldn't risk inflicting this regime on was Elvis. Elvis would not work to a strict three hours, all songs planned in advance, timetable. He turned up when he wanted to, which was usually later than planned, listened to songs in the studio and then decided which to record and how to record them. The session would carry on for however long it took. Crying in the Chapel for example was recorded at three in the morning. RCA were no doubt relieved Elvis was a night-time person, as this meant he could have the last session of the day, take as long as he wanted, and the likes of Jim Reeves could still come in for another thirty-song three-album set the following morning.

After Studio B we collected the cases and car from the hotel and headed out of Nashville stopping at the Opry Mills shopping centre. For an out of town shopping centre, Opry Mills proved again that America has to do everything bigger, if not better, than they do anywhere else.

For all the aesthetic, community, and environmental objections you can have about them, you can't help but see why people come for a clean, sanitised shopping centre experience rather than struggling into city centres and looking for an overpriced parking space for longer than they will spend shopping. It's just a shame they have to suck all the cinemas, shops, and legendary radio shows out of city centres at the same time.

Liz bought some clothes, I bought a couple of CDs, She Wants Revenge's self titled debut album and an instant live Echo and the Bunnymen CD recorded in Chicago. She Wants Revenge were a band I had seen a year earlier in London. At that time they sounded like a cross between The Killers and Interpol. By the time they made it to record they sounded like a bad Joy Division pastiche, which perhaps explains why their early London appearances were not the start of a transatlantic career. Meanwhile, the Bunnymen CD sounded like they were conducting a medical experiment with the aim of finding out just how long Ian McCulloch could sing with a very bad throat before he lost his voice or the audience begged him to stop. The experiment ran for about 90 minutes with neither event happening. The cost of the experiment was funded by ticket holders and people going into record shops, flicking through racks and thinking 'that looks like a rarity you can't get in the UK.' Not an album I'd recommend.

16 - Memphis

From Nashville we headed to Memphis. As well as being the Holy Ground of American music Memphis is also referred to as the Home of the Blues, and the Birthplace of Rock'n'Roll. The National Museum of American History declares that 'in the quest to identify the roots of American music, all roads led to Memphis.' In short, it is the Holy Ground of American music, and I was determined to get the full religious experience, so if you're not big on music you may want to skip on a few days.

The most famous musician to emerge from Memphis was, of course, Elvis Presley, and we were staying down at the end of Lonely Street at Heartbreak Hotel. Yes, there is an actual Heartbreak Hotel and it is down at the end of an actual Lonely Street. Of course the song came before the hotel and the street by some considerable number of years, but that wasn't important. The name and the description had been enough for me to know that we had to stay there.

The blurb told us it was across the street from Graceland, that the whole 1950s décor reflected the feel of the early Elvis era, that all of the 128 rooms had free Elvis movies, and that features included a heart shaped outdoor pool. The website told us how to stay in full Elvis style by spending the night in one of the Elvis themed suites, the Graceland, Burning Love, Hollywood, and Gold and Platinum Suites, each celebrating a different part of Elvis's life and career. Added to this the Hotel also offered the Jungle Room Lounge for food and drinks, a restaurant promising 'deluxe continental breakfasts' and incredible prices of around eighty dollars for a room, one hundred and twenty dollars for a suite, and a suite and Graceland tour tickets for two for a mere one hundred and seventy-four dollars. It sounded to good to be true, and sadly it was.

The one hundred and twenty-dollar suites were was not themed. In ours, the only things Elvis were two black and white photos on the wall. It did have a movie channel with Elvis films, but this lurked hidden and unannounced somewhere around Channel 58. The Jungle Lounge was nothing other than a small bar where we were hard pushed to find any reference to the Jungle outside of the name, and where the food was undoubtedly later period Elvis with the most exotic offering being a burger with chilli topping. The restaurant where the 'deluxe continental breakfasts' were served looked and felt like a large canteen, which at least lowered expectations ahead of a breakfast where the words deluxe and continental could have been replaced with crap and self service. The heart shaped swimming pool was smaller, older and far less loved than it appeared to be from the promotional pictures, and only the reception area looked as if more than cursory attention had been paid to creating a 1950s décor.

So much more could have been made of Heartbreak Hotel. People wouldn't mind paying more - or leastways I wouldn't - to get something decent, but instead it was a low budget motel, offering less than other low budget motels, and getting away with it by exploiting the name. The hotel rips off the fans who made Elvis a legend, and do it in a contemptuous way. Nip a bit further down the road and, for less money, you can stay at the Days Inn and get free Internet - Heartbreak Hotel doesn't have Internet at all - a better breakfast, and less of a feeling that someone is taking you for a fool.

Just up the road from the hotel, at the bottom of Lonely Street, there was a Kentucky Fried Chicken, which somehow linked early and late period Elvis in a way his image makers would despair at, and, in sharp contrast to anything else on offer, the China Garden Restaurant, which offered an oriental buffet. Drawn by the promise of this, we went in. I am not aware of any part of the Orient which has a buffet that consists of fried food and pizza at the expense of traditional Chinese items, but I have to assume that there is one and that it is celebrated at the China Garden. We decided to go to the shop at the petrol station next door and purchase hearty chicken and vegetable soup to take back to our room and microwave. After a beer and wine in the Jungle Lounge we returned to our suite to eat this culinary masterpiece and settle in for a night in front of the TV. We decided against an Elvis movie on the grounds that most of them were crap, and the one on Channel 58 looked amongst the worst.

August 22. I'd always pictured Graceland as some remote outpost, set back from the road in acres of its own grounds, but it isn't. Graceland sits on Route 51, a six-lane highway better known as Elvis Presley Boulevard. Unlike Heartbreak Hotel, Elvis Presley Boulevard did get its name during his lifetime. Must be strange to drive home down a road bearing your name, but then being Elvis Presley must have been unusual enough anyway.

Our trip to Graceland came a week after what is unofficially termed 'Dead Elvis Week.' Dead Elvis Week is the week when Elvis died. It is commemorated with vastly inflated prices at every hotel, and a sales boom for the never dormant Memphis wreath industry. More tourists than usual head to Memphis during Dead Elvis Week, and they all buy floral tributes to leave at his graveside. For once, we were glad to have just missed a big event.

Graceland one week later is a far better prospect for the curious visitor. There are still more people in the city than usual, which adds to the atmosphere, but you don't feel like you are part of some mass homage where worship of Elvis is compulsory.

We had booked on the Graceland Platinum Tour. Unlike Heartbreak Hotel, the rest of the Graceland experience is remarkably good value for anyone's money. We got an audio guided tour of the mansion and grounds, a self-guided tour of his two customised aeroplanes, and entry to the Elvis Automobile Museum, the Sincerely Elvis Museum and the Elvis after dark exhibition. We got on the bus for the short journey over the road, through the gates and up the equally short drive to the entrance to Graceland. The first thing we noticed, aside from it being on a main road, was that it was smaller than we imagined. From the outside it looked the size of two good semi-detached houses, albeit ones with very large gardens. Inside came another surprise. It was far more tasteful than we'd expected. Admittedly, given what we'd expected, that wasn't hard, but on the whole, in comparison to Beckingham Palace for example, it was positively understated. Not that there weren't some hideous bits of course. The worst, or best depending how you look at it, had to be the Jungle Room decorated in the seventies and inspired by Hawaii. It has brown furry walls, Astroturf for carpets, fake trees, plants and monkey sculptures. Maybe Elvis was on medication when he decided it had that Hawaiian feel. Running it a close second was the poolroom with wallpaper that could have been curtains, and a colour scheme that required sunglasses to get a proper look at. In third place on the hideous list was the side room off the main guest reception where an understated subtle black piano was nicely offset by gold lame curtains, a candelabra, and stained glass windows etched in gold with blue peacocks as a centre piece. Outside of these three areas it all looked fairly normal, however. Honestly.

The tour was limited to the downstairs and basement areas of the house, so the myth that Elvis is alive and well and living upstairs can continue. The death of Elvis was portrayed as a very sedate event. In what was the racquet hall room in the outside buildings, we were told he was singing a few songs, including Unchained Melody, around the piano on his last morning and later died of heart failure in a sitting room. There was no mention of him dying in a toilet, or having a burger in his hand at the time. Any suggestion to this effect is probably deemed as heresy, and I can't help thinking that if Elvis was alive he'd have reappeared by now just to prove the story was false. As the King of Rock'n'Roll you'd want people to think you had a more dignified ending than that.

In the grounds outside there is the Meditation Garden, which Elvis had specially constructed, and where he and his parents are now buried. The floral tributes left in Dead Elvis Week were still covering the garden but, them aside, it was simple, tasteful and understated, once more giving a different impression of Elvis from the one that has endured for so long. That said, the image of the Jungle Room came back whenever I started to think I might have been completely wrong.

After Graceland we went on to the planes. The Lisa Marie, the larger of the two, was more than just a plane, it was a travelling home and office, with bedrooms with blue suede headboard, gold bathroom, kitchen, games room and board room included. You could live in it and not realise it was meant to fly. We moved on to the Automobile Museum which included a car Elvis had sold, and which the new owner had been in the process of slowly restoring with the aim of returning to show him. Elvis died shortly before he'd finished it, which must have been really annoying after all the time he'd spent doing it up. Next up was the Sincerely Elvis exhibition, essentially a 1956 retrospective, which made me realise that that was the year that defined him. He was on endless TV shows and played hundreds of dates around the country. After that he only did three more live TV appearances and hardly toured for years. I could see what John Lennon meant when he said Elvis died when he joined the army.

In the evening we got the hotel bus into downtown Memphis. We were expecting to just get a bus ride, but the charming old man who drove the bus had other ideas. Looking and sounding like he was a driver in the original Elvis entourage, he was in the driver's seat when we joined the bus, but then opened the driver's door, left the bus, walked round it, and re-entered through the passenger door before introducing himself as our tour guide. Each sentence he spoke was said slowly and separated by long pauses that made us think he'd finished. His introduction lasted five minutes. After he finished it he left the bus, walked round it and got on again at the driver's door, before taking us into the centre of Memphis telling us where Cybil Shepherd and various other stars lived, in houses we'd long passed by the time he got their names out. There was something endearing about him that almost made me feel sad when we reached Beale Street and had to get off the bus.

Beale Street was the big area for jazz and blues in Memphis from the turn of the last century. It was a predominantly black area at a time when there was still segregation in the city. Through the fifties and early sixties, curious white kids headed there to hear things they couldn't hear on the radio. The influence of Beale Street grew and an Act of Congress in 1966 officially declared it, rather than Memphis as a whole, to be 'The Home of the Blues'. Sadly its decline started around the same time. The victim of its own success in bringing black music to white audiences it became of less importance musically, and the assassination of Martin Luther King, and the ongoing civil rights disputes that divided the city, contributed to it losing its role and importance as part of a multi-cultural city. Rather than preserving and restoring its buildings and communities, in true town planning style most of the street was torn down in the early seventies as the first part of an urban regeneration scheme. Again in true town planning style, the second part - putting new buildings up - never seemed to happen. Of the 1.8 miles of Beale Street, original buildings only remain at the far end alongside new buildings in the same style. Here you can still find blues music coming out of bars on hot summer evenings.

We left Beale Street to look for Sun Studio and the site of Stax Records. Sun and Stax were two of the three main Memphis labels. The third was Hi Records, which is the lost record label when it comes to city landmarks. Influential in the sixties, home of Al Green in the seventies and home of the studios where, in one of his last sessions in the city, Elvis recorded Suspicious Minds, it has nothing to mark its location, not even a cross on a map. Someone should start a campaign.

While we stopped to look at a map to find Sun and Stax, a guy from Fox News chatted to us and told us we shouldn't try to walk it at night, both because of the distance and the number of panhandlers in the area. From his hand gestures he clearly didn't mean that the panhandlers were gold prospectors. We decided it could wait till tomorrow, and booked a room for the following night at the Hampton Inn, before getting a meal in the Kings Palace Cafe and going on to a couple of authentic Beale Street bars. The musicians union were boycotting the area as old bar owners had sold up and the new ones insisted that musicians play for tips only. Older musicians wouldn't do this so the bars got younger less experienced musicians to bang out anything they could. In the first bar we went to an off-key version of Billy Joel's Piano Man was sung by two twenty something guys playing piano. Much as I love the original, I wished the boycott wasn't happening and took strange comfort from the fact that Beale Street had an eleven o'clock curfew for people under twenty-one so they'd probably have to stop then, and an old guy would get a paid gig instead.

We got the bus back to Heartbreak Hotel, this time driven by a guide who had little to say, and after the purchase of Elvis souvenirs including a CD of his first album with bonus tracks, and a postcard with one of his favourite recipes we went back to a room where there still wasn't a good Elvis movie on Channel 58.

August 23. Started the day chatting to a man on his third visit to Graceland. He talked a lot about the time he came with his ex-wife, oblivious of what the lady sitting next to him, who I assumed to be his current wife, thought.

His last visit had been for the twentieth anniversary of Elvis's death. He informed us that "this year was the twenty-ninth anniversary, next year will be the thirtieth", in a way that made this sound somehow revelatory in spite of being the inevitable conclusion of adding one to twenty-nine.

"The thirtieth anniversary promises to be the biggest year yet", he went on. I didn't know whether to see this as a promise or a threat.

When we checked out we tried to follow the simple route the bus had taken to reach downtown. We didn't manage it, taking a less scenic ride round the outskirts and backstreets of the city before spotting a road we recognised as one that would eventually lead us into the centre. Once there, we checked in to the Hampton Inn, and went back down Beale Street.

We stopped at Memphis Music, where we bought a CD, postcards, and a Beale Street blues mug. The CD, We the People by Guitar Shorty, was playing while we were in the shop. As I'd never heard of him, the owner of Memphis Music told me he was a sixty-plus years old blues veteran, which meant he probably wasn't playing in bars round there at the time, who still includes somersaults and back flips in his acrobatic stage routine. He played with the likes of Sam Cooke and Little Richard, and his wife was the half sister of Jimi Hendrix. Hendrix used to go to some of his gigs and was influenced by him, but not to the extent that he ever name checked him, unless the influence was a bit too strong to admit to and remain a pioneer of guitar music at the same time. The CD was one of those records that work best in their original setting. In Memphis Music it sounded superb, in a car heading to Arkansas it was okay, but after that there were very few locations I tested it out in.

In spite of his age, Guitar Shorty's fame seemed to be increasing in the States. In the UK, We the People got a release but failed to dent the top 75 by some considerable distance, and he remains undiscovered.

We grabbed lunch at the Blues City Cafe, a good diner style restaurant that has been there for years, where you can also pick up one of the Backbeat tours promising 'Rockin' Rides through Memphis Music History.' The tours are run on Miss Clawdy, a fully restored 1959 GM transit bus, with real working musicians as tour guides. They cover the main music sites in and around the city, and they leave at nine in the morning. Because of that last fact, I can't say whether the tours are as good as they sound, as it was after one when I found out about them, but I think I'd have liked it, which is all you need to be able to recommend something sometimes.

The tour we took instead was the Duck Tour. Duck Tours are an institution in American cities with lakes or rivers. The premise is simple, the tour takes place in a boat with wheels that travels along the road and then takes to the water. Add to this a wacky tour guide, a happy quacker for everyone on the tour, and some musical accompaniment to sound it to, and you're off. It should be naff, and it is, but it's also great fun.

We passed Elvis's parents old home, a small house in a small block which would have been very cheap at the time but has now been refurbished and turned into a gated development. We also passed the Lorraine Hotel on Mulberry Street, which could have been remembered as the hotel where black and white musicians came together during segregation and where 'In the Midnight Hour' was written. Sadly, the chance of that being its main claim to fame was lost when Martin Luther King was assassinated there. I'm not sure that a comedy boat is the best vehicle to pass such a site in. It is far more appropriate for passing the local state penitentiary, a landmark the tour guide introduced by turning the volume up and playing Jailhouse Rock – I bet the inmates never get tired of that.

From the penitentiary we headed down towards Mud Island, going five times round the roundabout that leads up to it - that's how wacky a trip it was. We were then meant to take to the river at Wolf River Harbour, where Jeff Buckley drowned in 1997. This wasn't mentioned on the tour, perhaps because it is not a good subject to raise on a comedy boat, even if it is okay to pass the Lorraine Hotel in one. Sadly in spite of a heavy downpour the previous evening, low water levels meant that the river part of the trip was cancelled, which meant that all we actually did that day was take a boat on the high street with a happy quacker to toot as and when we felt like it. Still, not a bad way to pass an early afternoon in Memphis.

After leaving the boat we went our separate ways as I continued the Elvis experience with a trip to Sun Studio. Sun Studio is a must-see place. Unlike so many other landmark sights in America it is the original building in the original location. The cafe at the entrance to the studio was originally a separate business and the upstairs was a bed and breakfast where many of the musicians using the studio would stay. The studio and reception are still as they were. The desk of Sam Phillip's Secretary, Marion Keisker, is in the reception area, with her name plate on it. The studio has a cross on the floor to mark where Elvis stood when he recorded That's All Right Mama, the first song in his first recording session. There is a microphone from that time that may or may not have been the one he sang into. The fact that they aren't sure suggests it probably isn't, but I still made sure I got my photo taken on that spot holding that microphone.

Sun Studio isn't just about Elvis, it has a history that both pre and post dates him. BB King played there as a session musician in the days when he was skinny - they have a photo of the slimline version before the paycheques came in and the waistline went out. Ike Turner acted as an A and R man for the studio bringing acts to Sam Phillips attention long before he knew Tina Turner. Johnny Cash, Roy Orbison, Carl Perkins and Jerry Lee Lewis all began their careers in the studio. In short, it oozes legends.

Sun changed locations in 1960, and the building remained empty for most of the next 25 years. For a while it was used as a barbershop, there was also a scuba diving shop at the back of the studio at one point, but in all the years it was vacant, amazingly, it wasn't knocked down or irretrievably refurbished. It was still capable of being used as a recording studio in 1985 when, alongside producer Chips Moman, Cash, Orbison, Perkins and Lewis, decided to go into it one evening and record some music. Two years later Sun Studio was officially back in business, and a whole range of artists, including REM, ZZ Top and U2 have recorded there since. U2 even got BB King to join them. The stuff that dreams are made of, at least it is if your name's Bono.

After leaving Sun Studio, and taking a quick trip to the Hard Rock Cafe to see what they had on display, I went back to the Hotel, joined up with Liz and squeezed in a visit to the Memphis Rock'n'Soul Museum on 3rd Street before it closed. With less than two hours to go, I probably shouldn't have dwelled too long on the parts tracing the early history of blues music from cotton plantations to the birth of radio and the Grand Ole Opry. They were good and informative in a historical recreation kind of a way, but I should have jumped straight to the fifties, and the sections where you find out about people like Dewey Philips, the DJ who gave Elvis his first radio play and then gave him his next nineteen plays all on the same show. The influence of Philips, and others at the time, was such that they could tell people a record was the nation's number one and everyone would believe them. The records would then become number one in Memphis and Tennessee even if they never broke nationally. Nowadays the sales they generated would probably get you the national number one too.

The same parts of the museum provided a great insight into how segregation affected the way music was recorded and performed. It was not unusual for session bands to have black and white musicians, but when it came to playing live a black band could play to a white audience and vice versa but the idea of a mixed band sharing a stage was frowned on and other musicians had to fill in. Amazing and

144

shocking to think this was less than fifty years ago. Restrictions on mixing socially even meant that musicians could not go the same cafes once they left the studio, which was where places like the Lorraine Hotel played their part by being somewhere where colour was not a barrier to mixing.

As it got to seven we found out that there was no leeway on exit times, and so, after discovering that Hi Records at least makes it into the Memphis Rock'n'Soul Museum, we fleetingly saw the parts of the museum covering the late eighties onwards. Probably the best bit to miss, as it seemed to mainly consist of endless quotes from artists on what Memphis means to them. The absence of much else suggests there is little happening in Memphis now that will draw similar quotes forty or fifty years further down the line.

We went for a meal in Isaac Hayes Soul Food Kitchen Restaurant and Nightclub in Peabody Place. It no doubt draws people in because of the name and the prospect, for South Park fans, of asking if the Chef has chocolate salty balls, but the quality of the food would bring you back and would be worth going for even if you had no idea who Isaac Hayes was. The food was superb and the service so brilliant that we even forgot it was in a shopping centre.

After a look at the Isaac Hayes memorabilia on the wall, we headed off a little heavier than before and passed a bar with a Young's Bitter sign outside it. Wondering whether the UK chain had got this far we went in and found out it was just the sign that had made the journey. Another pub offered the prospect of a quiz. Tempted by the prospect of seeing just how general any knowledge is outside of your own country, we nearly went in before deciding that an embarrassing last place, with a comedy team name suggesting we knew it was inevitable, would be the best we could hope for. We headed instead to a fairly high end bar with comfy sofas rather than tables - always a sign of a place trying to be classy - and had one drink there before heading back down Beale Street where blues acts of dubious quality and limited years played and a group of motorcyclists suddenly appeared, as if they were on a convention. We had one drink then went back to the hotel.

August 24. After a good breakfast, we checked out, left the bags in the hotel and went our separate ways again. I got a taxi to the Stax Museum of American Soul Music. The taxi driver was an old guy who had lived through the era of segregation and gave me a free history lesson that beat anything you'd get at a school. He told me what it was like to grow up on a street near to a school for white children only, and to have to get a blacks only bus every morning to a poorer school further away. He told me that at the time he and others at the school just accepted that that was the way it was. They had no sense of injustice and no expectation that things should be any different, even though their parents did. He said all of this without any sense of rage or anger. Nor was he angry with the white kids at the school who he said had been too young to realise the injustices of segregation that the different schools represented.

He went on to talk about the great changes that took place in the late sixties and what it was like living through a time when so much was happening that was meant to improve his quality of life and create equal rights. To him, the amount of activity going on then achieved a lot eventually, but this was tempered now with the knowledge that they were starting from a very low base. He told me he could see why black kids today were going down the gangsta rap and gun culture path, even though he didn't think it was the right thing to do, and why music is the way it is. He said the new generation hadn't lived through the changes his generation had and it was only with the benchmark of what they didn't have before the late sixties that what they had now could be seen as any approaching a good deal in many ways.

We carried on talking long after the taxi reached the museum at 926 East McLemore. The depth of his knowledge and first hand experience was something I could never hope to capture in two paragraphs, but will remain grateful for hearing forever.

The Stax Museum is in the exact same location that the Stax Records building was until it was demolished in 1989, more than a decade after the label went bankrupt. The exterior is an exact replica of the original, which began life as a record shop run by Estelle Axton and her brother Jim Stewart, on the site of the previous Capitol Movie Theatre. The name STAX came from the first two letters of their surnames. Like Beale Street, STAX brought together blacks and whites in Memphis. Estelle and Jim were white, but most of their customers were black. The people who came in to the shop to listen to records wanted to record stuff themselves and Estelle and Jim had always planned to put a recording studio where the cinema screen used to be, so it all came together with STAX becoming the label that launched local talent such as Isaac Hayes, Otis Redding, and Booker T and the MGs.

The Stax Museum tells the full history of the label, and the full history of black music in Memphis and America. As with the Rock'n'Soul Museum it begins long before record labels existed, with a history of cotton picking and gospel music, but at STAX it is a more personal account with a spiritualist church, complete with altar and font, moved brick by brick from its original home to the museum. Only in America would they move an original building into a recreation of another building.

Notwithstanding the church, the detailed story of Stax - its development, rebirth and eventual decline - remains the unique draw of the museum. It takes you through the link with Atlantic Records which ended with Atlantic owning the back catalogue and Stax having to get all its artists to record new albums, leading to 27 albums and 30 singles released in a month, a workrate nowadays only dreamed of by executives at EMI. It covers the death of Otis Redding and the assassination of Martin Luther King together with the changes in the Memphis music scene that followed and saw the label focus on black and African music. It ends with another dubious distribution deal that finally killed Stax. Al Bell, who joined the company in the mid-sixties, negotiated the deal with CBS and later became one of Stax's owners. It should have provided Stax with money and freedom, but Clive Davis, the CBS chairman who negotiated it, was sacked and the bits of the deal that weren't written down were disregarded. As these were the good bits, the end result was bad promotion, bad distribution and a spiral down towards bankruptcy. Estelle Axton had sold her shares in the company some years earlier, but Jim Stewart re-mortgaged his home to try and provide the label with working capital, and ended up penniless and a recluse. Al Bell, who took out loans in the company's name that added to its debt, went on to have a lucrative career that included a stint as President of Motown. Somewhere in there is an oft-told story of business failure.

The last place we visited before leaving Memphis had nothing to do with music. The National Civil Rights Museum on Mulberry Street is one of the few non-music attractions in Memphis, and probably the best civil rights museum anywhere. It could not have a better location. It is spread across two buildings, the Lorraine Hotel, and 418 South Main Street, from where James Earl Ray allegedly fired the shots that killed King. There can surely be no better use for either of the buildings and no better location for a civil rights museum.

The reason I say Ray 'allegedly' fired the shots is that, as with any major assassination or unexpected death, there are a variety of conspiracy theories about the events on that day and the days leading up to it. As if to add to the idea that things are not as clear cut as they seemed, the bathroom from which the shots were fired has been preserved as it was in 1968 but is closed off, with the doors and walls on the outside of the room replaced by glass. From the closest you can get to the window, it does look as if it would have been easier for Ray to shoot from his own room, but then I suppose someone is less likely to notice a gun pointing at them if it comes from an obscure angle.

The penultimate part of the museum is devoted to a dissection of the police investigation, the possible flaws in it, and the alternate theories of who could have killed King, or who Earl Ray may have been acting for. Whether or not there is a shred of truth in any of them, it was still fascinating, and I figured that, while they may have encouraged speculation by closing the room, a national civil rights museum would not trivialise the assassination, so they must believe there are at least some unanswered questions.

The rest of the museum set out the full history of the civil rights movement with sections on all the major landmarks in the struggle such as Rosa Parks and the bus journey that led to the end of segregation in travel, and the workers strikes in Memphis that ultimately led to the rally King was attending at the time of his assassination.

Alongside this are temporary exhibitions. We saw an excellent one looking at victims of gun crime, and not just focusing on the obvious stories. As well as the innocent lady walking down the street threatened by drug addicts, there were recollections from drug addicts and naïve novice dealers suddenly caught up in gang warfare. As well as abused wives and girlfriends, there were abused husbands and boyfriends, all talking about their shooting, what led up to it, and the effect it had on them.

We came away with the lasting impressions the exhibition clearly intended, which is that gun crime can affect anyone, how it happens may vary but the consequences will always be the same, and anyone who willingly carries a gun is probably not someone who should be allowed to have one. This was highlighted in particular by a college girl's recollection of how her paranoid boyfriend shot her when he thought he heard burglars, in spite of all the doors and windows being locked and knowing that she was in the house. It was not a light-hearted exhibition, and it is not a light-hearted museum, but, if you are ever in Memphis, you should make time to see it.

After the usual late lunch we drove out of Memphis. We'd missed the Gibson Guitar Museum, which I can't say I was too disappointed about, and also missed various tours to obscure locations such as Elvis's school, or his resting place before his body was returned to Graceland. I wasn't too disappointed about that either. For a non-worshipper there is only so much Elvis you can take in one trip.

17 – Little Rock

As Memphis is the only city to spread over three states - Tennessee, Alabama and Arkansas - we were in Arkansas before we left the city. We decided to stop in Little Rock mainly because it seemed to be the first, if not only, place of note on the map between Memphis and Dallas, roughly a third of the way between the two. Arkansas - pronounced Arkansaw - was the state where Clinton was governor, and Little Rock is its capital. If you don't know this before you get there, you soon find out.

As we turned off for Little Rock we saw the Holiday Inn. The Presidential associations were immediately clear from the full name of the hotel, 'The Holiday Inn Hotel Presidential Conference Center' - unlike Springfield and good old Abe, they haven't added the words William Clinton to the title so far. The Clinton Bar, near to the Camp David Restaurant, was the first hint of which president is connected to Little Rock.

Little Rock is another small state capital, although as Arkansas is a small state, both in terms of people and square miles, it is still its largest city. As it is small, you can stay at a hotel just off the Interstate and still walk into the heart of the city. Not that we did. The receptionist told us they ran a free shuttle bus to the centre, so we got that and went to the River Market district.

From a range of bars and restaurants, we drank at Markham Street Grill and Pub, a mock English pub complete with soccer on the TV and a row of dart boards on the wall, and ate at Boscos a good Italian restaurant on the riverside where smart dress definitely wasn't required to enjoy the usual generous helpings. Before that we walked along the river in both directions. To the east we saw the Clinton Presidential Center Museum, and to our west we saw what looked like a decent little town. Back at the hotel the maps in the Little Rock Travelhost magazine covered six different areas mixing restaurants, shops and historic old buildings, all of which convinced us that Little Rock could offer at least as much as Springfield and was therefore worth staying in for a second night. Or so we thought…

August 25. Before saying what Little Rock doesn't have to offer, it is only fair to say what it does, particularly because what it offers is good, just as long as you're not planning to spend a full day there.

The main thing to see is the William J. Clinton Presidential Center, to give it its full and correct title. The centre has full scale replicas of the Oval Office and the Cabinet Room, the originals of which are now off bounds to the public. The replica Oval Office has many of the personal furnishings Clinton had in it while he was president, while the Cabinet Room has interactive stations around the desk so you can see who everyone was in the Clinton Administration and what they contributed to cabinet discussions. If you could get in to see the real things you would, but as cover versions go they are better than anything that Westlife have ever produced.

The centre documents the history of Clinton's rise to power and time in office through photos, papers, press articles and policy exhibits along with a narrative which gives a detailed, although slightly slanted, appraisal of Clinton's presidency.

Looking at the footage from his first campaign made me feel nostalgic. In an almost fairytale way I was taken back to the time when the Democrats took back the country from the Republicans, promising a new era of hope and opportunity, leading to much rejoicing amongst all those who felt they had been shat on by the governments of the eighties.

Was it all a dream? When we were there it was less than six years since Clinton left office, and only fourteen since he won the presidency, and yet it all seemed such a long time ago. Looking around the exhibits and displays it became clear how much his administration accomplished, including the work they started on environmental protection. So much achieved, and yet so much pulled apart in such a short space of time, starting on that day in 2000 when the legal battles stopped and a state where the senator was the brother of the Republican candidate delivered the election result that created President George W. Bush. The evidence of what Al Gore has done since then, and what he had already begun as vice president, are all there is to even hint at what may have happened had there been a different outcome.

We moved on to the Old State House where Clinton stood on the night he was elected and said, "I still believe in a place called Hope," a pun on his birthplace that was missed by anyone who didn't know where he was born. The Old State House is inevitably dominated by Clinton. He even gives the introduction to the Clinton exhibit - on a videotape of course, he hasn't yet reached the stage where the only job he can get is a tour guide - which documents his use of the Old State House during his presidential campaigns. Clinton aside it has a lot on the history of the state, exhibits from all of its governors, various historically redecorated rooms, and a collection of gowns worn by various First Ladies.

All of which helps to idly pass another couple of hours away in Little Rock. After that, however, my advise for visitors would be to head out of Little Rock unless you want to embrace the law of diminishing returns in the most full on manner possible, by exploring the rest of the city. From the Old State House, we walked further along Markham Street believing we would be heading into a bustling city centre, but it never came. There was a vague hint that we could be near something when we reached the Hilton Hotel, but that was a false dawn. We looked for the city tour buses, and found an office. It was closed. You have to ring and book the tours in advance. For all Little Rock claims to be America's newest thriving destination, it is not busy enough for tour companies to be confident of getting a bus full of people to see its sights.

We stopped for lunch at a nearby Subways, and looked at the maps we'd got from the hotel. We thought about getting the trolley bus to see the rest of the city, but on closer inspection found that it just went round the downtown area we'd come through and then crossed into North Little Rock to take in its two 'attractions', the Ristorante Capeo and the Arkansas Queen Riverboat, which had started its last sailing of the day while we were still in the Clinton Center.

We decided instead to look for the Riverdale area of the city - which boasted a range of antique and designer shops - and then to go on to the nearby Historic Hillcrest District and The Heights, which both sounded like quaint little small towns in their own right. From the maps Riverdale looked like it would be just a short walk further down the road. Ten minutes later we still seemed nowhere near it - our map was to a scale that would have made the whole of the States seem smaller than England. After a couple more turns we decided to go back to the hotel, get in the car and drive. Near the hotel we found the tourist information centre, where the staff were very friendly and polite as they confirmed that if we wanted to see anything else the only way to do it was by car.

The Central High School, featured in the National Civil Rights Museum as the place where nine black students were denied entrance in 1957 creating a stand off that only ended after presidential intervention, was one place we could have visited. They were planning to celebrate fifty years of integration, a dubious celebration given that there would have been less to commemorate had it not been for the racist actions of the State's Governor, and the support of a thousand strong angry white mob, fifty years earlier. We decided to give it a miss and stick with our plan of seeing the idyllic communities in beautiful settings that would be Riverdale, Hillcrest and The Heights.

Even in the car finding them was not an easy task. Most of the roads in Little Rock are arranged in typical American grid style, but just when we thought we were reaching the road we needed we came to the railway line that dissects the city east to west offering no visible route across to the north. With the road we wanted tantalisingly close but completely inaccessible, we turned round and went back most of the way we had come. Back on the right route and the right side of the railway track, the turn off still proved elusive as all roads seemed to lead to the bridge into North Little Rock. When we could finally find no alternative we headed for the bridge and, a little too late, discovered the small exit just before it. We crossed into North Little Rock turned round, came back and finally headed down the right road, where we eventually discovered that all three districts did exist and weren't the fictitious invention of a mad cartographer. Aside from this discovery there was nothing else to suggest the journey had been worthwhile. They were nice enough in themselves, but amounted to little more than collections of old houses, small antique shops and a couple of cafes and restaurants. If you lived elsewhere in the city and had all of your life to see them, you probably wouldn't go out of your way to get there.

We drove back to the hotel, booked two nights in Dallas, and went for an upmarket meal at Vermillion Water Grille, a restaurant a short walk and a large bank account away from the restaurants around the River Market. We returned to the hotel concluding that Little Rock was worth a visit, but you don't need to spend two nights there to see it.

153

August 26. Marking the completion of more than 3,000 miles since we picked up the car, I took it into the garage opposite the hotel to get the oil changed. The woman in the garage was very friendly and told me her son was married to an English woman from Montrose, Scotland. I made a mental note to pass that one on to my Scottish friends.

Arriving back at the hotel I noticed the commemorative plaque outside it and realised that either Little Rock is a deeply religious place, or the Director of the Carpenter Hotel Group is. The plaque begins with a dedication that reads 'This building is dedicated to the glory and honor of our Lord Jesus Christ. He provided the resources, the vision and the wisdom to complete this magnificent project. May God bless this building and all who enter in.' In a slight exaggeration of just how wonderful the building is the dedication continues with the words 'I am also grateful to the following individuals for their faithful dedication to the construction of this phenomenal facility' followed by a list of people, last of whom are the ones who actually did the building, rather than provide the money or divine intervention. I doubt that I will ever see a greater, more over the top, or inappropriate, eulogy outside a Holiday Inn, or any other hotel, ever again.

18 - Dallas

We headed out of Arkansas and towards Texas. Black Horse and the Cherry Tree, the KT Tunstall song we first heard as we left Canada, was on rotation on almost every radio station, and every time we changed station it reappeared, ensuring it was the song we would remember the whole journey by.

Our last stop before leaving Arkansas was Hope, the birthplace of Bill Clinton, where we continued our Clinton homage. We started by going into the small museum in the old Railway Station, a great little place with photos and school reports from the ex-presidents formative years as Billy Blythe and then, after the death of his father and his mothers second marriage, Bill Clinton.

From there, we followed signs through the town for his birthplace in a journey that lead to a collection of small, predominately wooden, bungalows and houses, all of which looked identical to the house in the photos in the museum, and none of which had any commemorative plaque to confirm that they were where he had lived. Seeing the area and remembering he was the most powerful man in the world for eight years, I could almost have believed that America really is the land of opportunity.

When we came out of Hope, we rejoined Interstate 30 on a largely insignificant stretch of road, and crossed the state border into Texas. Texas is the state that gave George W Bush to the world and took John F Kennedy from the world. What more could you need to know about it by way of an introduction?

We reached Dallas late afternoon and followed the directions for the Hotel Indigo. We drove past the entrance once, not realising we had reached it, and drove round the block a further two or three times looking for the car park. Eventually we gave up, and pulled up outside the entrance to the hotel.

The Indigo is also part of the Holiday Inn chain but, unlike the Little Rock Holiday Inn, Our Lord Jesus Christ isn't acknowledged as providing any resource or support to build it. If He had been, his reputation in the building trade would be shattered. One thing the website had neglected to tell us when we booked was that Holiday Inn had only recently acquired the hotel and were still renovating it. We found this out when we entered the foyer and were greeted by the smell of paint and the absence of anything other than the reception desk and a small bar.

We pressed for the lift and waited an eternity before going back to reception where we were told that only the service lift was operational and we'd have to call through to reception anytime we wanted it. They called the lift and we finally made it to our room. It was long and narrow with two queen-size beds crammed uneasily into it. After manoeuvring the suitcases around the first bed and a desk crammed, equally uneasily, into a space in the corner I looked up and observed the room in its full glory. The bright blue beds with yellow and white headboards were truly a sight to behold, but they paled in comparison to the photo that filled the entire side wall and depicted nothing more than a blue knitted top blown up to ridiculous proportions. I had to sit down to really take it in and as I did I noticed stains on the sheets of one of the beds and decided to sleep in the other. I also decided to cancel our second night and look for somewhere else for tomorrow evening.

We called for the service lift and, after it eventually arrived, we went downstairs and asked for the complimentary shuttle to the West End Marketplace, home of the nightlife in downtown Dallas.

The Marketplace is a mix of restaurants and bars with a couple of nightclubs. As the name suggests it also has a few market stalls and some outside entertainment, but this was more of the DJ playing records variety than drama students doing fire eating. We booked the Hampton Inn, on the edge of the Marketplace, for the next evening and passed the, by now obligatory, panhandlers and alleged veterans on the short walk back.

The restaurants in the area were all fairly large anonymous looking affairs, so in the absence of anything unique we went to TGI Fridays, and then to a bar that doubled as a Mexican restaurant, before heading to Froggy's nightclub, the first nightclub we'd been to in America.

Froggy's was a strange hybrid of a nightclub. The DJ played a mix of cheesy old favourites and hip hop, and there was also Karaoke as part of

156

the entertainment. The Karaoke worked on a 'whatever anyone wants to sing, whenever they want to sing it' basis, so in between two house classics from the DJ, old men sang ballads in pained voices and a younger guy did Mr Brightside by The Killers, recognising this as an easy option as a good half of it can be spoken so tone and pitch don't come into it.

The crowd was equally eclectic with a mixture of all races and ages, although the later it got, the older the average age became. As a nightclub concept, it shouldn't have worked but somehow did. People danced to most things, switching from serious flirting to line dancing to house and even doing the full gymnastic routine of DJ Cha Cha when that came on. Only when they played anything lacking an uptempo beat did people leave the floor in droves. As for the sudden Karaoke interruptions, no one seemed annoyed or surprised when a middle-aged man singing a ZZ Top song followed Hips Don't Lie. There was an enthusiastic audience for whoever took the microphone. As a large lady belted out her rendition of Bon Jovi's Wanted Dead or Alive, the word Wanted was greeted every time by large groups of people, including us, singing it back in mock mid-western accents that were entertaining and hilarious for reasons that you had to be there to appreciate

We ended up staying far longer than we'd intended and drinking far more than we'd planned. Getting back to the hotel in a less than sober state meant that we weren't conscious of the smell of paint, or the décor of the room, and that can only have been a good thing.

August 27. We checked out of the Indigo and into the Hampton Inn, got breakfast and went to the place that most visitors to Dallas go to - Dealey Plaza and the book depository from where, in a room on the sixth floor, Lee Harvey Oswald allegedly fired the shots that killed Kennedy.

The depository is now home to the Kennedy Museum. Walking towards it, we bought the obligatory mock up newspaper covering the assassinations of Kennedy and Oswald, the Warren Commission investigations and the conspiracy theories, from a street vendor who looked as if he hadn't the slightest interest in any of it other than the two-dollar cost. Inside the museum, we went straight to the 6th floor. They have a great exhibition, covering the day of the assassination, the history leading up to it, the immediate aftermath, and the longer term investigations and official conclusions. The main draw, of course, is the window and room where the shots were fired. To paraphrase the late Bill Hicks, the room is exactly like it was when Kennedy was shot - there are boxes on the floor and Oswald isn't there. As we expected, you can't go in the room or get to the window. As with the bathroom in the National Civil Rights Museum, the room is surrounded by glass and the closest you can get to where the shots were fired is about six feet away.

You might think, so what, if you can't get to the 6th floor window, the museum is also on the 7th floor so why not look out from the corresponding window there. The answer is that you can't do that either. They run a film some twenty or so feet in front of the window and as a result it has been blacked out. They really don't want to disappoint the conspiracy theorists in Dallas, and the Kennedy assassination offers so much to keep them occupied. The Mafia, big business interests, the Cubans, even L B Johnson, have all been identified and implicated as people or organisations who may have benefited from the death and hence had some responsibility for it. The only organisation for whom Kennedy's death really delivered any long lasting benefit, however, is the Dallas Tourist Board. This is not to say the Tourist Board had anything whatsoever to do with the assassination, obviously and for legal reasons, but, in tourist terms, it must have been the equivalent of finding several theme parks had moved onto the same block and all the executives could take early retirement as a result. Dallas continues to benefit from the number of visitors Kennedy pulls in and this allows it to get away with offering precious little else in the way of tourist attractions. Its two biggest claims to fame are one dead president and one dead TV series, and the latter isn't even in the city.

The common strand in most of the Kennedy conspiracy theories is that the fatal last shot could not have been fired by Oswald because of the reaction Kennedy had to it - which suggested the shot came from in front of him - and the angle Oswald would have had to have fired from. You can test this from the 6th floor, albeit estimating what the angle would be if you were standing six feet further forwards or six feet further to the left. I did this, and at odds with common wisdom, decided that the first shot would have been the more difficult, and it would have been easier to shoot when the car came down Houston Street, rather than wait till it turned left. It would have been a straight shot forwards and down, and wouldn't have required a compass and protractor to calculate the angle of trajection needed to hit the car and avoid the nearby tree.

That you can do this experiment, sans bullets and guns of course, is as a result of two X's marked on the road on Dealey Plaza to show where the first and last bullets hit. As the road is fairly free of cars on a Sunday you can also join a whole host of people standing on the X's and taking photos up towards the sixth floor room. To continue the experience you can then go to the grassy knoll to see where it is widely claimed the shot came from. The views there aren't blocked by windows, but are slightly obscured by conspiracy theorists selling magazines and books to tourists, whilst hoping no one discovers that the angles from it are equally obtuse. All in all it makes for a fascinating, if ultimately meaningless, morning's entertainment.

Leaving Kennedy behind we headed for lunch at the nearby West End Pub which proudly declared itself 'A neighbourhood pub without the neighbourhood.' As descriptions go it's about as good as they get. While Dallas was bigger than some of the other cities we'd been to recently, and also had more money and more high powered offices than they had, it still looked like a weekday place where most of the restaurants and bars outside of downtown closed up for the weekend. Consequently while the West End Pub was a charming place, which with a few more regulars could have been the Cheers of the south, it had no neighbourhood to enable it to fulfil its potential.

Our plan for the afternoon was to take the trolley bus uptown, but that was the point when the Dallas heatwave finally and unarguably came to an end. As we started away from the West End Pub the temperature dropped remarkably, the sweltering heat disappeared completely, and the wind taking its place made the now normal temperature feel like it was created by turning the air conditioning up to overdrive. We debated whether to carry on to the trolley stop, decided we might not reach it before it started raining, and went back to the hotel to wait till it blew over. This was probably one of the smartest things we have ever done. As we reached the hotel the heavens opened, the sky turned black, and the rain came down, accompanied by thunder and lightning. Anyone we could see on the street looked wetter than a passenger on the Titanic, while we were inside and dry.

It was a good couple of hours before the rain stopped, and it was about 5:30 before we left the hotel and went to the trolley stop off Ross Street. The next trolley failed to appear, and we decided that the odds on there being any more trolleys were probably non-existent as a result of the rain. Associating bad weather with cancellation of transport services probably marked us down as English more than our accents did. We walked up towards McKinney Avenue to see whether we could walk all the way to uptown. We probably could have done, but the walk would have taken us past a large amount of nothingness and Interstate, so we turned round and headed back down Ross Street just as a trolley appeared. Proving once more that real life does not imitate fiction, we did not begin a frantic run only to see it pulling out just as we reached the stop. Instead we walked back and got on with time to spare.

The trolleys are a part of Dallas history rather than a modern gimmick, consequently they are very old vehicles, run on very old tracks, by very old volunteers who share a love of trolleys and very low pay. At almost every turn the cable on the trolley came off leaving the aged trolley driver to reconnect it only for it to come off again a few moments later. Out of a sense of pride he struggled on to complete the outbound leg of the journey, but the return journey came to an abrupt halt when the cable came off once more and the trolley was taken out of service. Defying the seemingly inevitable for the second time in an hour, we weren't thrown off the trolley a long walk away from anywhere we wanted to be, instead we were just a short walk away from a strip of restaurants including the imaginatively titled Mexican Pueblo Arriba, where we ate vast combinations of good Mexican food served at shockingly cheap prices.

Hunger satisfied we crossed the road to The Idle Rich, another pub that recreated the American version of English watering holes using a billiards table and dart boards. We played billiards and had a couple of drinks before heading back downtown. The trolleys had stopped running so we got a taxi outside the Hard Rock Cafe, which possessed the most impressive and yet sinister exterior of any Hard Rock Cafe you will ever see. At dusk with the moon behind it and bird sculptures to the left and right of the pointed roof it looked and felt like the entrance to Dracula's castle, at least until we looked down and saw the logo staring back at us.

Downtown was shutting up early. Froggy's was closed, so no dancing and Karaoke tonight. We went back to TGI Friday where the seven or eight customers included three local cops. This may have been an excessive police presence, but they were paying for their drinks and the landlord needed the custom. We left before it was just us and the police in there, and finding nowhere else open called a halt on a rainy Sunday in Dallas.

August 28. The weather had definitely broken, but as if to illustrate how warm Dallas had been, the temperature was still in the eighties. On top of the drop in temperature it was also raining with the rain predicted to last most of the day. None of this, however, would bother most of the people in the city as, with the exception of the homeless, most of them rarely set foot outside the subway and sidewalk network which connect most of the major buildings and plazas in the city so that your average environmentally polluting Texan businessman doesn't have to go outside in the sweltering heat they've helped to create.

Below ground level there is a veritable Aladdin's Cave of food shops, pharmacies, and specialist shops selling nothing in particular. At ground level there are glass panels separating the network from the sidewalk and leading eventually to plazas and courtyards that would once have been open to the elements but are now encased by high glass roofs. On a Sunday, with no businessmen near the town, access around the network is curtailed, shops and cafes are closed and things you take for granted, such as cashpoints, are locked away behind glass corridors. On a Monday access is easier, but it still makes the city seem a somewhat strange and unwelcoming place. While the city architecture is impressive, the place itself seems strangely soulless.

We wondered around the underground maze resurfacing to find it was dry once more, at which point we returned to Kennedy related tourism with a trip to the Conspiracy Museum, one of the few museums in the city that opens on Mondays.

The museum doesn't just focus on John F Kennedy - why should it when conspiracies are on every corner - it also gives you Martin Luther King, Abraham Lincoln, and, just to keep it in the family, Robert Kennedy. Its centrepiece was a grainy JFK related video of a Channel 4 dispatches show from the late eighties produced by Kevin Godley and Lol Creme of 10cc and Godley and Creme fame. The poor quality of the tape, and the fact that it is not widely available were presented in a way that suggested this was an underground film that the Government did not want you to see, rather than an old Channel 4 programme that, like any old programme, is naturally impossible to find nearly twenty years after it was shown, and any copies that do remain have inevitably deteriorated. Conspiracy theorists can miss the obvious sometimes.

Another display at the museum listed the links between the JFK and Lincoln assassinations. The evidence was clearly meant to expose some big over-arching conspiracy at the heart of American life, but instead it read like an exam answer where someone had been asked to come up with ten links and, after getting a few good ones, got bored and put down any old rubbish for the rest. But don't take my word for it. Here are the connections.

1.   Lincoln became president in 1860. Kennedy became president in 1960.

2.   Both had vice presidents called Johnson. In Lincoln's case it was Andrew Johnson, in Kennedy's Lyndon Baines Johnson.

3.   Both were shot on a Friday.

4.   Both assassins were killed before they could be sent to trial

5.   Lincoln was shot in the Ford's Theater, Kennedy was shot while driving in a Ford.

All good so far, but now it starts to go awry…

6.   Southern Democrats named Johnson succeeded them both. The Johnson's were opposed for re-election by Grant and Goldwater - men whose last name started with "G" - this may be true, but where the president is assassinated, you expect the vice president to take over, and the names of the VPs had already been used as a connection.

7.   John Wilkes Booth shot Lincoln in a theatre and was caught in a warehouse. Lee Harvey Oswald shot Kennedy from a warehouse and was caught in a theatre - only problem here is the warehouse in Booth's case was a tobacco barn, and the theatre in Harvey's case was a movie theatre.

8.   Both were shot in the presence of their wives - is this really so unusual? You would expect the wife of a president, or any famous person, to be with them in public sometimes. You could extend the link further and add John Lennon, seeing as how Yoko Ono was with him at the Dakota Building. Then again, they probably have done this.

9.   Each assassin was detained by an officer named Baker. Lt. Luther B. Baker was the leader of the cavalry patrol that trapped Booth at Garrett's barn. Officer Marion L. Baker, a Dallas motorcycle patrolman, briefly detained Oswald on the second floor of the School Depository - all well and good but the roles of the two Bakers are not really the same, and neither actually detained anyone. The Baker in Oswald's case briefly stopped him rather than detained him, and Booth was trapped, rather than detained, by a group of officers led by Lt.

Baker. That just leaves you with one Baker being vaguely involved in each case and, given the number of people with the surname, this is hardly unusual.

10. The names Andrew Johnson and Lyndon Johnson each contain 13 letters. John Wilkes Booth and Lee Harvey Oswald both contain 15 letters. The names Kennedy and Lincoln both contain 7 letters. All fair points, although it may be classed as cheating to count only the letters in the surnames for the presidents, and then to add forenames for vice-presidents, and full names for the assassins.

All in all, if I were running for president the only thing I might decide from this is not to ask anyone called Johnson to be my vice-president.

Since Kennedy, there have been no more Vice-President Johnson's. Maybe that's not a coincidence.

After the Conspiracy Museum, with the rain stopping and the day brightening up, we headed back to the West Village area of uptown for lunch and an afternoon trip round the shops. Although most of uptown seems to be under almost constant development, it is carried out so unobtrusively that it still looks relatively sedate and nothing like a building site littered with cranes and diggers. Also, unusually for America, the development isn't creating indoor big-box shopping malls. West Village is an old-fashioned tree lined residential area with apartments, houses, shops, restaurants, and even a cinema with less than five screens. People walk around in the open air, getting exposed to the elements in a way they would never do in the glass panel lined centre, and all in all it is fairly charming in a TV set kind of way. If you think back to the early days of Dallas, and the sort of stores and streets where Pam Ewing worked or Sue Ellen shopped, then you'll have a pretty good idea of what uptown looks like. And, believe it or not, that is not meant as a criticism.

When we get back to downtown it was 5 o'clock. The glass-covered shops were starting to close. People emerged from their hermetically sealed glass pods, leaving little more than a passing impression on the street landscape as they did the brief dash across the road to the nearest Dart station stop to take them home away from the city. Downtown Dallas was not like the TV show. There were no oilmen and no one wore big hats.

In the evening the West End Market Place was even emptier than it was late Sunday. We had a truly dreadful spaghetti in the Spaghetti

Warehouse, a fitting name given that the food tasted like it had been in storage for years, and then went on to a couple of bars. In the second the barmaid told us she had just moved from Boston for this job. I assumed and hoped she was the manager, not wanting to think that anyone would come all this way just for a bar job. She told us that unless there is a game on - the baseball and NFL stadiums are just a few blocks down the road - the area is dead in the week. We decided that as we were in an empty city we should at least be in a place that makes light of it and headed back to the neighbourhood pub without a neighbourhood for a last couple of drinks.

August 29. Just as we couldn't go to Dallas and not see the 6th floor book depository, we also couldn't go to Dallas and miss Southfork, the home of the Ewings.

Like Graceland, Southfork ranch is not as big as you expect, probably because very little of Dallas was actually filmed there, and what they did film was shot from wide angles to make it seem larger. The owners of the ranch insisted that, apart from Ms Ellie's kitchen, only exterior shots could be filmed, and all the shots had to be completed during the summer, out of term time, so their children wouldn't be distracted. They eventually sold the ranch for a vast sum of money at the height of the shows popularity. Their timing could not have been better. Shortly afterwards, the exterior shots ceased to be filmed at Southfork, and the new owners went bankrupt soon after. Forever Resorts, the hotel division of Forever Living Products, the world's largest grower, manufacturer and distributor of Aloe Vera-based products, bought the ranch for next to nothing in 1990 and recognising the marketing potential, recreated the interior as it was on the programme and turned the ranch into a tourist attraction. A year later Dallas was cancelled but, instead of making this seem a misplaced investment, visitors continued to come, and several years on Southfork still draws in the crowds.

Exiting the shop and museum at the front of the ranch, we went into the house where a talk about the ranch and TV programme were drowned out by a loud demonstrative child whose mother eventually realised that she was not going to be quiet long enough for her to hear it, and so took her out so that the rest of us could. The talk ended soon after she left, and we were set free to explore the house.

As re-creations go it's almost as good as the Oval Office in the Clinton Center, only the absence of JR drinks cabinet in the lounge will be noticed by anyone not looking too hard to spot continuity errors. After sitting at the pool, sitting at the outside dining table, and seeing Ray Krebb's house, we stopped at the site of the annual rodeo. The 'no entry' sign on the steps to where you get on your bull and ride had been moved, so I pretended not to see it and climbed the steps to get another wacky photo before we headed into the museum and, like star crossed fans, spent almost as much time there as we had at most of the heavyweight museums we'd been to in the last few days.

As we drove out, past the entrance with the distinctive Southfork Ranch arches that cars drove in through on the series, a German couple asked us to take a photo of them, and then returned the favour for us, and with that we left TV land behind and headed on to Interstate 35 and Oklahoma.

19 – The Road to New Mexico

The route to Oklahoma was a scenic one, taking in mountains, rocks and black coated hills. It was so reminiscent of the landscape in Cowboys and Indians films that I expected to see people hiding out in the hills, looking for the enemy, and preparing to ambush them. Eventually the landscape flattened out, and the hills were replaced by low lying fields and ranches that looked more like I imagined Texas would look than Texas itself did.

We'd decided to stay away from the centre of Oklahoma for two reasons. The first was that what we'd read of the city didn't bode well. The legacy of Timothy McVeigh and the 1995 bombing of the federal building meant that the city was still re-establishing itself several years later. The literature all spoke of the revitalised downtown area and businesses coming back to the city, which made it sound like most of the other supposedly big cities we'd been in since leaving Chicago. The other reason for avoiding the centre was that, trawling through hotels on the internet, I had discovered the Marriott Hotel overlooking Lake Hefner and this sounded far too good to pass up for a night in a faceless hotel in another city with an allegedly vibrant downtown and sod all else.

Sadly it turned out that the lake the hotel was meant to overlook had been overlooked. It was nowhere to be seen. Instead of a lake, it overlooked a car park, which overlooked a Borders store, which overlooked a petrol station, which overlooked houses, which overlooked more houses which overlooked nothing else for as far as the eye could see. Our room was on a high floor, but, if there was a lake, it was not on that side of the building. I walked down the corridor and looked out of every window I could find, at every angle I could think of, searching for a lakeside view that never appeared. Maybe if I'd gone on the roof and squinted I'd have spotted it somewhere in the distance, but I hadn't and I didn't.

Absence of lake aside, it was a tremendous hotel, but that's a bit like saying that apart from having no fans anymore the Spice Girls are still really popular. With nothing else in the immediate area and no desire to start driving again we contented ourselves with a three course meal and a few drinks in the bar. For the second time in a matter of days we found ourselves in a Karaoke evening. A collection of locals and business people on away days got up to sing. When there was no one waiting, the hostess sang to spur others on. Maybe it was the drink, maybe it was the feeling that this was something you have to do once in your life, and doing it in a room full of strangers is better than doing it in front of friends, maybe it was realising that being a good singer was a hindrance rather than a blessing for the average Karaoke star, or maybe it was none of these, but there was something that made me decide this was my moment. I got the songbook and sat with Liz looking for a song I might not massacre completely. I chose Tempted by Squeeze, and gave a performance that proved that wasn't the song.

Like TV quizzes where people say, "I always do really well when I watch it at home," it is far easier to sing karaoke in your mind than on a stage. I was destined to murder the song, and I met my destiny head on. Only a couple of chance coincidences, where my pitch and tone matched the pitch and tone of the backing, saved me from complete disaster and suggested that I could have done a better job. Not that anyone would have wanted me to try, of course.

Like everyone else, I was applauded at the end, but, also like everybody else, it was an applause borne partly out of pity, partly out of recognition of courage by people far too wise to do anything so daft themselves, and partly out of pre-meditated planning by the next set of singers who realise that if they clap you, you'll clap them. The one thing it wasn't borne out of was a recognition of talent. But at least I could cross Karaoke off my list of things to do, and could leave in the knowledge that I would never have to face any of the audience ever again, which was probably more a reward for them than for me.

August 30. Started the day with a trip to the gym, working off the embarrassment of last nights vocal exercises, then headed over to Borders where I bought a book and the soundtrack to the movie Garden State. In the film, the music sounds excellent. Strip the music of the dialogue and it becomes one of the wimpiest soundtracks ever, and not something to drive across the desert listening to. Another great CD purchase.

Shortly after leaving the hotel we were back on Route 66 for the first time since St Louis. Route 66 in Oklahoma has retained its identity as a road and also retained the business and the life it had prior to the Interstate. It has a number of small towns, each of which have their own small claims to fame. First off was Yukon, where the entry to the town bears the words 'Home of Garth Brooks' and where there is a road named after America's favourite nineties country star. All of which suggests there has probably never been a president, or anyone else of note, born in Yukon. El Reno was next. Its claim to fame is that it has a motel that was featured in Rain Man. Sadly for El Reno, the Big Eight motel was relocated to Amarillo in the film. As a result El Reno doesn't attract many tourists.

After Route 66 got submerged into Interstate 40 we turned off on to US Highway 281, and stopped at a park in a canyon with red rocks, which was imaginatively named the Red Rock Canyon State Park. A short while after leaving the park, we passed the equally imaginatively named Red River, which was a river where the water ran red. I wondered how they came up with the names.

We were heading to Indian City USA in Anadarko, the only authentic reconstruction of American Indian dwellings in the United States. Built on the site of the massacre of Tonkawa Indians by Shawnees and other mercenaries in the civil war, the city has reconstructions of seven authentic Indian villages, including the Navaho, Comanche, Choctaw, Tonkawa and Apache. The tour round the site was given by a Native American, a practising tribesman for whom this was a part of his life and not just a hobby or a job. With real interest in his subject matter, he told us the history of the tribes, how the Plains Indians lived and how their life was reflected in the designs of their houses.

The type of buildings each tribe lived in would reflect its intended use and the nature of the tribe. Tribes that followed buffalo made homes that could be taken down and moved in about ten minutes. Tribes that moved with the seasons built settlements appropriate to whatever season it was, and tribes that stayed in one place built homes with doors on the top to protect them from unexpected attacks - a good security system, but unlikely to be revived in the foreseeable future. All the buildings

168

made imaginative use of the environment. Mud and clay were used to keep them cool in summer and retain the heat in winter. Ventilation was provided by twigs in the roofs and by the wattle in the body of the buildings that stopped shortly before both floor and roof to create gaps for air. If only town planners of the nineties had put as much thought into their buildings as this, we might not have been hearing as much about the energy crisis as we do.

You can go into the buildings, although, in the two smallest and darkest ones, you do so at your own risk. We were told the darkest one had a snake in it the last time anyone looked. No one was brave enough to go in, but I was stupid enough to. This was more out of a general long-standing desire to look into any small building I pass, than a hope that I would come face to face with a snake. Inside, it was so dark I could see nothing, until I turned round and looked above the entrance where, in front of me, a mere matter of inches away, was………nothing at all. I felt disappointment and relief in equal measure.

After tipping the guide at the end of the tour and noting that, somewhat unusually, very few others did, I was taught a small part of an Indian Tribal language, as he responded with "Iho babi" and told me it means "thank you my friend", which was better than finding out it meant "is that all you are giving me you tight arse."

After leaving Indian city we decided on a long drive round the area to see more of the scenery and find somewhere to stay for the night. The drive was scenic in places and deserted throughout. Whenever the radio signal disappeared, which it often did, we heard cracking noises which sounded like stones chipping the window, but turned out to be flying insects hitting the car. The only towns we passed through were Roosevelt, which had nothing, and Blair, which had a few cafes, but, aside from these, also had nothing.

I had seen an advert for Lake Altus in a magazine the night before. I knew there was somewhere to stay there, and was determined to find it. After a couple of hours we made it to the Quartz Mountain State Park and the Quartz Mountain Resort on the lake, a lake we could see, with no car parks, Borders stores or Interstates to block the tremendous view out towards it and the mountains. The Quartz Mountains have long eroded to the point where they no longer deserve the name mountain, but as two very tall hills in plains country they still offered a scene of genuine beauty.

We checked in for the evening. The hotel and rooms had the feel of a mountain lodge not a hotel, and every room had a superb view. In spite of having the word 'resort' in the name, Quartz Mountain was not a big tourist, or timeshare, location. It had a conference centre that no one was using, but other than that it seemed much further away than the twenty or so miles it was from the city of Altus.

Outside, the feeling of nature was added to by the absence of any noise other than insects and birds. The air was fresh and there was wildlife to watch – we saw a deer and a racoon who came up to the outside of the restaurant window in the evening. There were trails leading off from the hotel, and a circuitous route down to the beach and the lake via a footbridge and the side of the mountains. Set into the grounds higher up there was an amphitheatre in such a fantastically rugged and remote location that even the worst drama group would be able to create some kind of atmosphere if they performed there.

In the evening I looked on as the sky changed colour and the sun started to set. The view and the atmosphere made me think of when the Native Americans lived there at one with nature, marking the passage of time only by the changes in the position of the sun and the moon, without any of the trappings of modern day life. It reminded me how much of modern life is false, and how free we could be if only we let ourselves appreciate what is around us rather than competing for prizes in an ultimately meaningless rat race. Sitting by Lake Altus as the light faded for the day, the world made sense and was all the better for it.

August 31. I took a run around the grounds of the park first thing in the morning, then headed to the cave trail, walking through rocks and peering into caves like a curious child. After breakfast, deciding that the landscape was too big to capture by photographs alone, we charged up our ancient video camera, loaned to us by my parents, and filmed around the grounds of the resort, and a short way further round the lake where there was a small shop and a campsite for the hardier travellers.

And then it was back towards Route 66 which we rejoined at the wonderfully named Elk City, a city which has no Elks and is probably too small to really claim to be a city. Elk City does have two claims to fame however. The first is that it is the home of the official National Route 66 Museum. The second is that it is also the home of Susan Powell, Miss America 1981. These two claims tell you all you need to know to correctly gauge the size and stature of Elk City.

We stopped at a Days Inn Motel to ask for directions. The receptionist told us the city was "a large but spread out place," a description that was inaccurate on both counts, with the centre seeming to consist of little more than two large roads with a group of chain motels and shops at the bottom of one, and four museums and a park in the middle of the other.

The four museums are the Route 66 Museum, the Transportation Museum, the Old Town Museum, and the Farm and Ranch Museum. You can get into all four for one admission, and they are all conveniently situated next to each other to make sure you don't lose interest or get lost while looking at all that Elk City has to offer. We started off with Route 66. While there are lots of Route 66 museums along the road, most of them only cover their stretch and some are little more than shops. As the official museum, Elk City's is one of the few that covers all of the Mother Road, and throws in an old pick up truck, like the one used to take the journey west in the Grapes of Wrath, for good measure. A large map plots the route across the country so that you can see what you have done and what there is still to do before you reach the end. It's a good little museum, although it doesn't have as much as you would expect from an official museum. If you had gone out of your way to see it you would probably be disappointed, but, as a Route 66 museum on Route 66, the odds of anyone having gone out of their way to see it are small.

The other three museums provided good trips into a long forgotten past. The best was the Old Town Museum where we nipped into the mock old railway station, the mock old sheriff's office, the mock old courthouse and the mock old shops. We also went into the mock old two story Victorian house where, alongside displays on the lives of the pioneers, cowboys and rodeo riders there was also a display on Susan Powell, presumably because they could find nowhere else to put a celebration of their most famous daughter, rather than because 1981 is deemed to be way back when in Elk City. For those of you wondering what has become of Susan, she is now an actress, acting was her first love, and she is getting a fair bit of work. No doubt she is also pleased that no one else from Elk City has become Miss America since 1981 so her place in the city's memory and museum remains secure for now.

On leaving the museums I realised that I was not sure which of the two main roads became Route 66 as it was tangled up with the I-40 at this point, and the museum was on the crossroads. To make sure we had the right road I walked back into the Route 66 Museum to ask for directions. Our next stop was Amarillo. There was only one question I could ask, and I had a genuine reason for asking it. Sadly, fearful of the response "oh god, another English tourist who's heard that sodding record and thinks it's funny," I wimped out and asked simply whether this was the westbound Route 66, missing the once in a lifetime opportunity to legitimately ask "Is this the way to Amarillo?"

After it was confirmed that this was Route 66, and it was indeed heading west, we headed out on the Mother Road, following what we could of it as it took its own route before merging once again with the I-40. At several exits along the way there were turn-off's with a historic route 66 sign or an I-40 business loop sign which normally meant the same thing. Each time we came to one we took it to explore the old road. The towns we passed through were some of the most deserted you will ever see. Texola was the most deserted and derelict of all of them. On the border of Texas and Oklahoma, which partly explains its name, the few buildings that remained included a gas station and a few houses with no signs of life coming from any of them. Maybe the houses had previously been rented, or their owners had died leaving no relatives and no one else who could be bothered trying to sell them. Either way, it felt like a ghost town.

I had read in a book that the only signs of life emanating from Texola were the shouts and swears emanating from the combined pool hall and beer bar in the large metal shed on the south side of the old highway. Even these appeared to have disappeared, and nothing but silence remained.

Inside Texas, towns like Shamrock, McLean and Alanreed were not completely dead, but looked as if someone should be reading them the last rites. They all had variations on the motel, gas station, and burger joint combination that denote towns that were once on a major road, but in each case it looked like it had been a long time since they had any passing trade. McLean is, or was, headquarters of Texas' Historic Route 66 Association. They were trying to preserve the town in prime condition around the turn of the century. Unless I missed something, they appear to have given up on their mission.

The most interesting town on this stretch of Route 66 was, without a shadow of a doubt, Groom. With a population of 613 in 1990 and 587 ten years later, it is safe to say it is not a thriving town, but it does have three things of note. The first is a water tower that leans like the tower of Pisa, and yet somehow remains standing. The second is a gigantic white stainless steel cross, 190 feet high, visible miles before you reach it, and guaranteed to scare the hell out of any sinners driving past unawares on a dark evening. The third is the Blessed Mary's burger bar and restaurant, which offers 'Burgers, faith, hope and love', as opposed to 'fries, mayonnaise and a soft drink'. It closes its doors at five o'clock each day, opens every day of the year regardless of custom or weather, and has no prices on the menu and no cash register on the premises, preferring instead to have a big jar by the door and a sign asking you to pay what you can. Any profits are donated to charity. Its owner, Jim Moraniec, was told to do this by the voice that guides all of his business decisions. It goes without saying that the voice is God's.

Jim, by the way, is a 71 year old Michigan native who worked as an engineer at the nuclear bomb factory in Amarillo for 31 years. Say what you like about radiation and the hazards of nuclear power, it clearly hasn't affected Jim.

On reaching Amarillo we booked into the Holiday Inn just off the Interstate. In the evening we went into town and discovered that Amarillo is yet another city that has been bypassed by big-box developments. On the main street there were a fair few bars and restaurants, which were all reasonably busy in a workers night out kind of way, but, beyond this, city life came quickly to a halt with nothing signifying the victory of business over entertainment more than the Paramount Building, which used to be an old cinema but was now being revitalised as an office block. In that wacky, 'we are a business, but we also have fun' style, beloved by executives with no discernible sense of humour, the businesses about to move in were advertised as if they were future cinema attractions. Sadly none of them were worth watching so we had a meal at Zen, an excellent local restaurant, and then went to Bodega's where we had a drink and listened to a band playing covers. It was a good evening, but not one that you couldn't have in most other cities.

Back at the hotel, an Indian barmaid was doing her best to bore an old couple senseless with inane conversation about an ass killing a lion to protect a boy. I was desperately trying to follow the story but failed miserably as she changed topic and started to talk about her anti-drink stance, always a good move for a barmaid. She said she had never drunk and had never wanted to. She continued talking, in spite of their obvious lack of interest, proving that you don't need to be drunk to talk crap and bore people rigid in bars.

The bar closed up around midnight and we went to have a look around the rest of the cavernous lobby of the hotel. There was a games area with a Pacman machine and other games that looked like they had been acquired as a job lot from a bankruptcy sale for the local fair. There was a general air of neglect about the place, which could apply as much to the city as the hotel.

The visitor guide suggested there was so much here, but closer inspection showed that most of it was someplace to the north, south, east or west of the city, and there was nothing in Amarillo that the literature had neglected to tell us about.

Is this the way to Amarillo? Thanks, I'll take a different route.

September 1. We had decided that the room was fairly dirty and unloved shortly after checking in, and as I woke in the morning, following the most uncomfortably hot and sticky night I had spent in any hotel, I discovered it was also a haven for all manner of creature, and I now had several mosquito and flea bites. This was not the only unwelcome intrusion to my life as I woke in the early hours of the morning.

Travelling had become a way of life, the point at which it ceased to feel like a holiday had long passed. Living in Kingston seemed a distant memory, home was a succession of hotels, and my occupation was driving between them and sightseeing. Against that background, I neither expected nor wanted to hear Jeff Stelling talking about transfer deadline dates on the Sky Sports News channel, but, suddenly and unexpectedly, he was there, in my room, on my TV.

For a while I wondered whether I was back in England or just hallucinating as a result of venom released by one of the many creatures that had bitten me. Eventually I decided it was real, mainly because I could flick up and down the channels and come back to it. It was probably the only thing about the hotel that would endear it to any Brits who had made pilgrimages here off the back of a Peter Kay video. Finding little else of interest on any other channels, I tuned back in and the soothing tones of football talk eased me back to sleep while the fleas stayed awake determined to continue feasting.

The thought of breakfast here was faintly repulsive, so we checked out and went down the old San Jacinto area of the city, also known as the Route 66 historic district on 6th Avenue. It used to be home to honky tonk joints and motorbike bars, but now also boasts diners and fine antique shops. This may seem an odd combination until you realise that when they say antique shops what they mean is junk stores with stock from house clearances. The most interesting shop in the area wasn't an antique shop, it was a costume shop with a window display that featured Pink Panther and Scooby Doo costumes alongside more traditional ghosts and vampire gear. I imagined leather-clad bikers going into the store and emerging as popular cartoon animals a few moments later.

We went for breakfast in one of the many small cafes which all resembled biker bars or the American equivalent of greasy spoons, and consequently guaranteed a fantastic breakfast so long as you didn't worry too much about cholesterol levels. We had bacon butties, tea and coffee, a decidedly English breakfast in a decidedly American setting. Walking back down the road we passed Record Joint which looked like it could have been an excellent second hand shop, but no longer existed, the antique shops probably having cornered the market in buying and selling old records.

After that we left Amarillo, never to return, and rejoined Route 66. This stretch of Route 66 would have been completely unworthy of note were it not for the very small town of Adrian. The very small town of Adrian would have been completely unworthy of note were it not for it being the exact midpoint of Route 66.

The population of Adrian was one hundred and fifty the last time anyone bothered counting. The 'Welcome to Adrian' road sign tells you that this is Route 66 and Los Angeles and Chicago are both 1,139 miles away from you in opposite directions. Elsewhere Adrian has a cafe, which is logically, and for the avoidance of doubt, called the Midpoint Cafe; a motel which, in a sardonic reference to the Interstate that bypassed it, is called the Fabulous 40 motel; a post office that has no name; and, Billy's tires, which is presumably owned by a man named Billy and most definitely fits and sells tires. Apart from these, it has a couple of Aermotor windmills, some factories and little else - were it not for its position it would probably have gone the same way as Texola and closed up completely.

The Midpoint Cafe is an excellent cafe with a great little museum and shop at the back of it. The roadside sign for the cafe is a mix of bright colours, angular shapes and the words Midpoint Cafe. Standing at the end of a thirty-foot poll, and set against a backdrop of endless empty flat plains that create a splendid sense of isolation, it looks like it should be an iconic image for any road traveller.

On the day we were there all the customers so far had been European, with a large group of Norwegian bikers turning up earlier and a group of Germans who, living up to stereotypes, had rang earlier to say they were coming and to make sure they got chairs. The manageress chatted to us with a genuine interest in where we were from, how long we'd been doing Route 66, and where we'd been. She'd seen more of Route 66 than we had, but we were still ahead on how much of the rest of the country we'd seen.

We passed an hour in the museum without realising it, and then said farewell, heading back round the corner to where we'd parked the car. We were probably the only customers not on motorbikes. While taking a car along the Mother Road is not forbidden, the car should probably be something rebellious, dynamic or iconic. A Ford Fusion ticks none of these boxes, which is why I was pleased the car was out of view when the manageress asked how we'd got there, and why I hope she wasn't looking when we left.

After Adrian, Route 66 leads back to Interstate 40 and the next time it reappears is at Glenrio which sits on the border of Texas and New Mexico. Glenrio is unusual for a town that crosses Texas borders as it does not have Tex in its name. If Texas were a person it would sew its name tag into its clothes, just so everyone knew who they belonged to. Texola and Texhoma sit on the borders with Oklahoma, Texico is on a border with New Mexico, and Texarkana sits on the border with Arkansas.

There are perhaps two reasons why Glenrio doesn't have Tex in its name. The first is that Texas probably doesn't care enough about it to claim it. It consists of a few derelict houses, a cafe and an old burnt out van, making Texola look thriving in comparison. The second reason is that with Texico already taken, the only remaining name for a place that borders Texas and New Mexico is Texmex, and that wouldn't be the first name you'd choose for a place.

Following Route 66 out the other side of Glenrio was a bad idea as, a couple of miles in, it turned into an old dust track with nothing to convince us it would lead back to the Interstate or anywhere else with a 'Historic Route 66' marker. Tempting as it is to go far back in time to discover long forgotten stretches of road, the heyday of Route 66 was in

176

the forties and fifties, and ranching towns bypassed before then can offer only knackered suspension and long drives back after you realise the road has become a series of potholes, rocks and little else.

Returning to the main road, and another part of Route 66 that is now Interstate 40 we were in New Mexico and Tucumcari, also known as 'the town that's two blocks long and two miles wide' a description that could have applied to Elk City if they took away the two miles wide part of it. Tucumcari used to announce itself with signs proclaiming 'Tucumcari Tonight - 2,000 Motel Rooms.' This was revised down to 1,500 and then 1,200 as the number of motels decreased. It doesn't seem to make any claims now, which is probably a good idea as monitoring the decline of an area through road signs isn't a good form of self-publicity.

Plenty of motels have survived the decline however. The Blue Swallow Motel, described as 'the last, best and friendliest of the old-time motels' by the Smithsonian Magazine, is the most notable. Had it been later in the day we would have booked a night there to see if it could live up to this claim, but, as you can't fill an afternoon and evening marvelling at how good your Motel is, and the rest of the town didn't seem to offer much else by way of distraction, we carried on and drove through Montoya, Newkirk and Cuervo, another place where Route 66 ceased to be a road by any popular definition of the word, before reaching Santa Rosa, where we decided to stop ahead of the short drive to Albuquerque the following day.

Santa Rosa is another motel town that stretches for a few blocks. It has a downtown area just before you reach the end of town. The main distinctions between it and the rest of the town are that the shops and bars are smaller, there are diners rather than chain restaurants and the motels are privately owned. We stopped at the other end of town and booked into the Best Western. People talk about how the chains have taken over the motel business leaving you with faceless towns where the same names continually appear in slightly different orders. While there is a lot of truth in this, the Best Western somehow retained something of an individual charm and friendly personalised atmosphere, alongside the pre-requisite free Internet and matching king-size beds of course.

We chatted to the manager, who told us he had lived in the UK in Harrow until he was twenty-four, then moved to LA for twenty-four years, and had now moved to Santa Rosa to run a Best Western franchise. It seemed a strange career trajectory, but he liked it.

It was the start of the Labor Day public holiday weekend that marks the end of the summer. In true bank holiday style the weather was atrocious. Had it not been for the roadworks along the sidewalk that made us decide not to attempt to walk downtown, we would have been caught in yet another deluge as the rain and thunder began at 5:30 and continued unabated till late evening. We put our plans to see the Blue Hole, an eighty-foot wide, two-hundred and forty-foot deep artesian well filled with water so clear it draws scuba divers from all over the western states, on hold for the day deciding that if a well that size would still contain less water than us after thirty minutes, it could wait. We spent the late afternoon and early evening using the laundry, and booking our next hotels instead.

When the rain finally slowed we walked along to the nearby Dennys and got our evening meal. We had had lunch there earlier, so it's fair to say we didn't really see all Santa Rosa had to offer on the food front. Full credit to Dennys however for being more than the burger chain we thought it was. Proper meals at decent prices, and tasty enough to have come from somewhere far more illustrious, we could see why it is a beloved institution for over-fifties travellers. As we left Denny's, the motel, which had been nearly empty earlier, was filling up with seasoned road travellers who had crammed as much driving into a day as possible and then stopped late on ready to start again early the next morning. Even though we arrived several hours before them, they had probably seen the same amount of the city as we had.

20 – New Mexico

September 2. We got up relatively early, and found out that all of last night's late arrivals had already gone. We had breakfast and said our goodbyes to the manager. He told us he hoped to see us again next time we were round this way, and added that he occasionally returned to the UK, prompting us to return the gesture and tell him to get in touch next time he was over. Neither of us expected ever to meet again, I'm sure.

The weather channel was dominated by the possibility of Hurricane Ernesto hitting the mainland, and the storms that were happening in Washington, Philadelphia and New York. It seemed like a long time since we had been in any of those cities, which was more a consequence of the number of places we'd been to since, than the actual time that had elapsed.

Because of the rain we missed the second and final chance to stop at the Blue Hole, but did just about see the other main site in Santa Rosa, the famous Fat Man logo. The logo, the smiling face of a fat man in jacket and tie, used to belong to the Club Cafe and was emblazoned on signs for miles in both directions from it. Because it was such a friendly face it drew customers in by the shedload. It lives on now at Joseph's on Will Rogers Drive, but has changed slightly from the old days. In an age where obesity levels are causing concern, the change hasn't been to slim down however, instead the fat man appears to have had a bit of a hair transplant. I'm not sure what that says about America's biggest preoccupations looks or health-wise.

Leaving Santa Rosa, we followed Interstate 40 into Albuquerque. Staying in Albuquerque was a late decision. Months before, when we first started planning the route and began looking for stops, it was on the itinerary before Flagstaff and the Grand Canyon. It was there not because we knew anything about the place, but simply because it was name checked by Prefab Sprout in The King of Rock'n'Roll. It had come off the list after a friend told me it was an ugly city and we should avoid it and head up to Santa Fe instead. If only he'd been to Amarillo, we might have avoided going to another place on the basis of a record.

Albuquerque came back on to the itinerary courtesy of a good write up in a tour guide and the fact that we had not realised how popular Santa Fe would be on a bank holiday weekend. We couldn't get a hotel there till Monday so we booked two nights at the Hotel Albuquerque in Albuquerque's historic old town. The hotel was massive, but had the feel of a rambling 17th century villa deep in the heart of Spain rather than a large hotel in America. Checking in early we got a suite on one of the top floors, which also didn't resemble anything from a large hotel, with wooden floors and furniture, Mexican styled artwork on the walls and great views out towards the mountains. Only by looking down to the car park was the image even remotely shattered.

Leaving the hotel and walking into the historic old town we were taken completely by surprise, even though the style of the hotel should have given us a hint as to what to expect. The old town is not just a collection of old buildings, it feels like it belongs to a different era and continent entirely. Reflecting New Mexico's Spanish colonial past, it is a village laid out in the classic Spanish style of a central plaza surrounded by a church, homes, cantina-style eateries, saloons - as opposed to bars - small shops and a town hall.

The buildings are made with adobe bricks, protected with mud and cement, and have traditional flat roofs and curved edges, made possible thanks to the hot weather and limited rainfall in the area. While most of them are old, newer buildings have been constructed in a similar style and, whilst looking a bit plastic in comparison, are still completely different from your average American home.

Stay anywhere else in the city and you leave with a very different impression, something we discovered when we got the downtown trolley to the new part of Albuquerque, the part of the city that comes closest to deserving the description of ugly, but is better served by the description unloved. The downtown civic plaza dates back to 1972. A large open space, it doesn't have the charm of the old town, but could be part of a nice walk to work or a place to sit and eat lunch on a weekday break from the office. On a Saturday afternoon, however, it is an empty part of an anonymous city centre, and the preserve of the homeless and the drunk. We were approached by another supposed veteran who looked far to young to have fought in any war where you could acquire the veterans tag. We contemplated stopping at a bar, but a look inside it brought to mind a weekday afternoon at a pub in Walsall, which wasn't really the type of thing we were looking for. Nothing else even remotely grabbed our attention save for a gentleman's club – for which, read strip joint – which had a sign listing what was on offer inside that ended with the words 'discreet rear entrance'. We assumed and hoped that there was an entry towards the back of the club that was not easily visible to the public.

We headed back through a suburban landscape of tree-lined roads that gave no hint of either the old or new towns they linked. At the hotel, a large wedding was taking place, and the wealthy of Albuquerque were out in force, making the garden out of bounds for anyone whose name was not on the guest list. We went to the Q-Bar, the hotels chiq designer style bar, and then to the High Noon Restaurant and Saloon. In spite of not being an area dripping in wealth, the High Noon, like most restaurants in the old town, was on the pricey side, but the interior and exterior of the two hundred year old building created a setting worthy of the bill. Once again, we felt like we were somewhere from a different time and place compared to anywhere we had stayed before. We certainly weren't in the same era that Dennys in Santa Rosa was, that's for sure.

Finding anywhere to drink afterwards was not easy. Most of the places were aimed at people wanting to eat, so after one relatively long stop we ended the evening at the Q-Bar, where the second petty crime of the trip occurred.

As with the accidental taking of a map in New York, there was nothing deliberate about this crime but, as with most inner-city crimes, it was alcohol related. When we first sat down, the waitress service was good and it was just too easy to carry on drinking as they came over and took our order every time our glasses got low. This continued till shortly after midnight, when they all seemed to suddenly disappear and we spent ages waiting to get another drink or settle our bar tab. Tiredness made us want to leave, and alcohol made us forget that there was a simple option, which was going to the bar rather than waiting for the bar to come to us. Having failed to realise this, we did the only thing that came to mind, and went back to the room without paying.

I woke up the next morning worried that the hotel bar staff would be waiting to arrest me when I went for breakfast.

September 3. Liz slept on while I suffered pangs of guilt and the feeling of imminent reprisals for not settling the bar tab. I put these behind me and wrote a long e-mail to friends until Liz woke up. It became a very long e-mail, and eventually with nothing more to say and only the faintest of stirrings from the bed, I decided to go to breakfast. I made my way downstairs. No one looked at me as if I was an arch criminal, so I decided not to confess, but just to leave the money in the room when we checked out. I ordered a Mexican style breakfast that consisted of most of the ingredients of an English style breakfast but with hot chilli sauce on top for that distinctive Mexican touch.

When I got back to the room Liz was still asleep, making me wonder just how many drinks I hadn't paid for. Rather than ponder on this I decided to go round the corner to the Albuquerque Museum of Art and History, on the edge of the old town. Liz woke briefly and decided not to join me, but promised to be up by the time I got back. As that was likely to be a couple of hours away, it seemed an easy promise to make.

The museum was excellent. Before I went inside, I spent a good half hour in the Sculpture Garden where sculptures of New Mexican history were thoughtfully arranged rather than slung together in a 'the arrangement doesn't matter, these people are famous' style.

Inside, I was asked if I was from New Mexico. I said no and was told I would have to pay an admission charge. When I followed this up by saying I was from England, I was told that in that case it was okay and I could get in for free. I took this as a sign that it's not just people from outside Albuquerque who find little to remind them they are in an American city, if the only people they charge to enter a museum are Americans from outside of the state.

The museum contains almost exactly what it says on the tin - art and history from New Mexico, if not from Albuquerque itself. A wall of fame, which is more like a corridor than an actual room, begins the museum, commemorating individuals who made a big contribution to the past and present of Albuquerque. After that, the Four Centuries galleries trace the origins of New Mexico from Spanish rule through self-governance, American territorial rule, and on to Statehood in 1912. Then, with you now fully dosed up on the history side of the deal, the art side of the museum commences.

The art galleries cover modern and contemporary paintings alongside paintings by native Americans rooted in tribal history and customs and combining styles across centuries and cultures. The depth and variety of work is all the more impressive for being relatively, or entirely, unknown outside New Mexico. I felt like I was stumbling upon undiscovered artists, which made for a very enjoyable and rewarding experience.

A temporary exhibition on migration drew the art and history sections together with an excellent collection of montages merging together photographs, household objects, and other mementoes of migrant families from before and after they moved to New Mexico. An excellent argument in favour of hoarding obscure possessions and never throwing anything away, all I have to do now is take my own junk out of boxes and I have a major exhibition.

In the afternoon we got a taxi over to the Casa Rondena Winery on the outskirts of the city. It seemed an eternity before we reached the winery. Once we were there the first of a few illusions I had about wineries was shattered. I had imagined you would be able to take tours round them, walk through fields of grapes and look at barrels slowly fermenting. Turns out that generally speaking you can't, and the Casa Rondena was a winery that fitted the rule rather than the exception.

That said, the promotional material still offered the prospect of strolling through the great hall with its cathedral ceilings, antique oak fermentation tank and Indian-carved sandstone-shaded windows before enjoying a glass of wine in the Vineyard Garden replete with bubbling fountains, rose bushes, mountain views, a pond and a vine-shaded arbor. This would have been good were it not that it was clearly wedding weekend in Albuquerque and all of the above had been taken out of commission by another happy couple's big day.

My next illusion was shattered when I discovered that tasters were not the size of a full glass and you do not get enough free ones to make driving impossible. Each of the five taste wines seemed to be measured out using estimates on how many mouthfuls they would take to swallow, rather than anything recognised in imperial or metric systems. We drank the three or four small mouthfuls of each before leaving.

As there was nothing much else within walking distance, we had taken a long taxi ride for what was basically a tasting session, at the end of which I was still sober enough to drive. With the time it took to get a return cab, it would have been quicker taking the car even if I were drunk and had to sleep in it till I sobered up.

The Taxi Company must have decided to send us a taxi driver with no sense of direction, no Satellite Navigation, and no idea of how to read a map. An initial twenty-minute estimated time came and went with no appearance. Two irate phone calls to check on his whereabouts didn't manage to locate him, but did manage to use up the last of the credit on my cell phone. After a call to add more credit, a third irate call revealed that he was somewhere in the area, that he didn't know where the winery was, that the road he was taking was very busy, and that he was on his way and should be there soon. Soon was not defined. Eventually, almost an hour and a half after our twenty minute tasting session, the taxi appeared. The driver greeted us in a jolly way, proclaiming "the roads are a bit busy and this place is difficult to find." No shit. And, needless to say, no tip, when we finally arrived back at the hotel.

It was nearly 5 o'clock, I had had no food since the morning, and Liz had had no food all day, so the first thing we did was find somewhere to eat. Chicken Quesadillas were devoured in record time with more time spent over a Mexican beer and a glass of wine. A few hours later we ate at Cristobals, the main hotel in the restaurant, which, as with most places in Albuquerque, served Spanish Mexican cuisine. I had a Pork Burrito that consisted of a mountain of shredded meat lurking under a mountain of cheese and further mountains of vegetables and burritos. Realising I had no chance of finishing it, I felt less compelled to try than I would have, and gave up after a quarter of an hour, piling what remained onto a corner of the plate to make it look like I'd ate a lot more than the meagre amount I actually had.

We worked the dinner off with a walk around the old town, which had gained an extra serenity from the absence of people. There was a group taking the Old Town Ghost Tour, hoping to see the towns thirteen ghosts. If all of them had appeared at once, they would have outnumbered the tour-goers. After a drink in a quite saloon bar we went back to our room to drink one of three bottles we'd brought at the Casa Rondero. It felt like we were drinking in a small intimate cafe rather than spending Sunday evening in a hotel room, and at least tonight there was no question of not settling the bar tab.

September 4. Labor Day morning. We took the camera round the old town and the sculpture garden and filmed the mountains that surround the city. The mountain view is another thing that makes the historic old town special. Downtown the skyscrapers obscure the view, but from the old town you can look out beyond the city and understand why New Mexico calls itself the Land of Enchantment.

With the bank holiday travellers heading home we drove to Santa Fe heading out of the city on Central Avenue, part of Route 66 which takes you through Nob Hill, the other fashionable area of Albuquerque. Nob Hill looks like you expect Route 66 to look more often than it does. Driving along it you can imagine how the ghost towns that line the road would have looked years ago, and can understand why so many thousands of people were drawn to the road. It's lined with brightly coloured motels, restaurants, bars and shops. The neon lighting outside the old style diners and motels welcome you into the area and see you back out of it. The classy sits alongside the tacky, galleries follow adult video stores, and strip joints follow theatres. We drove the whole length of it, soaking in the atmosphere, before turning round and driving back again. This wasn't because we had a desperate urge to see it a second time, it was because the turn off for Santa Fe was at the start of the road.

Santa Fe was not part of the final incarnation of Route 66, but the original road did run through it, going from where the I-25 corridor branches off from Route 66 and heading straight into the city, where it turned east to Santa Rosa along what is now US Highway 84. The city was left behind by the road when the development of the railroad meant it could be by-passed, and the shorter road that links Santa Rosa and Albuquerque was developed.

If you want a short description of Santa Fe, the city takes Albuquerque's Historic Old Town, trebles the size of it and ditches all of the non-historic parts so that there isn't anything that looks remotely modern. Whilst it might have lost its place on Route 66, Santa Fe remains the state capital of New Mexico - another state whose capital is not its largest city - and remains a popular tourist destination, nestling at the edge of the Santa Fe National Forest with the Sangre De Christo Mountains to the north of it.

We had booked into the Inn of the Governors, a name that sounded like an east end pub run by old Sweeney style cops, rather than a historic inn and hotel on West Alameda in the heart of the city. Half of the rooms were inside the main body of the independently run hotel while the others were outside, down corridors decorated with bright coloured plants. These captured the Mexican feel more than the inside ones, but I would say that seeing as how we stayed in one of them.

Santa Fe is awash with money and celebrity homes, which are occupied for varying amounts of time. Oprah Winfrey has a house in the hills, Shirley Maclean wanted a house on the hills, but laws limiting how high any building can be in comparison to city landmarks, meant she didn't get to build as high as she wanted and now only visits occasionally. Val Kilmer, meanwhile, is a regular visitor and even preaches at his local church on Sundays when he's in town.

The historic buildings that frame the city are all built in Spanish Mexican style with the exception of the Cathedral Basilica of Saint Francis of Assisi, which, for no apparent reason, was built in a French Romanesque style. Pope Benedict XVI elevated the Cathedral to a Basilica in October 2005, perhaps fitting in a city whose name translates as Holy Faith. The Cathedral was unfinished for a long time. Concerns over the building materials, style, and cost meant that the one hundred and sixty foot steeples planned for the two towers never got made, and, even after completion of shortened versions, the left tower was, and remains, one row of bricks lower than the right one. Not that you would notice this if you weren't told by a tour guide. Not that there is any chance of a tour guide not telling you.

We took the one o'clock trolley round the city, and out into the hills. The existence of vast amounts of money was clear from the number of galleries throughout the city. There are around thirty on Canyon Road alone. All of them have sculpture gardens outside, applying varying levels of quality control, so that next to excellent and innovative sculptures thoughtfully displayed, you get something that resembles the garden section of Homebase. Prices are high irrespective of quality. If you are buying art, go to Albuquerque, if you are selling art, go to Santa Fe.

There is also the Santa Fe Arts Festival that takes place over Labor Day weekend. By Monday, the market stalls covering the large historic grass plaza are all that remains of the festival, but Santa Fe doesn't rest for too long as the following weekend brings Fiesta. The original theme of the fiesta was the re-conquering of New Mexico by the Spanish in 1692 after the pueblo revolt of 1680. In 1924, to prevent the religious elements of the festival damping down the exuberance, they added the burning of Zozobra, a fifty-foot tall marionette with a black bow tie and white frock-type costume who represents Old Man Gloom. Burning him is a symbolic banishing of gloom.

The burning is accompanied by a firework display helping to further banish the gloom, unless you don't like fireworks. A mix of pagan-like jubilation and catholic reverence, the closest the UK comes to it is the yearly Lewes bonfire celebrations. Both are influenced by Catholicism, the biggest difference being that in Lewes you normally see at least one burning pope, something that wouldn't happen in Santa Fe. As to just how similar the two are I couldn't say, as we left town a couple of days before the burning of Zozobra, in much the same way as we arrived just as the Arts Festival ended. A notable double whammy in a trip characterised by single whammies.

Back in the Inn of the Governors, for an afternoon treat, complimentary sherry and biscuits are served in the lobby and around the pool. Sounds stuffy and formal but is anything but, sherry being just a nice afternoon drink round here. Sporting a Tennessee T-shirt and shorts, I was approached by a guest from Tennessee who wrongly assumed that I was wearing the T-shirt because it was my home state and I needed something to remind me of the fact. Misunderstanding cleared up, he joined the list of Americans to have seen less of the country than us, but as he had been to the Grand Canyon he offered us some useful tips including recommending a restaurant and advising us to book early. The friendliness of strangers in America once again made me realise what a lot of miserable buggers people English people can be.

People from Tennessee are clearly keen to track down their fellow state-folk. Going round the shops later, another man from Tennessee working in a gift and clothes shop also asked about the T-shirt. Once more I had to disappoint him and tell him I was from England, although he didn't tell me I'd seen more of America than he had. Instead, after doing an English accent so bad it would have got him a job in a sitcom, he explained he was from Nashville and had come to Santa Fe to further his acting career. Not the first place I'd have chosen to pursue a career in film, but, as he'd already completed a part in one small movie and was working on another, he didn't seem to be doing too badly, even if it didn't pay the rent yet. His name was Jason Shepherd and his movie had a working title of Western Movie. It was going to be a 'Scary Movie' style spoof of the western genre. I wished him luck and we joked that I could sell the story of how I met him before he was famous. Even now I can find nothing to suggest that the film has been released, and nothing about the actor Jason Shepherd, so I guess I can't retire off the back of that meeting just yet.

In the evening we went to the Atomic Grill, a nice cafe type restaurant serving good tuna salads, before looking for a lively bar for a drink. After a couple of hours it seemed that Santa Fe was in a quiet spell after the excesses of the arts festival, so we headed back to the hotel and into the Del Charro Saloon that joins on to it. We found out that it was the liveliest place in town, a title it may still have taken even if the rest of the town had been busy. A saloon in all respects, except for the absence of cowboys and swinging doors, and not a hotel bar in any sense of the word, it proved that sometimes what you are looking for is on your doorstep all along.

September 5. Our Santa Fe walking day. We started off following the narrow stretch of the Santa Fe River in front of the hotel, then headed to the New Mexico State Capitol building and on to the Loretto Chapel and the legendary miraculous staircase. The staircase is probably only legendary in New Mexico and some neighbouring bits of the States, but once you've been there or read about it, it becomes legendary to you too. The chapel was constructed in 1882. The architect designing it died suddenly, and only after he died was it realised that he hadn't included a stairway to the choir loft in his plans. The builders, in time honoured style, hadn't picked this up while he was alive - you can almost picture them saying the Spanish equivalent of "bleeding typical, he misses one of the main bits out, then goes and dies just before we noticed. What are the odds on that" - and on discovering that the chapel was too small to take a standard staircase, in equally time honoured tradition, they picked up their tools and left rather than try and solve the problem. "Sorry Sister, you've seen the plans, we've done all we were asked to do and there's another chapel down the road we've got to be at on Tuesday," probably came into a conversation somewhere along the way.

Left with no way of getting upstairs, and no builders or architect to help out, the nuns who ran the church prayed for a solution to their problem for the next nine days. At the end of this time a passing carpenter turned up and offered to try and build a staircase, but asked for total privacy. After three months a staircase had been built. Nothing odd about that you may say, except that the staircase is not supported by anything other than its own weight. It completes two revolutions on its way up to the choir loft, more than twenty feet above, without the use of nails or any central support. There is no apparent reason why it stood in the first place let alone continues to stand over one hundred and forty years later. The carpenter never asked for payment and left before the Mother Superior could even as much as offer him a cup of tea. You can probably guess who the carpenter was supposed to have been but, just in case the nuns were completely stupid, he left them a big clue in the only thing he ever told them about himself, which was that his name was Joseph.

Had the Lord answered their prayers and sent Joseph to build their staircase? Was it the confession of a shamed architect trying to get through the gates of heaven – "Have you sinned my child?" "Well not sinned as such, but there are these nuns who asked me to build a chapel." – whatever it was, the nuns never needed to pray for funding thanks to the donations of visitors coming to see the miracle. Fast forward to the present day and even the Lord's work gets appropriated by private companies, as the nearby hotel that acquired the chapel in the late eighties began charging $2.50 to see it. Joseph should send them the bill.

After visiting a few more old buildings, we headed down South Guadalupe Street towards the railway station to take the Royal Gorge Railroad. Trains normally leave once a day at one o'clock to take travellers through the Royal Gorge and past scenery, wildlife and panoramic views from which you can see a thousand feet down, deep into the Canyon. It sounds so splendid that no trip to Santa Fe could be complete without it, and yet on September 5, 2006 no one else shared our view and the train was cancelled through lack of interest. Was there no one in the city that hadn't been on it before?

After stopping for lunch we tried to book places on the city ghost tour. All we had seen of this was a leaflet with a phone number, which, on ringing, turned out to be an answerphone. We asked the hotel if they knew anything about it. They didn't, but left a message on the mysterious tour company's answerphone. They eventually rang back from a different phone number, leaving a message for me to call them. I rang and was told they were not sure if they had enough people to take the tour - Santa Fe was clearly having problems generating interest in anything that day. They said they would only run the tour if they had enough definite takers and asked for credit card details to reserve our place. The request to give bank details to a company that had no address, who may or may not have been running a tour that evening and who had a published phone number that was an answerphone they didn't ring back from, would ring alarm bells with even the most naïve, trusting or stupid people, so I politely declined and suggested they ring me to tell me if they got anyone else naïve and trusting and stupid enough to pay in advance.

After that, we took a trip round the Palace of the Governors. The Palace is the nation's oldest continuously occupied building, built in 1610, and, as you would guess, was originally the Palace where the Governors of Santa Fe lived. The Palace is an impressive building, but the museum could be a whole lot better. What you don't get from the Palace of the Governors, in contrast say to the Doges Palace in Venice, is any sense of what the building itself was used for. The first half of the Palace, with artefacts from Native American cultures, Spanish settlements, the Civil War and more, was informative but fell some way short of its billing as the best history lesson you could ever imagine, mainly as it wasn't all that interesting. Compared to the second half however, which was all about the Santa Fe printing industry, it was positively gripping. We learned that Santa Fe has for centuries had a small printing industry which continues to use some interesting print methods to this day, and that was about it. Even if I had been interested enough to begin with, my interest would have started to wane somewhere into the second hundred years of the history lesson. Finding out that the Palace had its own printing press, and that you could buy books from it at the end of the tour, provided an explanation if not a justification for the tedium of the whole thing.

Back at the hotel, to my surprise, the Ghost Tour Company did ring back later but only to tell me the tour was cancelled. Maybe I had been wrong about them and they were honest people. If I am ever there again and get the chance to give them my credit card details, I won't see it as a less than elaborate con. I still won't do it, of course. They may be honest, but I wouldn't bet on it.

21 – Durango

September 6. Started the morning by booking two nights at the Strater Hotel in Durango. Hampered by Internet problems and a website designed to prevent all but the most determined visitor from staying, this proved to be far more difficult than I was expecting. Navigating the booking system for rooms at the Grand Canyon was easier, even if their website seemed keener to tell me why it was the one to use rather than actually let me use it. With rooms booked for the next three nights we left Santa Fe.

Somewhere along US Highway 84 I failed to notice a sign showing the road branching off and before I knew it we were heading along the very scenic State Highway 68. The only problem with this what that it headed north-east and we needed to head north-west. At least it was going north. We pulled in to look at the map and decided to drive through Taos and then go west to rejoin the road to Durango. There are normally few joys to be had from taking a wrong turn, but, fortunately for us, what joys there are can be found on Highway 68.

The drive into Taos took us through the Santa Fe National Forest and along some steep roads through dry rocky mountains with signs warning us to beware of falling rocks, and netting by the roadside providing woefully inadequate protection from them. When the mountains dropped away on the left I could see the Rio Grande. I tried not to look, there being no safer way to ensure you crash down a mountainside than to stare at the bottom of it. The land became flatter, and the drops less severe, as we approached Taos.

Taos is a thriving little town with more than enough small independent motels, restaurants and shops to make it distinctive. It nestles between the Santa Fe National Forest to the south and west and the Carson National Forest to the north. With the San Juan Mountains further over to the north west and the Rio Grande running past the edge of the town, it boasts fantastic scenery at every turn.

When you leave the town it gets better still. The photographers in the distance were the first hint we had that there could be something big ahead, but it was only when we found ourselves going over the bridge and looking down at the sheer drop that we realised we were crossing over the Rio Grande Gorge. All there was was grey rock stretching further than the eyes could see. I couldn't even see the river, but this still didn't stop my brain from moving into its customary, awe-struck, mode when confronted by the unexpected and the spectacular.

After that we turned on to US Highway 64 where the things we saw fell into two categories, weird and downright bizarre. We passed a small community of underground eco-houses with bright multi-coloured roofs and upper walls poking out above ground level. The rounded constructions resembled something out of Yellow Submarine. Beyond these we started seeing cars, and more cars, and even more cars. They spread out over a mile with no caravans, trailers or houses anywhere near them. Whether this was a road where Americans dumped cars and claimed to have had them stolen, or where getaway cars got swapped and abandoned, I couldn't say. Either way an insurance firm or parts dealer could have cleaned up on a visit out to it.

Driving through Carson National Forest we were back amongst the mountains, although in places the area resembled a desert more than a forest, with sandy ground, dry grass and deep red rock. There was still the occasional ranch, one of which had a hanging man effigy at the gates and a sign saying 'we do it the old way.' We decided this wasn't somewhere to stop for a photo.

We travelled for what seemed an eternity without passing anywhere where people lived. Sometimes we could see for miles in all directions only to find there was nothing to look at, at other times we were cutting through mountains and forests with the road rising and falling, and the ever-present rocks biding their time before deciding eventually to tumble.

The wild untamed nature of the scenery remained incredibly impressive but, with no run down old towns to see, the long drive through nothingness eventually made us long for a petrol station, a motel, a diner, or anything else to tell us that we weren't the only people left alive, and that civilisation continued to exist. But nothing appeared, all there was was a road cutting its way through the forest, telling no one where it was heading.

You can understand why the pioneers, heading west with their wagons and horses, went stir crazy. No distinctive landmarks, no way to know which way they were heading, no way of knowing how long it would be till they found something, and no guarantee that there was something to be found in the first place. Even the most direct of routes must have taken weeks, and we were starting to feel the symptoms after a matter of hours.

Eventually, shortly after rejoining the road we had mistakenly headed off several hours earlier, we passed the town of Dulce. Dulce is the tribal headquarters of the Jicarilla Apache Reservation. Its population is about two thousand and six hundred, made up almost entirely of Native Americans. It boasts a Best Western Hotel, some restaurants, a couple of garages, some small shops and a few houses, all dotted around over a mile or so. It was a one-off rather than the start of a group of towns and soon we were back in the forest, with no more signs of life till we reached Chucks Joint, a solitary diner on a deserted road, which proudly boasted that it served the best burgers around. Given that it must have been at least thirty miles from Dulce, and a further twelve miles to the next place with anywhere to eat, this seemed a somewhat hollow claim.

The place that appeared twelve miles on from Chucks was Bloomingfield, a small town on US Highway 550 that looked like it might be a nice place to live in, but that could have been because it was the first place we'd seen that could fit that description for several hours. Relatively soon after Bloomingfield we reached Aztec, which was slightly bigger but looked like a business park rather than a nice little town, and after that there were no more towns, and nothing much by way of scenery, until we approached Durango, at which point not only did the scenery improve but there was also a notable increase in traffic. Not that Durango is a big sprawling city, its population is less than thirteen thousand, but that was still probably more people than we'd passed since we left Taos.

The Strater hotel is in Durango's historic old town, most of the city is. The hotel was built in 1887, and was designed to look like it came from an era that had long gone even then. The few owners it has had have all maintained that style. It has a Wild West theme typified by the Diamond Belle Saloon, where waitresses squeeze into figure enhancing basques, flowing skirts and fishnets, and barmen wear old style waistcoats and shirts. It's fair to say that the guys have it better than the girls do, whether they are customers or staff. Just like the Wild West really. When we first looked in, a honky tonk piano player was taking requests while a group of men wearing cowboy hats sat at a table playing cards. All that was missing was a swinging door, and silence descending as we entered through it.

In keeping with the theme, the rooms had heavy wooden chairs and desks and thick carpets throughout. To further add to the character, our room, at the top and back of the hotel, overlooked the steam train line where the last trains of the day were tooting their way back as we arrived.

After a drink in the Diamond Belle we ventured out on to the streets of Durango. We passed the Gaslight, a small cinema on a corner where a man stood on a ladder carefully taking down some letters and re-arranging others as he changed the title of this weeks film. We walked past the photo shop, where you can dress up in Wild West costumes and get sepia tinted photographs in old brown frames, and we looked at restaurants, saloons and bars that added to the atmosphere. All of which made our eventual decision to eat at the North Italia Restaurant something of a mystery. The restaurant served nice enough food but it was far too modern and Italian for the city and far too overbearing to make anyone want to go back unless they liked simpering waiters. I still can't think of a good reason for going there.

After eating, we crossed over the road and went into the Hoe Bar, a spit and sawdust kind of bar, which had a sign saying it welcomed bikers and looked like, in days of yore, a few wrong words would lead to wooden chairs being smashed over peoples heads. We then went back to the second of the hotel bars which still looked like something from the Wild West, even though it didn't have a honky tonk piano player. By that time the Diamond Belle Saloon had also lost its honky tonk player – the requests for songs drying up before the bar did, and a halt to the evening being called earlier than ever happened in the bad old days.

September 7. Every room at the Strater has a guest book, and guests are encouraged to write down stories of their stay rather than just the usual 'bed nice, breakfast could have been better' comments. From this I learnt that our room allegedly had a ghost, although most of the comments said they hadn't seen or felt anything, which made me wonder where the claims had come from. The first person actually claiming to have witnessed a ghostly going-on was a lady who wrote of being taken over at six in the morning by a presence which led her to get up and do a ballet dance for no known reason. I hadn't been woken by a presence making me want to get up and boogie, but was woken up by a steam train pulling out of the station and tooting at no one other than the guests in the Strater.

To most people the sight and sound of an old-fashioned steam train in a historic old town would be somehow heart warming, but it seems that not everyone feels this way. Reading further through the guest book I saw the entry of one man who stayed at the hotel on his honeymoon and for whom it was the culmination of a bad first day of married life. It began with his wife laughing at him when he ordered a desert with a raspberry compost. He didn't find this amusing, but when they got back to the room, in spite of being in a mood, he was still confident of being able to consummate his marriage, notwithstanding a failed attempt earlier in the evening when she had decided to watch her favourite programme instead. This time she fell asleep. When he awoke early the next morning, he thought this would be the moment as, in his words, his wife was still asleep. Just as he was about to do the deed, presumably expecting that she wouldn't wake up until it was over, which, from the picture I was forming of him, seemed more than likely, the train with its annoying hoots woke her up and, as he so eloquently put it, he got none.

Somehow I can't picture them returning to the Strater for their anniversary. Not that I can picture them having one now I come to think about it.

The steam train that so annoyed him would have been on its way to Silvertown, an old gold mining town fifty miles north of Durango. We attempted to go there but found that there is only one train out of town a day - how Wild West is that - and we had, of course, missed it. Rather than taking a less scenic and far longer bus ride we decided to go for a walk along the Animas River which runs through Durango and the San Juan National Forest. The hills and mountains behind us framed the river landscape to create a beautiful scene. As the river widened out we watched a group of men fishing, knee deep in the middle of the river with their rods cast, catching nothing. It was an image from a place relaxed and at ease with itself. It may not have been a trip to an old mining town, but it was good enough for us.

When we finished walking we headed back to the city and went for lunch. The rain started as we got into the Diamond Belle and finished shortly before we left. Our timing could only have been better if we had got up in time for the train.

Durango is an expanding place. New apartments were being built at the end of Main Street, a block had gone up in 2004 and more building was about to begin. The new buildings were all in the old style so while we felt we were seeing a place that would be a lot larger in a few years, we didn't feel like we were seeing a place that was about to lose its character.

We went into an art shop where we tried to work out shipping costs for a painting in a gold-edged support frame. After a long time trying to get estimates from people who all seemed to have left for the day, the guy in the shop gave up, but promised he would try again the next day and gave us his e-mail address. I lost it a few days later, so never found out whether he succeeded or not.

A bit more shopping included another random CD purchase. This time I went for Todd Snider and The Devil You Know. Todd Snider is a rocking country guitarist in the Steve Earle mode. A sticker on the CD proclaimed him as one of America's best undiscovered talents, a title that by its very name is hard to award definitively. The album sounded like a clear attempt to turn him into a discovered talent. Very few people seem to have heard of him even now, from which you can draw your own conclusions on whether this approach worked.

We ended the afternoon by wondering along back streets and stopping for coffee and ice cream, something that is far more enjoyable than words can convey. In the evening we went to the Diamond Circle Melodrama and Vaudeville. The melodrama has been a feature of summers in Durango for the last 45 years. Two plays and vaudeville revues are performed each year from the end of June to the end of September.

Tonight's play was 'A 4 legged fortune' a melodrama set in London at the turn of the last century where the fate of a town, a hero, and the woman he loves all depended on the outcome of a horse race, and the crooked antics of the villainous Grindley Goodge. It was excellent. Guaranteed to keep you on the edge of your seat and hissing, booing and cheering with the best of them, a truly wonderful piece of locally produced entertainment. The Culinary Cabaret that made up the

Vaudeville Review, with songs and sketches about fast-food waiters, drunken chefs and e-numbers, was equally entertaining.

In the interval and after the show we got talking to the Walkers, a couple we shared a table with at the theatre. Both of them shared a great love of Europe, borne out of extensive travelling; a supreme hatred of George Bush, borne out of a sense of taste and decency; and a dislike of the US media's failure to report news from outside the US, borne out of the media's lack of interest in the rest of the world, and in the case of some local media, the rest of the country. They had a point on this. After a couple of months here I'd realised just how little I'd heard about what was happening anywhere else. Even big stories like North Korean nuclear testing plans had barely registered, and stories that didn't involve the US or national security were generally only to be found in the international section towards the back of the quality papers, assuming they were anywhere at all.

Our new friends aversion to America and patriotism was not something they shied away from. They didn't stand up when God Bless America was sung in the interval which, whilst creditable, did make me worry that people at other tables would call us commies, and in another state - Texas perhaps - might mean we'd be lucky to escape with our lives.

At the end of the evening, while other American traditions may not have been respected, the tradition of friendliness was, and they invited us to stay at the Palm Springs house they were in the process of refurbishing. In case it would otherwise be a deal breaker, they promised us that they had a swimming pool. I returned the offer, letting them know they could stay with us if they were ever in Kingston, although with a two-bedroom flat, I couldn't promise swimming unless the drains were overflowing.

Back in the Diamond Belle Saloon things were livelier tonight and a few drinks brought the curtain down on our stay. It would have been good to have stayed another day. The Tribal Fare was starting and promised a tepee making competition and a duck race, but as tomorrow was my birthday I wanted something a bit grander. With that in mind, we were going to the Grand Canyon.

22 – The Grand Canyon

I woke up on September 8, another year older. Actually I was only another day older, or to be even more precise, as we were seven hours behind GMT and I was born at 6:30 in the morning, I wasn't even another day older as I had been that age when I went to sleep. I had a dream where we were driving and to the side of me a somewhat menacing and strange voice kept telling me that there were five miles to go. I looked round and saw that the menacing and strange voice belonged to an equally menacing, but not quite so strange face. The hands that belonged to the face, that belonged to the voice, tugged at my shoulders. It felt like a real tug. I woke up, and wondered if I had felt the presence of the ghost, and if I had, why he couldn't have just got me to do a ballet dance. It was my birthday after all.

We headed out of Durango on US Highway 160 to Kayenta. Following advice we were given the day before we skipped the chance to stop at the Four Corners Park, the only place in the US common to four state borders - Arizona, New Mexico, Utah and Colorado - on the grounds that it's nothing more than a plaque in the middle of a road, and you have to pay to see it. We went instead to Monument Valley, a Navajo park of canyons and rocks.

Everyone has seen Monument Valley even if they've not been to America. It was used regularly in Westerns from the forties and fifties. Of late its use has declined, the last film of any note to be shot there was Back to the Future 3 – the one where Michael J Fox nearly died filming a stunt.

The technical, geological description of why the valley is the way it is goes as follows; Materials eroded from the early Rocky Mountains were deposited over earlier layers and cemented into sandstone. Wind and water eroded the land and uplift generated from pressure below caused the surface to bulge and crack. The cracks deepened and widened into gullies and canyons. The wearing downs of altering layers of soft and hard rock slowly shaped the mesas and buttes that now pepper the otherwise barren landscape.

The non-technical, non-geological description of the valley is; it is a weird looking collection of massive funny shaped gravity defying rocks, located in the middle of the desert. You have to get up close and personal to them, even though it is unbelievably hot and arid whenever you set foot outside your air-conditioned car.

To see Monument Valley you can either take a jeep tour or, if you're feeling brave, you can drive the seventeen-mile loop yourself. We figured we wouldn't have time to do the full tour so we took the self-drive option instead. The jeep tour man laughed, or possibly sneered, when we told him, and he pointed to the start telling us he'd see us in two days.

While it is only seventeen miles, and two days is an exaggeration, it wasn't a drive you could do in an hour. The road is not only unpaved it is also uneven, narrow, and full of small hills and blind turns at the top of them. Once you get over the initial fear factor, and realise that there are very few opportunities to turn round, it's enjoyable and almost exhilarating, even if you are in something as unsuitable for off-road adventures as a Ford Fusion. The scenery is outstanding. There are eleven main sites, the distances between them making the panoramic view as impressive as the individual structures. We did about half of them before deciding we were running out of time. When we returned we smiled at the jeep tour man. I like to think he was wondering how we had done the whole thing in an hour, but he probably had no idea who we were anymore.

We went back down to Highway 160 and resumed the journey to the Grand Canyon. The highway passed through Navajo reservation land. Shortly before joining State Highway 64, we crossed the Painted Desert and slowed down behind a school bus. Twenty children got off and ran in all directions towards mobile home style buildings literally in the middle of the desert. It was strange to think of children growing up in settings such as this and still getting a formal state education with a bus picking them up and dropping them off everyday. It felt like I was looking through a window into another world.

Elsewhere there were far more familiar sites amidst the desert scenery as we passed casinos and trading posts. The Native Americans have been good at seizing the opportunities presented by the return of land from the American Government. Out of town casinos are a big feature in Arizona and surrounding states, they operate outside of any state or national restrictions, and have helped the Native Americans to finally get the gold that was taken away from them when they lost the land. Better still, they haven't even had to dig for it.

Most people head into the Grand Canyon from Flagstaff. Coming in from Durango, we were on a route that was less well known but much more spectacular. As we drove from the entrance of the Canyon to the heart of the South Rim we found ourselves as close to the edge of the canyon as it's possible to get in a car, taking a first look into its deep vast brilliance, albeit through snatched glances, whilst concentrating on mastering the twists and turns of the road that made the twenty-five mile drive seem far longer than that. On the other side of the road from the Canyon, and as if to highlight the wonder that is nature, the dense trees and woodland of the Kaibab National Forest provided a complete contrast, nearly eight thousand feet above sea level.

Of course, even at one of the worlds seven natural wonders, you can't get too far from the day to day irritations of life, which manifested themselves in the queue to check in at the Maswik Lodge. Not only had we managed to arrive at the same time as almost every other guest, we also seemed to be there on the same day as the most intellectually challenged crowd of the year. As we had an extra hour to play with, thanks to moving unknown into the Pacific time-zone, we went into a cafe until the check-in no longer resembled the queue outside a new Ikea store. A few coffees later, we returned.

The rooms at the lodge were fairly basic but surprisingly large. After unpacking and changing for the evening we took a leisurely stroll over to the restaurant, looking out across the south rim. I was amazed at how the view from any two points could be so different. I had expected the Canyon to have a fairly sheer drop down to the bottom, but instead it makes a slow but dramatic descent down across its width and length, meaning you only need to walk a few metres, and face out at a slightly different angle, to see so much you hadn't seen the last time you looked.

The El Tovar Restaurant was in the hotel of the same name, the whole thing looked like a posh mountain lodge for rich skiers. The food was excellent and the table was in about the best position you could get, with a view out across the canyon as the sun set.

We decided we had to try and stay another night so that we could see as much of the canyon as possible without having to worry about moving on afterwards. We asked if there were any rooms in the hotel and found they had one left. We reserved it and headed back to the lodge. With the sun having set, the canyon looked different again. It was the most spectacular sight I had seen in my life, and you can't really ask for much more than that on your birthday.

September 9. We took the desert view bus tour round the east rim of the canyon. Our guide lived in the park, as most of the people who work there do. He was a former lecturer who decided he wanted a change and, as he had always loved nature, went for a job in the Grand Canyon National Park. The appeal for him wasn't just the canyon, it was the forest, the wildlife and the nature. Once you have lived and worked in the canyon for twenty years, you can also be buried there. He had been there for nineteen and, provided he is still there as I write this, will be there for all time. As well as knowing everything about how the canyon was created, he also knew what wildlife lived in the park and what to look for. Thanks to him pointing it out, we caught a rare sighting of a Javelina. Javelinas are like small hairy pigs. They are one of the most unpleasant and grumpy species of animal you're ever likely to come across - great to spot but lousy to get on with.

We stopped at various viewpoints. From the first one we could just about make out the mules making the daily journey down the Bright Angel trail to the bottom of the canyon. At the second the Colorado River became just about visible in the distance, and by the third stop we could see it clearly and notice its reddish-brown colour.

Further round we were shown Snoopy Rock, so called because it is said to resemble Snoopy on his kennel. The tour guide pointed to it, but we were not alone in being unable to spot anything that looked like the famous cartoon dog. Feeling sure it was out there somewhere, we filmed and took photos to search for it later, deciding that looking for one obscure piece of rock was not a good use of time when there was so much else to see.

The buttes, temples and shrines that cover the Canyon offer up different views depending on the time of day and weather conditions. The weather can change rapidly and unexpectedly. As the light shifts or the clouds clear something previously hidden gets revealed, and what was comparatively indistinct suddenly shows colours and contours you never knew it had. While the heavy storms that appeared from nowhere mid-morning could have been annoying, without them, as the clouds lifted over Grandview point, we would never have seen various peaks and rock formations suddenly appear and light up.

It really is a scene of beauty far more impressive than you can imagine without seeing it. Layer after layer of rock has been exposed and uplifted to create an intricate and colourful panorama of greens, reds, yellows, browns and golds. If it were designed by man you would wander how they came up with the idea. That it was carved out without the slightest bit of intervention from mankind, and what you see represents a work in progress stretching back more than two billion years, just makes it all the more incredible. Words can not describe it, so I'll stop trying to.

The furthest distance between the north and south of the Canyon is just fifteen miles, the shortest is about ten. At its lowest point the canyon is only a little over one mile deep. That may not sound much, but when you add the fact that canyon is so wide that to drive the short distance between the north and south rims takes about five hours you start to get a better idea of the scale of the thing. To walk to the bottom of the canyon, you can either take the eight or so mile Bright Angel Trail or the South Kaibab Trail, which is a mile shorter. Again, this might not sound a long distance, but again it is misleading, and official advice is that you should not attempt to walk to the bottom and back in a day.

Amongst the reasons for this are the drastic variations in temperature, the inner gorge being on average about twenty degrees warmer than the rims making dehydration inevitable if you don't take lots of water with you; sudden rainstorms; flash flooding; rockfall; bootpacked ice; encounters with wildlife; and the risk of getting kicked by a mule if you pass one on your way down. Meanwhile at the Colorado River you can add hypothermia, due to the river's consistently cold temperatures; trauma, due to collisions with boulders in rapids; and drowning, to the list of things to watch out for.

So what hardy soles do the trail? Eighty year old men it appears. Our tour guide told us about a guy called Maverick, who lives in the canyon and turned eighty in 2006. To celebrate he had decided to do eighty different hikes in and around the canyon and park. By the time we were there he'd already done sixty-one and was likely to reach his target with room to spare. Hearing this, I decided I would return at some point to spend another birthday here, but this time hike, starting at the Bright Angel Trail on the South Rim, spending the evening in the lodge at the bottom of the canyon, and walking back up to the North Rim the next day. Knowing someone can still do this at eighty means I can put it off for a few years, but I probably still need to get in a bit of training to make it look like a serious plan.

That night we watched the sunset at Hopi point. Hopi Point is recommended as one of the most romantic places to see the sunset, not just in the Grand Canyon but anywhere in the world. As the sun started to descend it cast new light on the canyon and across to the north rim. The sky looked like a snow-covered lake with a small band of clouds underneath a thicker band looking like boulders rising out of it. The clouds and sky changed colour slowly as the sun gradually disappeared from view. We watched mesmerised as it finally dipped below the skyline. And then the serenity was shattered by large groups of people applauding as if the sun had performed a trick for them and, if they thanked it, it would come back up for an encore. I almost expected to see them stamp their feet and call for more before eventually drifting away.

The beauty and splendour of the day ended there. We ate in one of the canteen style restaurants in the lodges. From the opulence of the El Tovar to a hardy backpacker-type diner. The room at the El Tovar was also disappointing, a small room on the ground floor that lacked any real charm and was a shoebox in comparison to the room at the Maswik Lodge. We headed for the El Tovar bar, and rounded the evening off with a few drinks, the magical romantic potential of sunset at Hopi Point now just a distant memory. Beauty has never been so fleeting.

September 10. The Park honours many people associated with the discovery and exploration of the Canyon in many different ways, various Spanish and American explorers have buttes named after them and lodges take names from Native American tribes. Whilst people who were neither Spaniards nor explorers are also commemorated, Ralph Cameron, a pioneer and prospector who extended the Bright Angel Trail to reach the Colorado River, is not honoured anywhere. What did he do to be shunned in this way? Basically, it all comes down to money and greed.

In the days before the park was even a National Monument let alone a National Park - and in case you wonder what the difference is, I don't know either - Cameron registered land on the edges of the canyon in his name for copper mining. He never found any, and knew he never would, but the land he registered included the start of the trail, so whilst there was no chance of him finding copper he did, metaphorically, strike gold. He named the trail 'the Cameron Trail' as if to make sure there was no doubt it was on his land, and kept renewing his stake in the land, claiming he was sure there was copper in them there hills, and reaping a considerable income by charging people to enter the trail.

It didn't end there either. Cashing in on the rail line stopping on his land, he built a hotel adding further to the income he got from land that others felt should be public property.

Hitting back at Cameron, the Park developed the Hermit Trail, began construction of the South Kaibab Trail, and moved the final stopping point of the Santa Fe Railroad so that it didn't even reach his land, let alone stop outside his hotel. And yet he still made money, which still annoyed the locals and the park staff. There were frequent attempts to take the land from him, although this being the turn of the twentieth century these were legal challenges rather than posses of cowboys coming in with guns-a-blazing, which may have been more successful as it turned out. Although Cameron appeared to be universally unpopular, he proved himself canny enough to turn the attempts to recover the land to his advantage and got elected to congress campaigning that, in the land of the free, it was wrong for the state to take land away from someone who was making the most of his opportunities. He held on to the land until 1937 when he sold it to someone else entirely, and the new owners gave it over to the park.

Cameron is buried in the Legion Cemetery in the park and so still has a presence in the land people wanted him out of. If stories of how rangers keep his grave watered are true, he may have rested better outside of it.

Returning to September 10, while Liz slept, I decided to go for a stroll, past the Kolb Studio, which had a great exhibition of photos from within the Canyon, and on to the Bright Angel Trail. I looked ahead to what appeared to be a sharp turn with a steep drop, and decided that would be as far as I'd get. Then I reached it, and suddenly around the corner was another long stretch that looked easily manageable so I decided to carry on. And so it continued. As each stopping point was reached I decided to head on to another one. At the start, some distance ahead of me, I could see the mules on their way down. It had seemed miles away, but as I walked past it, while the mules remained some distance ahead, I realised it was either nearer than I thought or I'd walked further than I'd intended.

By the time I eventually decided to turn back, the route down to the bottom, hidden at the start, was visible, and my surroundings had changed considerably. The inside of the canyon was nearer to me, there was more above me and less below. I was tempted to go further still. Only the lack of sturdy walking shoes and breakfast prevented me from doing so and becoming one of those people who discover they've walked too far only when it's too late to turn round.

If I'd remembered to bring sensible footwear and a picnic basket it may have been a different story.

23 - Sedona

We headed out of the park towards Flagstaff. Unlike the road in, we saw motels and diners almost as soon as we left the park. We got a fantastic breakfast at a roadside diner, and then a short while further along found the unexpected treasure that is The Flintstones Bedrock City Theme Park, an AAA approved campground, where a yabba dabba doo time is guaranteed for all.

The theme park is one of those weird and wonderful sites that you expect to stumble upon on a road trip. There is no apparent reason for it to be there. It isn't an official Flintstones/Hanna Barbera enterprise. It opened in 1972, and has a Flintstones theme for no other reason than the owner was a big Flintstones fan who decided it would be a good idea. He died some years ago, but showing a love for her husband that transcends any idiosyncrasy he may have had, his wife continues to run the park to this day.

The park has life size models of Fred and Barney's homes, the Bedrock City Jail, the Bedrock Bank and the Post Office. As if that wasn't enough to fill an hour of any grown man's life, an assistant asked us if we wanted a ride in Fred's car. Needless to say we took up her offer, and got driven round a small track by a woman who showed no signs of finding it unusual that we accepted in spite of being two grown adults with no children in sight. It's probably a regular occurrence here.

We passed on the chance of a Dino Dog or Chickasaurus in Fred's Diner and headed down the 180 through more of the Kaibab National Forest. We passed the San Francisco Mountains and Humphreys Peak, which at 12,633 feet is the highest point in Arizona, and then reached Flagstaff, from where we headed south towards Sedona, which stands at a mere 4,326 feet. Much of the 8,000 foot drop came in the last thirty miles of the journey, where the road winds through and down Oak Creek Canyon.

It is a road you can't drive down in a hurry. It drops away dramatically to the right, towards the lake, and rises equally dramatically, towards the mountains, on the left. We looked to our left and saw a landscape of trees, plants and shrubs. We looked to our right and saw dry red sandstone rocks, and monuments that nature had carved out of stone. At the bottom we saw Sedona.

Sedona is a strange mix of a place. It's known for the uplifting power of its Vortex meditation sites. Vortexes are where ley lines converge. There are seven different types of them throughout the world. Most places have none at all, a few places have one, Sedona has all seven. This makes it a spiritual retreat to many, but to others it is a western movie paradise, thanks to monuments such as Coffee Pot Rock, the Cow Pies and the Rabbit Ears, and an old style town to boot. Sedona was a popular setting for movies long after Monument Valley lost its appeal. If you've seen a John Wayne movie, chances are you've seen Sedona.

The mix of styles results in a strange hybrid of shops and restaurants in the uptown area. Alongside small shops promoting spirituality, fighting depression, and removing negativity, you get movie shops, stalls selling cowboy gear, and a traditional cowboy style restaurant. The additional shops and attractions created by the ever-growing tourist trade adds further to the charm and quirkiness, catering for every kind of tourist, and leading to fine art at high prices next door to the best or worst excesses of mass-produced souvenirs. It shouldn't work, but somehow it does.

Looking for a place to stay we found a similarly wide choice, ranging from picturesque traditional holiday homes and remote lodges on the approach to town, through hotels and timeshares uptown, and ending with a strip of chain motels at the far edge of town. The motels defied all natural laws and managed to turn beautiful surroundings into something resembling a faceless Interstate, so, as you may expect, they were where the area the assistant in the tourist information centre recommended us to stay.

We rejected them upon sight and returned uptown to the Best Western Arroyo Roble Hotel. A chain hotel with a timeshare section it may be, but, in spite of that, it is still the best place to stay in Sedona, at least if you manage to get a first floor chalet with a patio offering a view directly into the forest, layers of red and orange rock visible between the trees, mountains rising up in front of you, and monuments standing proud at the top of distant peaks behind them.

When we could bring ourselves to leave the view behind we headed uptown and took one of the many jeep tours on offer. As with the shops, the jeep tours cater for every kind of tourist. Rugged types can go for the just slightly off-road adventure, the long way off-road adventure, or the 'drive yourself, as if you would risk it' adventure. The more spiritual can take the vortex sight seeing tour, while the neither rugged or spiritual can take the pink jeep tour, a nice on-road tour stopping at various rocks and mountains and run by a group of ladies with, no surprise here, a collection of pink jeeps. After some deliberation we went with them. As frequent passengers on sightseeing tours we were used to seeing man-made buildings and hearing about the people that lived there, but here the dominant themes were nature and natural history, with only a passing reference to films. It was far more fascinating than any tour we'd been on before.

After the tour it was back to the hotel to change and then out for a meal and a drink, followed by an early night with the aim of an early morning to follow. You could live a contented life in Sedona.

September 11. Five years since 9/11. The media had been making such a lot about this being the fifth anniversary. The risk of terrorism following the Heathrow bomb attempt was still seen as high, but in Sedona all was quiet. We sat and watched as small Lizards jumped in and out of a nearby flowerbed. A Texan couple sat next to us. The man kept a toothpick in his mouth as we chatted about the Geckos that came in and out of their house, and watched the little critters, as he called them, fascinated by their movement. Throughout the conversation, no matter how much he talked, the toothpick never seemed even remotely likely to drop out.

Completely unprompted by anything other than my accent, he admitted he had always had a stereotypical view of other nationalities until he took a cruise with "people from the UK, Australia and Wales." I decided not to point out that Wales was part of the UK as he was clearly describing a revelatory experience, admitting his surprise at the differences between the three nationalities. I offered back a statement of equal surprise on the differences between people of different states in the US, even though that hadn't surprised me as much as finding a

Texan admitting his initial view of something was wrong. We then went back to watching lizards in the Arizona sun until their bus came and the international bonding session came to an end.

Our main activity of the day was another jeep tour. This time we decided to combine the rugged and the spiritual by taking the off-road vortex tour, run by hippies with jeeps.

We were the only people on the tour. It started in an on-road and non-spiritual way, passing the celebrity homes of Al Pacino, Robert De Niro, Sharon Stone and Madonna. We probably saw more of their homes than they did that summer. Pacino is apparently the most frequent visitor mainly because he keeps his collection of antique cars there as the climate stops them from rusting.

After a while the driver took us off-road, or so we thought. After getting a long way from anything we'd define as road he announced "we're going off-road, so do up your belts." A heavy downpour started as we took a bumpy dust track up small hills and through the parched red stone and sand. It felt like one of those Agatha Christie movies set in the desert where Peter Ustinov is met off a plane and driven to an archaeological dig. When the jeep finally stopped I expected to see a party of people dressed up for an expedition. Instead we got an experience straight out of the best western movies.

The rain was getting heavier but our craggy looking guide was not deterred and told us to get out of the van and put on some ponchos as he was going to take us for a walk. It didn't sound like we had a choice in the matter. As he reached down to the side of the driver's seat, and emerged with a piece of carpet wrapped around something long, slim and gun-shaped, the merest thought of objecting disappeared. He pointed to a steep hill, and a wet dusty path lined by just a few cactus plants and trees. We were told to follow him to the top of it. My imagination went into overdrive and said to me, over and over again, "oh my god, he's a madman, that's a gun and we've been brought to the middle of the desert to be shot."

As we walked up the hill I started thinking of how we could escape, imagining that any moment now there would be a struggle for the gun and we'd make a break for it, only for him to get back up and start to chase after us, leaving us running for our lives, looking for hiding places to try and lose him until he ran out of bullets and we could safely reach town and the nearest swing door saloon where we would recount our tales over a shot or two of Bourbon.

We reached the top of the hill and looked out across the landscape from a place known as the mystic vista. The long slim object remained wrapped in the carpet as he took a stick and drew a magic circle in the earth to illustrate ancient sacred ceremonies that still took place there. Had he spoken in a slow and moody way, I would have thought this was a precursor to us being sacrificed in a ritualistic killing, but my paranoia dissolved as the rain stopped and the view out across the hills and rocks became clearer. The distinctive rocks were closer and larger, the Colorado plateau was further away but still marked out the untamed terrain, and the hills seemed like mountains. They combined to form a majestic red rock scenery bordered by evergreen vegetation. It was a view to make you believe in the healing powers of nature and how it can be used to deliver inner calm and positive energy. It was a view that no one should seek to disturb, and so, inevitably, it was a view that is not so gradually being destroyed.

The guide pointed to the next hill, hill being a term that was hardly fitting for something of that size and structure. He told us it had been sold to developers some years ago. Sedona residents fought against the sale, and then fought against the development plans. Nothing happened for years, but now the development was finally going ahead, and soon the view across an unspoilt landscape where the passage of the sun and the seasons had been worshipped for centuries would be compromised by the addition of timeshare condos and an eighteen hole golf course.

Not that this would be the first blight on the mystic vista landscape. The Enchanted Resort was already there lower in the canyon, far less visible but part of a growing timeshare industry which has led to some parts of uptown turning into resorts where timeshare hawks offer prizes and special offers to get tourists to go to sales pitch presentations.

One look at the official tourism site of the Sedona Chamber of Commerce tells you all you need to know about their likely position on the preservation or exploitation of the land debate. The 'Relocate to Sedona' page proudly makes the following claim; 'At the moment, due to the diligence of courageous developers who found parcels of land previously not known to be for sale…Sedona and the village of Oakcreek are sporting a selection of the finest, new residential communities found anywhere in the world….some of these communities feature clubhouses, parks, hiking trails and resort-style pools, others appeal to residents who are not concerned about such things, opting instead for maximum privacy.'

Or, as I would have put it, 'developers with no real claim to being courageous have scoured every last bylaw they could find to work out just what they can buy and build on regardless of the natural landscape. Any land they want is theirs, and if you want to join us, but don't want to share the view with the locals who've been here for centuries, don't worry, we'll put up big fences so they can't get in.' Mind you, I doubt that would get as many interested buyers.

I'm not against progress, but surely there has to be some respect for the centuries of Native American history enshrined in the area. Saddened by the selfishness of it all, we walked back down the hill and got back in the jeep without the carpet ever having been unwrapped to reveal its contents. The drive back felt less like an Agatha Christie film and more like the English Patient with us heading to a makeshift hospital to deliver medical supplies. Looking back on it, maybe the heat was playing tricks with my mind.

After lunch we checked out a few galleries before taking a walk behind the hotel and down to the dry creek where we ended the afternoon admiring the scenery before heading down a small stretch of road the guide had recommended to us for seeing the sunset. It was less spectacular than sunset over the Grand Canyon, but also less discovered. There were only about five of us there, and no one applauded the sun for doing what it does every day without fail and without choice.

Back uptown we ate at the Cowboy Club Bar and Grille and drank at their saloon bar, before buying a small cactus and assorted stones with assorted powers that probably worked against each other if you wrapped them in a bag and slung them in a suitcase. The city seemed to empty out in the evening, the timeshare residents returning to their exclusive bars and restaurants, leaving only the hotel and motel people walking around in the night air. A few shops remained open, but when we tried to buy anything we were invited to come back the next morning when they might be able to do a good offer if we went along to a presentation. I didn't know whether to be pleased or disgusted to discover that unassuming shops could be part of a timeshare enterprise. We retired to a bar where we didn't debate this for the rest of the evening.

September 12. Started the day with breakfast and a walk around uptown with a video camera to capture everything we'd already taken photos of but could now get in a panoramic setting. We left just after eleven and started the drive back up the canyon to Flagstaff, stopping at a few vantage points to do yet more filming of yet more dramatic scenery. The fact that we had probably filmed the exact same thing or something very similar a bit earlier didn't matter as a childlike sense of wonder drew us to stop at every opportunity.

At Flagstaff we rejoined Interstate 40 and took the Route 66 loop through Williams, where you can get the train to the Grand Canyon between March and December. Williams exploits its Route 66 heritage, but also retains it. The downtown streets have old-fashioned street lamps, the motels are mostly privately owned, and Rod's Steak House has been in business since 1946. It's distinctive and classic in an old road movie kind of way.

Williams is a small place with a healthy amount of Old Town America in it. It was the last town to be bypassed by Interstate 40 and held out until the bitter end, which came on October 13, 1984 after many court battles. To mourn the passing of the old road they held a celebration-cum-wake with a performance on the Interstate overpass by Bobby Troup, the first singer associated with Route 66 in the States. The death of the road briefly revived a career that was itself moribund.

A bit further along, past Ash Fork, there is a turn off for another, far longer, stretch of Route 66 which runs parallel to the I-40 as it takes you through Seligman, and then departs off to the north and out of sight of the Interstate for a couple of hours until the roads eventually merge again at Kingsman.

Seligman is another place that retains its Route 66 associations. Smaller than Williams - its population is just over five hundred, Williams is just below three thousand - it still boasts some memorable sites and places including the Historic Route 66 Motel and the Black Cat Saloon where Nicholas Cage has allegedly been known to stop for drinks, although the odds on catching him there are probably too small to make it worth stopping at on the off-chance.

Even if you're not hungry it's worth eating in Seligman, both because the cafes look good and because they are the last places to eat that you'll see for some time. When Route 66 leaves Interstate 40 it takes an evocative ride through the desert, which means the few towns you pass along the way are all but abandoned, and don't inspire you to pull over even if you do spot a working diner.

The only place of note comes about half way along, just before the town of Nelson. The Grand Canyon Caverns are a massive system of underground caves and passageways formed in Limestone and covering around eight hundred acres, two hundred and ten feet below ground. It has a motel and campsite, so you can stay overnight there, but it's hard to see why anyone would.

Fittingly, on the longest independent stretch of Route 66 we had been on, for the first time since we started out we found a Route 66 radio station with a playlist that consisted almost entirely of old driving songs and soul classics from the sixties. These were occasionally interrupted by adverts, including one from a republican candidate in the mid-sessional elections who promised to protect US borders by making illegal entrants build a wall to act as a secure border between the US and Mexico. Highlighting just what illegal immigrants prevented American citizens from accessing he reeled off the old favourites of jobs, hospitals and schools, but added, in a strange take on the nationalist card, that they were taking places in prisons that should be used for America's own criminals. I wasn't too sure what level of support this line would have amongst the criminal fraternity, but he clearly thought it a point worth making.

The longer we listened to the station and its non-stop mix of musical nostalgia, the more we got to like it, so it came as a disappointment when it suddenly and totally faded out of range, and the nothingness outside the car was joined by a nothingness from across the airwaves. When even a themed radio station ceases to broadcast on the road it takes its theme from, you know you are somewhere long since deserted.

We eventually reached Kingsman and re-joined the I-40. Kingsman has a population of more than 20,000 and is apparently a fairly good Route 66 stopping place, but all we saw of it was a petrol station and a few roadside diners that looked like they belonged to chains that had never really taken off. We stopped at one of them before heading on to US Highway 93 where, with a characteristic lack of awareness of our surroundings, we stumbled unexpectedly on the Hoover Dam.

One of the man-made wonders of the world, the Dam is nearly 1,500 feet long and 750 feet high. The size and depth of it make it so vast you have to see it to believe it, and the setting in the middle of the Mojave desert, with the Black Mountains to one side and Muddy Mountains to the other, adds to the experience. An added sense of unreality is created by the array of roads and bridges in varying states of construction, which make up the Hoover Dam Bypass project. They will eventually divert traffic 1,500 feet downstream of the Dam. The project is set to be completed in June 2010, in the meantime the whole thing looks like something out of a Bond movie. Being near Vegas is the perfect location for it, and Vegas was where we were heading.

24 – Las Vegas

We hadn't pre-booked anywhere in Vegas. There were two reasons for this. The first is that there are always hotels available, particularly mid week, the second is that finding the entrance to any of them is near impossible. Even if you do spot the turn off, unless you see it well in advance, your chances of getting off the road and into the hotel are small to the point of non-existent.

We decided to turn off for the MGM Grand, but as the small exit for its car park was about half a mile up the road and seemingly nowhere near the hotel we sailed past it and on to the more obvious exit for New York New York.

In the knowledge that we might not get as near as this to an exit for anywhere else that day we went for it. After about half a mile we reached the front of the hotel, where we guessed that without a booking the valet would either tell us to move the car or would drive it off somewhere where it would be lost to us forever. We drove on to the car park, twice finding ourselves heading out of the hotel's own unique ring road and back on to the strip, and once finding ourselves in a goods lane heading towards an obscure destination at the back of the hotel which, in a seventies cop show, would have been where the hoods beat up anyone who had been a bit lucky on the card tables.

Eventually we reached the car park and parked near some lifts, figuring it was an easy place to reach if we had to come back. The lifts promised to take us to the hotel, but actually took us to one end of the casino from which there was a long walk to reception. As the casino was like a small town in itself, with almost every aspect of Manhattan life recreated courtesy of diners, bars, restaurants, cafes, and even replica landmarks, it was almost as difficult to find the reception as it had been to find the car park. We booked for a couple of nights. I asked if the concierge could take the bags to the room, and was told they could but only if we used valet parking. Deciding this was better than walking two suitcases and a large bag through a casino we headed back to the car, and drove back to the entrance where, some thirty minutes after we'd pulled off the road, I handed the keys to a valet and we took the elevator to our room on the 15th floor.

The room was enormous and lavish in an over the top way. But for the absence of a body and a team of forensic investigators it looked every inch like a murder scene from CSI. At less than a hundred dollars a night it was remarkably cheap, but then the rooms are a small source of income in comparison to poker, roulette, slot machines and Celine Dion.

Outside our window there was a live working roller coaster. Things like that tell you you have made it to Vegas, and the size of the hotel confirmed this. New York New York's exterior recreates many landmark buildings from the city. Each of them are the size of a hotel in their own right and, combined, they form one massive hotel a whole block long. New York New York is apparently the biggest hotel in the world. Somehow I doubt you have to go too far to find the remainder of the top ten.

We got changed and left to experience Vegas. If you don't want to leave air conditioned interiors of hotels it seems you can cover most of the uptown stretch of the city just by using the walkways which link most of the casinos together and also cross over the five lane highways that spring off in every direction meaning that traffic lights with pedestrian crossings are rare, presumably discarded in the knowledge that drivers are too busy looking for the entrance to their hotel to spot something as irrelevant as a stop light or a pedestrian.

We chose to sample the fresh air, even though the dry Nevada air seemed anything but fresh. We emerged on Las Vegas Boulevard, AKA The Strip, where large numbers of continental men of varying ages held collections of cards that they clicked against each other and offered to passers by. It could almost have been Edinburgh when the festival is in town, except that the cards were for escort girls and strippers. Prostitution is a big industry in Vegas and it's a competitive one. Cards and magazines boast that you will either get the girl on the card or one that looks very similar, and, if you are not happy with the one you get, you are under no obligation to keep her. I can't help wondering how many girls get sent back and what it does for their self-esteem. It's never nice getting knocked back, particularly by a fat bloke in a hotel.

Looking for somewhere to eat we settled on the Paris Casino's Chinese restaurant – Paris being internationally renowned for Chinese cuisine - and got a table outside, opposite the Bellagio. At eight o'clock there was a thundering roar and fountains shot water into the air as the distinctive opening bars of Elvis' Viva Las Vegas emerged. The next song was Celine Dion with the theme from Titanic which, as a song about a shipwreck, somehow didn't seem to work as well when accompanied by plumes of water.

This was Vegas, the glamour and the extravagance, so over the top as to be unbelievable, but also unforgettable. There are a lot of reasons to hate Vegas but it remains a place that's alive any time of day, and somehow draws you in to its strange surreal world in the middle of the desert. We savoured a bit more of the atmosphere walking further down the Strip before heading back to New York New York where the machines and tables were all doing a roaring trade. We headed into one of the many bars and had a couple of drinks before going to bed while Vegas carried on regardless.

September 13. We started the day finding the one show we fancied seeing that evening- comedienne Rita Rudner - had finished, and there was nothing else worth paying a vast amount of money to see. At a weekend you get more one off gigs, Guns'n'Roses were the main draw in a few days time, but in the week it is normally just the long running shows. Barry Manilow was the only other show that carried any sort of appeal, albeit a cheesy one, and as he was having hip surgery following too much dancing at the Copacabana, he was taking a break.

After breakfast we explored the hotel casino - it was large enough for a walk around it to be called an exploration. After that we went on to explore the strip and the interiors of most of the other casinos. Our self-invented tour took in the Luxor, Mandalay Bay, MGM Grand, Excalibur, Paris and a couple of others I can't remember the names of. Along the way, a few misconceptions I had about Vegas casinos were proved wrong. The first, from Oceans 11, was that you can't film or take photos in casinos in case you find out where the security points are. In the casinos we went into, cameras were common place and no one objected to them.

The second was that people sat at the slot machines with buckets of tokens while other people waited to get their money as soon as they got up. I think this came from an episode of Friends when they all went to

Vegas to find Joey. In reality no one sat with a bucket of tokens, no one even had buckets, they just had tokens or coins.

The last misconception was that tables were always separate from slot machines, with the slots being in a down-at-heel room at the start. This one came from a trip to the Casino at Monte Carlo. The reality in Vegas is that there are no poker, craps, or roulette rooms, and no separate rooms for slot machines. The tables appear in one section of a vast space otherwise filled by a dazzling array of machines that are almost identical to one another. Casinos boast of having more than five hundred different types of slot machines, and it's true that they have five hundred machines with different names, but that's about it as far as differences go. All the machines are variants on the same theme, requiring only the spin of a reel, and providing 1,5,9,15 or 20 line combinations for wins. Very few go as far as to provide options for gambling up and losing your winnings without spinning the reel again, and yet people seem to believe that each machine is in some way unique. Their obliviousness to the similarities must be a constant source of delight for the manufacturers who get an endless source of income by simply coming up with a few new names every year.

The machines all make their own little noises while they wait for people to play or tell people they've lost their money. They combine together to make a somewhat eerie sound, which reminded me of the last track on Queen's Made in Heaven CD which ends with a strange endless bubbling noise that sounds like Brian May left his guitar in the bath. On record it is monotony personified, but re-produced by thousands of slot machines simultaneously, it was strangely soothing, like a piece of mood music played in the wrong place but working because of the incongruous setting. That said, after half an hour or so it permeated every fibre of my being and reverted to being irritating beyond belief, which may explain why everyone eventually leaves the slot machines even if they are winning.

Later in the day we took a trip up the Eiffel Tower. Not the real one of course, this was the one that starts off inside the Paris Casino and ends up outside of it. It's far smaller than the real thing, Las Vegas doesn't do life-size replicas, but also far easier to get to the front of the queue for. People who visit it don't always keep their expectations in check. As we were going up we passed a woman complaining that it was a rip-off as there was nothing much to see at the top. I wanted to explain to her that while they can recreate the tower, they can't recreate the Paris skyline, and if you are looking out across a desert you should probably expect miles of flat barren land, but I thought better of it.

We moved on to the MGM Grand where they have taken the recognisable symbol of the MGM lion, and put real ones in a glass cage for the dubious benefit of the paying public. For the sake of balance, and to avoid any possible legal claim, I have to say that they treat the lions well. They bring them in for a short period of time from a natural habitat they have created where they have more space, forest and trees than they would get in any zoo, and the glass cages in the casino are also very large and green, but, even so, I still can't see why it is in any way necessary as an attraction.

Down the other end of the Grand they offered free tickets for previews of new CBS shows, which sounded promising till we saw something that looked far more like animal cruelty as people sat behind desks on computers completing the after show focus group survey as if it were a multiple choice exam that their whole future depended on.

Concluding that we had probably seen most of what the south of the strip had to offer we decided to head downtown. Vegas' glorious past was recalled in the names of the roads to the east and west of the strip - Dean Martin Drive and Frank Sinatra Drive on one side, Duke Ellington Way on the other.

After passing the last of the large new casinos we reached the wedding chapels, the other thing Vegas is famous for. The notion of anything vaguely romantic or extravagant about a Vegas wedding is expelled by a look at the exteriors of the chapels. Most of them are run-down, old looking, buildings with adult video shops or strip-clubs nearby. Some of them offer satellite services so your friends back home can see the wedding live, but as that requires a level of forward planning that isn't a feature of your average Vegas wedding I can't see it being a much used facility. All in all, unless you want Elvis to marry you, Vegas isn't a place to tie the knot in.

A couple of weeks before we arrived it was on the national news that the days of on the spot weddings were over, as the place granting the licences to marry would close between midnight and eight. The closure was for financial reasons, it cost too much to open twenty-four hours. Too late for the likes of Britney of course, but anyone else drunk on a sudden unexpected win at a casino would no longer be able to rush off and marry whoever happened to be next to them at the time they won. I couldn't help but think that they should have looked at the bigger financial picture before doing this. Yes, they would save on wages, but what about all the divorce fees and court work they'd lose when the happy couple sobered up and realised what they'd done. Las Vegas lawyers must have lost an awful lot of work as a result of this decision.

Past the wedding chapels, we reached old style Vegas and the likes of the Golden Nugget where the northern end of the strip meets Fremont Street and the neon lights of the new casinos give way to traditional rows of red and gold bulbs. Downtown has a different atmosphere to it, more edgy and less sanitised. It's Vegas before it became a resort. Inside the casinos we even noticed a few old ladies with buckets of tokens, proving that you can find most things if you look hard enough.

After a drink and some random expenditure on nameless machines, we got the trolley back to the top of the strip with a driver who seemed to break wind each time he began to talk, much to the amusement of upper deck passengers who weren't near enough to know whether this was a quirk of his microphone or a bad case of flatulence.

Back on the strip, we had a 'traditional' Irish meal outside Nine Fine Irishmen, and listened to an 'Irish' band play a set including The Irish Rover and Pogues classic Fiesta, while an old couple stood listening and looking so contented and happy that it made others hope they would be like them at their age. After that we headed back to our room, got changed and hit the casino for a night of hedonistic gambling, or half an hour at least.

Knowing how games work and how to bet ought to be a pre-requisite for playing them, but that would have limited my options considerably, so I watched at a few tables and noted what the minimum bets were before deciding I'd have a go at the craps table. The minimum bet was fifteen dollars, so I got sixty dollars worth of chips and planned to spread my four bets out to make them last that little bit longer. I put three five-dollar chips on 8. The dice were rolled and came up on something other than 8. I decided to sit the next roll out. 8 came up this time, and some chips were put in front of where mine had been left. The next roll, which I still didn't bet on, came out as a 9, and then there was another 8. More chips were put where my original bet still lay. The man next to me helpfully asked me whether I knew all these chips were mine. My surprised response of "are they?" told him all he needed to know. I duly picked up my winning chips, leaving the original three where they were and putting another three on top.

A little while later I placed a further fifteen dollars on 6 at Liz's request. We carried on watching as 6 and 8 came up with surprising regularity. Fifteen of my original sixty dollars had still gone nowhere near the table, and the pile of chips of indeterminate value, that constituted my winnings, was building up. Wondering whether they were as much as my stake, and assuming that I had broken even if they were, I was further surprised when the game finally ended and my original stake was returned to me.

I picked up my chips and looked over at a Roulette table where the minimum bet was ten dollars. There was no space at the table and no one seemed about to move. Eventually I decided that holding an unknown amount of cash in my hands was not a good idea, and I cashed in my chips. I got one hundred-and-nine dollars, a forty-nine dollar profit. I had won more than I'd bet. Of course, if I'd been shrewd, or had a vague clue what I was doing, I might have reinvested some of my winnings as I went along, and I might even have bet the last fifteen dollars, but, either way, I had still won in Vegas, and few people get to say that.

Partly to keep this achievement in tact, and partly because there was nothing else where a stake lasted longer than one spin or turn of a card, I didn't bet on anything else that evening. The closest I got was at another Roulette table when I realised a ten dollar bet could be spread widely rather than going on one number only. I watched as two people cleared up, and a third man lost every time. Liz repeatedly asked what was happening and said it didn't make any sense. Partly to avoid having to attempt to explain a betting system I had only a limited grasp of, and partly because of a fear of losing my winnings, I decided against joining in and we went for a drink at a coyote ugly type bar where a tribute band played Jefferson Starship and Journey songs. We rounded the evening off with Liz playing Wheel of Fortune, a game with no wheel, where you can't win a fortune, and then went back to the room a little richer than we were when we left it.

September 14. Leaving Las Vegas seemed easier than getting into it. The valet brought the car round to the front of the hotel, and we headed towards the strip, ten feet and one mile away from us. From there it seemed like no time till we were on the I-15, heading towards Los Angeles. Strong winds were blowing across the desert roads as we crossed into California and a badly secured large tin sheet blew off the top of a van and bounded across the middle of the road narrowly missing us and several other cars.

That was about as lively as the journey got for a long time. The radio signal disappeared somewhere around the border, although it was still there long enough to hear Black Horse and the Cherry Tree several times as we drove past assorted dry lakes, distant mountain ranges and the occasional Indian reservation identified by those two well known Native American traditions - casinos and discount shopping centres.

Eventually we saw signposts to Peggy Sue's 50s diner, the first place to eat for more than a hundred miles, located in Yermo (population 1,092) on the Ghost Town Road, a name that tells you all you need to know about the location. Peggy Sue's looks nothing special from the outside, but on the inside it's awash with fifties memorabilia, with a bit of the Blues Brothers thrown in for good measure. Shortly after Peggy Sue's we reached Barstow where Interstate 40 ends and Route 66 makes a thirty-six mile reappearance.

Barstow was a large place, but looked scruffy and closed down. I had read a description of it as being slightly scary in the way railroad towns can be, and as descriptions go they don't come much better. Further along came the small towns of Lenwood, Helendale and Oro Grande. Oro Grande's main features were a still running huge cement plant and lots of roadside junkshops. Lenwood couldn't even boast that much. Helendale, however, did boast a genuine visitor attraction in the form of Exotic World, the only museum in America devoted to the art and craft of Striptease.

Retired dancer Jennie Lee started collecting burlesque memorabilia when she owned the Sassy Lassy nightclub in San Pedro, California. After she was diagnosed with breast cancer, she moved with her husband to an abandoned goat farm, where she intended to create a burlesque museum, found a burlesque school and run a bed and breakfast. After Lee died in 1990, Dixie Evans took over the farm and turned it into the Exotic World Burlesque Museum. Evans, a burlesque dancer from the sixties, decided to give each visitor a guided tour of her collection of costumes, posters, photos, props and rare movies, and while the thought of a woman in her late sixties showing you round an exotic museum may sound as comfortable as your Gran talking to you about sex, it didn't put people off going to the museum.

If you're want to know how I found the experience you'll be disappointed, because when I said Helendale did boast a visitor attraction, that's exactly what I meant. In late 2005 Lee's widower, and

Evans' assistant, Charlie Arroyo died, and storms damaged the facilities. As a result, the museum ceased to be, at least in Helendale. It has now relocated to Las Vegas, where somehow I suspect a burlesque museum is not nearly as unique an attraction.

And that's about it for the Old National Trail Highway, as this stretch of Route 66 is known. We rejoined Interstate 15 at Victorville, home of the Roy Rogers and Dale Evans Museum, which had an unfeasibly large and not to scale concrete copy of Trigger at its entrance. Sadly we didn't have time to go in, as at five o'clock we had to hand over the keys of the car, and the car itself, to the Hertz rental office at LAX airport.

We negotiated the maze of interstates and highways flowing in all directions around LA, helped by long stretches of near stationary traffic that made spotting exits and getting over to them easy. We made it to LAX with half an hour to spare. The sign for rental car returns greeted us like an evil bailiff coming to take away our possessions. The Ford Fusion, so uncool and yet so practical with all its added extras and large boot space, had been a feature of the trip for so long that handing it back made it feel like the holiday was nearly over, even though we had almost a month left. We parked the car, an assistant appeared, checked the tank, took a credit card imprint and headed off, leaving us to attempt to empty the car before his return. Ten minutes later we had finished, but he was nowhere to be seen so we took the keys to the office.

The lady in the office remarked on how many miles we'd done and I recounted our journey to her. It came as no surprise when she said that we'd seen more of her country than she had. I paid the drop-off fee of five hundred dollars and claimed back the money for the oil change. She worked out the balance, added the tax, and then took an extra fifty dollars off because we had, as she put it, "done all that travelling and should get something for it." She also rang for a taxi to collect us and take us to Redondo Beach where we were staying for the next three nights. What a nice person.

Part 4

California Dreamin'

25 – Redondo Beach

Redondo Beach is the southernmost beach on the west coast of LA. It was described in the brochure as being equidistant from all of Los Angeles' main attractions, which meant it was miles away from anywhere. It was another place I'd chosen off the back of a song title, this time a Patti Smith song. I knew it as one side of a Morrissey double A-side, the side that didn't get played, and so not a song I'd ever heard, but still enough to draw me in.

On our arrival we tried to book a tour round LA, but were thwarted by a concierge who went on a long break shortly after telling us to come back later. We decided to take a walk along the beach instead. It seemed to be buried somewhere between the marina and the harbour. We gave up looking after a while and walked along the ocean front, eventually stopping at a row of bars and restaurants near a large car park, where we got a great Caribbean type meal at Lou-Elueys - say it fast and you can hear a song - a small bar and restaurant offering good views out across a sandless stretch of the Atlantic. The people who cooked the food were the same people who served it, and the place had a good laid-back feel to it, diverting our thoughts from the possibility that, thanks to Morrissey, we were in a small place, miles away from anywhere, with no beach apart from the one in its name.

We wondered what joys lay in store for us over the next few days.

September 15. After a late start we managed to track down the concierge and book on a tour on Saturday before walking up the coast. It was as warm as Vegas, but thanks to fewer buildings, no skyscrapers and an ocean, it felt a whole lot fresher. We stopped for a breakfast/lunch at the Cheesecake Factory overlooking the ocean. Even in a chain diner miles from central LA, the clientele seemed vaguely glamorous and the waiters and waitresses acted as if they worked at one of the finest high class restaurants around. Needless to say, there was no scrimping on the portions, the club sandwich was vast, and served with fries and salad as if it were a challenge to see just how much you could eat. I got about three-quarters of the way through. Proud of my achievements, I still declined the offer of a box to go for the remainder.

We continued up the coast and, a few minutes later, discovered the beach. It wasn't Redondo Beach, which remained hidden, but was a beach all the same, Hermosa Beach to be precise. We looked out across miles of sand and a few people playing beach volleyball. Off a small pier a group of old Phillipino men were catching the dishes of the day for the local fish restaurants. A bit further down, a row of cafes and bars coming off from the beach offered satellite TV and English soccer matches amongst their attractions. People sat outside soaking up the sun, drinking and joking without a care in the world. This was the archetypal laid-back West Coast place I didn't think really existed. It was what beach life should be like. It was what all life should be like. I wished I had been ten years younger and ten times richer, or alternatively had just been born here in the first place.

Beyond the beach there were a few small shops, more cafes and restaurants. While we drank iced caramel coffees we saw another sight that framed this as Los Angeles - a large white lady with large blonde hair and large breasts, wearing a white top and a pink skirt, on a pink bicycle with a small Jack Russell in the shopping basket at the front. Where else would this pass as normal?

Dogs are everywhere in LA. Earlier we had witnessed the curiously English looking scene of a dog barking at a postman, at the cafe we were joined by a couple of gay men with large St Bernard's, and on our way back to the beach we passed our first dog walker, a lady in T shirt and shorts, with eight dogs walking on leads in front of her. Dogs are just one of life's essential accessories it seems.

Heading back to Redondo, we walked up the side road from our hotel and eventually worked our way back down to the front past a couple of parks that brought us not too far from where we had stopped walking the previous night. We walked past the car park and, a few feet further on, by a large two-tier pier, discovered the beach that stretched for miles to the south and west of us.

Above the pier there were a couple of rows of small offices and buildings including the Los Angeles Superior Court Redondo Beach Courthouse, a single storey building, which looked like a large beach hut with white wood panels and pale blue wood window frames on the outside. It almost cried out for a TV series to be set there. On the Pier itself there were more fishermen, several market stalls, little cafes, an Irish pub, and, on the upper level, a large seafood restaurant and a pole with signs pointing to major world cities, telling us how far we were away from them. We were 5,462 miles, and one lifetime, away from London. We had travelled a similar distance since we picked up the car in Boston. New York was 2,461 miles away, and it seemed a long time since we had been there too.

We walked along the beach, heading back as the sun slowly disappeared out of view behind the ocean. The sky was clear and changed slowly to a creamy colour as we looked down to the bottom of the now empty beach. Even if everything else in LA is fake, the sunset on Redondo Beach is natural and beautiful.

Back in the hotel I flicked through the TV channels. In the absence of party political broadcasts, political advertising is big in the States during elections. Governor Schwarzenneger was bidding for his second term in office, and a Democrat advert played on almost every ad-break. It began with a clip from an election rally for George W Bush with Arnie beside him proclaiming "lets go out and re-elect President George W Bush." It then ran through a list of the things Bush had done to harm California, each item on the list punctuated by a repeat of Arnie saying the words George W Bush, and ended with the question "Arnold Schwarzenneger is for George W Bush, is he for you?" A great advert, but the people of California still decided, on the whole, that he was for them, and re-elected him.

We headed back to the Cheesecake Factory for an evening meal. Spinach was off the menu following an outbreak of what was an, as yet, unknown form of food poisoning, from an, as yet, untraced consignment of spinach. All that was known was that the spinach was thought to come from California, which was more than a tad unfortunate as the state provides the US with about eighty per cent of the stuff. Not that Redondo Beach residents seemed too stressed by this, and even without spinach the portion sizes were still enormous. Liz rose to the challenge I had declined and took a box for her dessert at the end of our second feat of endurance. We headed back to the Crowne Plaza, ready for an early start on Saturday, thoroughly in love with LA, or at least this bit of it.

September 16. Just as it was starting to look like the Democrats would gain control of the Senate and Congress, there were stories circulating that new polling machines and a lack of computer training amongst most of the over seventy-two year olds who man the stations would lead to the same sort of disputes and problems there were in the 2000 presidential election. It came as no surprise to find that the risk was greatest in key seats for the Democrats. A couple of weeks later, it was reported that ID requirements had been brought in in many states, and the only two pieces of ID that would be accepted were passports and driving licences. Seventy per cent of Americans don't have one of these and ten per cent have neither. The ten per cent fall disproportionately within the poorest groups of society, who by and large are not Republicans. As a result, the Democrats had to look again at how winnable some marginal seats were, while bookmakers lengthened the odds on there ever being a problem that lost Republicans votes.

Our daytime activity consisted of a trip round LA, Hollywood, and the homes of the stars. We got the complimentary minibus that rounded up participants from the area and took them to LAX airport to meet up with other rounded up participants from elsewhere, and organise them into new groups destined for different tours. The military precision this required was beyond the tour planners abilities, so we found ourselves sat on a small minibus with two others waiting for no one else to appear. Eventually we were put on another bus with another tour and sent on our way.

The first stop was the Muscle Beach area of Venice Beach. Muscle Beach was a big place to hang out in the sixties, but got its name from the later influx of body builders and workout equipment permanently sited at the edge of the beach. We were told it was a great place to see later in the day, which begged the question of why we had stopped there at eleven in the morning when it resembled a run down beach front, and the only things of interest were a house Jim Morrison used to live in – which had his image painted outside, possibly so he could find his way home - and a strange old man who, for no apparent reason, whistled and clacked out tunes against his throat using his fingers to change the tone.

After a stop for lunch we moved on to Hollywood Boulevard, home of the Hollywood Walk of Fame, which, far from being the lavish attraction it's made out to be, is actually just a collection of paving slabs with stars in the middle and the name of an entertainer written on each one.

Anyone hoping to get their own star should note that your place on the walk is not determined chronologically, and there are a large number of stars all over the place waiting for names to be added. There are plusses and minuses to this. On the plus side, you could end up next to a Hollywood legend, but, on the minus side, like Elvis and Marilyn Monroe, you could find yourself commemorated outside a shop selling plastic Oscars and maps of where famous people met untimely ends.

A better place to be seen outside of is Grauman's Chinese Theater, where there are imprints of the hands and feet of stars. With less space than on the Walk of Fame, inclusion says more about your star status, although including the prints of Donald Duck does rather cheapen the exercise a little bit. The hand imprints are allegedly the result of a fortunate accident, caused by an actress tripping up on the wet cement when the theater was nearing completion and using her hand to break her fall. Sid Grauman saw the imprint, had an idea, and everyone was happy. They were simple times. If it happened today the end result would probably have been a lawsuit for not making the hazard clear.

Next stop was Mulholland Drive. Turning on to the legendary road and recreating the opening of the David Lynch movie was reason enough for being there, but the purpose of the stop was to look at the Hollywood sign way off in the distance. You can't get to the sign anymore, as so many people weren't content with a photo that they tried to get pieces of letters as souvenirs, and it was closed off. It is now guarded over by security cameras and a rapid response anti-trespass unit, a name that sounded like it should belong to a unit protecting something more vital to national security than nine white letters at the top of a hill.

At Universal Studios we joined up with the Homes of the Famous tour. The tour went round exclusive streets with celebrity homes in Bel Air and Beverley Hills. Both areas only allow tours in unmarked mini vans, so that the celebs don't realise that the managing agents of their gated communities let the plebs see where they live.

Our new guide did his best to make us feel like sad celebrity stalkers with a dismissive attitude to anyone famous, a complete disinterest in where they lived, and a thinly veiled contempt for the people who do the tour. I would have said he was in the wrong career, were it not for the fact that this was not his career. He had moved to Los Angeles from St Louis to pursue a career in music. Later in the tour, by popular request, or at least the request of a Hispanic couple with boundless enthusiasm and a limited grasp of English, he shared some of his music with us. After twenty minutes of twee ballads notable only for the number of variants on the line 'your warm tender hand makes me want to give you all of my heart' I decided I could still say he was in the wrong career. His dad had written some of his songs, so I could also say that I really did blame the parents.

In the evening we went back to Hermosa Beach and the imaginatively titled 'Comedy and Magic Club.' A quick look at the forthcoming attractions revealed no reason for including magic in the name, and every reason for sticking with comedy. You may think a comedy club by a beach, miles away from anywhere would not attract stars, but you'd be wrong. Jay Leno is the regular host on a Sunday, and other stars make occasional appearances.

Deciding that Leno is no David Letterman, we had intentionally got tickets for Saturday evening, for once not missing something by accident. The headliner was Louis CK whose show was doing well on HBO. He was very good, as was the compere, a local comedian, and two guys from New York. None of them, however, came close to the performance of the surprise guest, a former star of a TV sitcom who had done very little since, but still held a place in LA's heart judging by the rapturous reception he received before, during, and after, his set. He deserved it, with classic material about being arrested for jaywalking when he couldn't cross the road quick enough, and trying to buy fashionable trousers only to find fashionable now meant hanging off your arse. He delivered his set in an old-slacker style that made it funnier still, and left to a standing ovation and a group of people only partly joking as they bowed before him and chanted "we're not worthy." Surely this guy would soon get the international recognition his talent deserved. What could go wrong with material of this quality? If I say that his name was Michael Richards, AKA Kramer in Seinfeld, you may know the answer to that one. Just two months later on November 17 he achieved the international fame he deserved, but sadly it came courtesy of a racist outburst at a group of hecklers in another LA comedy club which effectively ended his career.

On September 16, 2006, I wished I could remember his material because it was hilarious. Now I wished I could remember it so I could pass it off as my own - someone ought to make a living from it, and it isn't likely to be him.

September 17. We spent most of the day on the beach, consequently there isn't much to say about the day. We began with an excellent breakfast of Corned Beef hash and orange juice in a cafe on the pier where all attention was focused on a group of fishermen who had caught something large enough not to need exaggerating about when they told their friends. Almost two feet wide and three feet long, it was slowly filleted and gutted while more and more children and their parents gathered to marvel at it. Simple natural pleasures in an artificial place once more.

On the beach I started reading Benjamin Kunkel's Indecision, one of the most acclaimed first novels of this century. Critics fall over themselves to say just how surprising the ending is. Not giving anything away, but whilst it is a good book, you can read biographies of people you've been life long fans of and be more surprised by the ending. Anyone who reads it and can't guess what's coming would find the conclusion of Columbo episodes unexpected.

The sun was out in full, and I failed to put suntan lotion on at the regular ten-minute intervals proclaimed as essential. The consequences of this were less surprising than the ending of the book. Various newly exposed bits of flesh got burnt and sore by the time we took an afternoon stroll down the beach and the pier.

The bars on the pier were full in the afternoon, and still busy by the time we returned for a meal in Kilkenny's in the evening. The American Football season had started and several screens were showing live games. Football has a far greater hold on the American public than Baseball. Baseball can be on in bars and just a few people look up at it between beers, but when Football is on everything stops. Unlike Soccer in the UK, American Football is still on terrestrial TV and is the highlight of a Sunday night. Women support the game as passionately as men, which means you don't get patronising adverts where they show a lack of understanding of the game or ask about the equivalent of the offside rule.

Scores and action were debated in the studio and in the bar. At the end of the games the crowd thinned out, as if that was the reason for their night out and now it was over the evening was too. We left when they did, but that was because I had stomach ache from too much sun, rather than because the football had finished. We took a last stroll along the pier and went back to the Crowne Plaza. Redondo Beach had been a real surprise and a great place to stay. I'd happily go back and spend the rest of my life there if only I had the money. I can but dream.

26 – Hollywood

September 18. We got a taxi in the morning and made the short move to the Hyatt on Sunset Boulevard, half an hour's drive away.

The hotel was used in the Spinal Tap film, it was the hotel of choice for Led Zeppelin, who frequently wrecked the rooms, and was also where Keith Richards and Keith Moon threw TV sets off balconies, possibly in frustration at the absence of anything other than celebrity news shows. We had a sunset view room. In the Hyatt this means a view of Sunset Strip rather than a view of the sun setting. On the balcony there was a sign saying, 'Throwing or dropping items off the balcony is a felony and will result in prosecution.' It was enough to put me off, but if I was a rock'n'roll legend I doubt I would have been deterred.

When we booked the holiday we intended to stay a couple of nights in Hollywood, then take a leisurely trip up the Californian coast by train, stopping at places along the way. Since then we had managed to get tickets to the filming of Two and a Half Men, the American sitcom starring Charlie Sheen, at the end of the week. We debated whether to extend our stay and take the train direct to San Francisco, or to stick to the original plans. The hotel confirmed they could offer us the same room for an extra three days, the concierge checked for trains and told us there was one on Saturday at a very reasonable thirty-three dollars each. We decided to stay, and any chance of seeing Carmel County, where Clint Eastwood was Mayor, disappeared.

Having extended our stay we went down the Strip and stopped for lunch at Mel's Drive-In, a fantastic diner that dates back to the sixties when, as Ben Frank's, it was frequented by The Rolling Stones, Andy Warhol and Jim Morrison. With the sixties styling remaining, eating there is like eating in rock'n'roll history. The diner is one of a group of places along the strip where actors who want their egos massaged sit outside hoping to be spotted. Behind us two women talked about a film script and the reaction of the woman it had been sent to. Across from us, an attractive pale skinned woman, who could possibly have been Nicole Kidman but in all probability wasn't, sat quietly eating. It felt like a place to be.

Just up the road was Chateau Marmont where John Belushi overdosed on March 5, 1982, where Jim Morrison fell out of a window, and where James Dean climbed through a window to audition for Rebel Without a Cause. More recently Britney Spears was allegedly thrown out for smearing food across her face and yelling. In a place where Led Zeppelin escaped unpunished for riding motorbikes through the lobby, getting thrown out for smearing food and yelling says something about the changing nature of celebrity and morality, or maybe it just says something about Britney Spears.

On the other side of the Strip was The Standard Hotel, co-owned by Leonardo Di Caprio and Cameron Diaz, and the House of Blues, co-owned by Dan Ackroyd. Further down the road was Whisky a Go Go, the legendary club where The Doors were house band in 1966, the Rainbow Bar and Grill, where Marilyn Monroe and Joe DiMaggio had a blind date in 1953, and the Viper Room, until recently owned by Johnny Depp, and forever known as the place where River Phoenix died. The list goes on, and every street is only a short distance from a famous hotel, or small place someone rented when they were starting out. Even the most cynical would find it hard not to be at least a bit in awe of all the showbiz associations. It may be shallow, but at the same time, there is something addictive about it.

To stand out in LA is difficult, but we managed it, not by being English or having no plastic surgery, but by walking, rather than driving, down La Cienega Boulevard to a shopping centre around Wilshire Boulevard, a relatively unglamorous part of the city. The cinema there was showing Woody Allen's Scoop. We passed again on the chance to see it, heading instead to the Farmers Market and Grove. The Farmers Market did actually start off as a farmers market before large supermarkets existed, but now has no farmers and instead is a collection of market stalls and cafes. The Grove is a swanky upmarket shopping area, which also has a cinema. We went to see the Black Dahlia, a film about the most notorious unsolved murder in LA, which seemed the right film for the setting. The woman in the cinema told me she really loved my accent, which just went to show that outside

England all regional dialects are lost and any accent becomes clipped and posh.

We ate a healthy Salmon Nicoise with a bottle of wine outside the Marmalade Cafe and then had a walk around the Market, one of the few places you can get UK newspapers a day after publication. I looked at one and discovered that Portsmouth were top of the Premiership. I double-checked the date on the paper. Back at the hotel we had a couple of drinks and returned to our room for the start of the new season on TV.

American TV starts to wake from its slumbers at the end of August, and becomes fully alert during September when all the big shows start back. Tonight, as well as the return of Two and a Half Men and CSI Miami, there was the premiere of Studio 60 on the Sunset Strip from Aaron Sorkin, creator of The West Wing. It was one of the most eagerly anticipated shows of the new season with Matthew Perry in his first big role since Friends. In the third episode, one of two I saw while we here, the fictional show in the programme sees its ratings rise, and someone says it will be downhill all the way from there. Life imitated art, only didn't wait till episode three, and viewing figures crashed from twenty-one million for the first episode to seven million by Christmas. The show was cancelled after one series. Funny really, because aside from Michael Richards return to fame, and the inevitability of a Woody Allen film getting an English release, there was nothing I'd considered a more sure fire bet all the time we'd been here.

September 19. After breakfast we walked up to Hollywood Boulevard, a walk that takes longer than it looks like it should do, probably because the person who drew the map has never actually walked it and missed most of the side streets as they drove past with a pen and paper.

Our first tasks were to buy a fake plastic Oscar for one of my nieces and to get some stamps for Liz to continue sending postcards to her sister. The former was easy to achieve, loads of shops on the Boulevard sell them, the latter proved more difficult. We trawled around various convenience stores until someone directed us to a post office where we finally completed our quest just before I screamed "do we have to get them now, we are here till the end of the week."

We booked a tour round the Kodak Theater. The Theater is sponsored rather than owned by Kodak. For seventy-five million dollars their name appears on the outside of the building, although on Oscars night a banner with the words 'Academy Awards' goes up in front of it. As this is the night most people see the building it could be argued that the value of their investment has been reduced somewhat. The front of the building isn't the only thing that changes on Oscars night, the road does too, which is just as well given that it doesn't look fit for purpose usually. To create the glitzy street scene you see on the night all the buildings to the east of the theater are covered up to disguise their status as shops, and the red carpet and other trimmings are added on the street and steps leading up to the Theater. Nothing seems to be done to the road to the west, which is probably why no one ever enters from that direction.

Being the proud owner of an Oscar, albeit a fake plastic one, I seized my moment and had a photo taken with it at the top of the steps before we started the tour. Inside the theater we got to stand on the stage and look into the vast auditorium where various cardboard cut-outs were dotted around the front few rows of seats. These are a key early part of rehearsals for Oscars evening. The organisers know who is meant to be sitting where, but don't know who is going to win, so they put cut outs in the seats and run through each and every possible winner to work out the lighting, cameras and anything else that would be needed just in case an obscure movie should happen to win an even more obscure Oscar.

The next stage of the planning involves getting stand in's to sit in the seats and pretend to win the Oscar and walk up to the stage to accept it. The whole movement from seat to stage is practised to make sure the spotlight can follow every moment.

Of course if stars happen to swap their seats before the event a sense of panic emerges as producers have to work out where they are now, and whether they have swapped places with another nominee or someone who wasn't up for anything at all. If it's the latter the panic grows as a whole new walk from seat to stage has to be planned for, just in case.

One of the yearly jobs on offer for would be actors in Hollywood is the role of seat filler. They employ more than a hundred people a year for this. When someone leaves their seat, be it to get an award, a drink or a comfort break, they take their place so that there never appears to be an empty seat in the house. They give them specific seats to watch - thereby preventing an unholy rush of wannabes heading for a seat every time an actor goes to the toilet - and there are back-up seat fillers just in case more than one person nips out at the same time - a seat filler sprawled across three out of four seats, with an actor buried underneath, wouldn't be a pretty sight.

All of this meticulous seat filling means that programmes or films with scenes where the search beam lands on an empty seat aren't authentic. The worst you would get is the spotlight falling on a budding actor sat in a seat waiting for a star to come back - which might be the closest to fame they will ever get.

Oscar winners normally won't re-appear after getting their award, and the crummier awards are given out at the end of the evening, so that the big stars don't have to stay all night. After getting an award they get lead off backstage. In order to prevent the immediate backstage area getting cluttered with journalists and drunken movie stars, no press are allowed and no drinks are served in this area. The drinks follow at the end of a less glamorous walk along a corridor, and the interviews take place in the Renaissance hotel next door.

And that's all you need to know about the Oscars, or at least all I can remember about them. The tour lasted an hour, after it we made a brief stop at Virgin on Hollywood Boulevard where I finally bought an album that was big in the UK, but as it was Kasabian's Empire, which had been number one in the UK about a month before and had now finally got a US release, it didn't really count as a discovery.

In the early afternoon we took a trip on the LA Metro to downtown LA. Downtown LA is a strange place. Overall it's worth a visit, but it's never going to be the highlight of your stay. It's not particularly run down like a lot of other downtown areas but it is a very different type of place from the rest of the city. Macy's Plaza and the area around it are drab and unappealing, while other shopping streets have charm but are mainly lined with small independent discount stores and Mexican handicrafts and food shops that feel like they belong in the suburbs rather than a city centre. Over the other side of downtown the Music Center, Walt Disney Concert Hall, Los Angeles Times Building, Supreme Court Courthouse, open spaces and wide roads, combine to make a far more appealing area, where you can spot buildings and scenes from TV series, many of which were not set in LA. You can probably find more buildings that featured in Dallas than you can in Dallas itself.

We completed our travels on the Metro with a trip to the Vermont/Beverly stop from where we estimated it should be just a short walk to Melrose Avenue, a big retro fashion shopping street we'd passed during Saturday's tour. It was indeed a short walk to the Avenue, but as all roads in Los Angeles are very long and Melrose Avenue is no exception, the distance to the part with the shops was still longer than the entire length of an average UK road. We took a bus and reached the row of shops, which was also longer than an average UK road in spite of covering less than a quarter of the street. You could spend an entire day there, going up one side in the morning and coming back down the other in the afternoon.

The small shops are almost all independent ones, some are second hand, but most sell underground retro fashion, the sort of thing that designers pick up, replicate as ironic and increase the price ten-fold. It's the place for goth girls and rock guys to get their clothes, and the place to come if you don't want designer gear, but also don't want to look as if you've been dressed by your mother. That may make it sound like it should be the preserve of the young, but, being LA, this isn't the case, and for every dozen teenagers you'll get at least one Tommy Lee wanting to look every inch the LA rock star.

The World Famous Vintage T-shirt shop is worth stopping at even if you don't want to buy a T-shirt. The 'world famous' description may be over egging its fame even by American standards, but it does get frequented by the stars and is a place where you can pick up second hand tour T shirts from gigs you wished you could say you'd been to. Britney Spears visited shortly after her wedding to Kevin Federline. There is a graffitied note written by her on the wall, with an accompanying photo of the happy couple taken inside the store. The badly scrawled semi-illegible note talks about being here with my great husband Kevin on our honeymoon, proclaiming we're having great fun and he is just the hottest guy ever. One day it could be a rock'n'roll landmark, although for now it's probably a long way behind a certain tattoo shop in Britney related tour stops.

A shop worth avoiding is the second hand record shop, unless you know exactly what you want, and don't want anything but that one record. It should have been a record hunters paradise, with two large rooms and several thousand records to look through, but the owner didn't seem to appreciate the art of browsing, and pushed me for the name of the particular artist I was looking for, until I said the first name I thought of just to get him to leave me alone. Sadly it didn't work and he went on to point to every record even vaguely connected to them as I struggled to pass a quiet half-hour.

After completing one side of Melrose Avenue, Liz ended up with a couple of things to buy, and I found a pair of gold and black jeans that looked like they could be good until I put them on and found they looked indecent and could only be carried off by a rock star on a stage. We got a bus back to the hotel, marvelling at how good the LA public transport system is considering it is meant to be the sole preserve of the few unfortunates who can neither drive themselves or have a chauffeur.

For our evening meal we took a short walk down the road to Yatai, an Asian tapas bar, where the food was excellent, and we easily polished off two bottles of wine during the course of the set meal. We headed back to the hotel bar, which tries to look like a cool late night place to drink and would have succeeded if it hadn't closed down around midnight. It would never have happened in Led Zep's days.

September 20. Leaving downtown and retro shopping areas behind, we went where the beautiful go with trips to Beverly Hills and Santa Monica. The contrast between the aspirations and the reality of life for so many people in LA was illustrated at the bus stop, where a seriously camp and glamorous man bemoaned the fact that he had had to get off the last bus because it had no air conditioning.

"Can you imagine breathing in other people's air in that heat?" he asked us, and I had to admit that I couldn't, mainly because I'd never really thought about the passage of air from someone else's mouth to my lungs in any heat.

On the bus, he was joined by an old guy with the whitest grimmest pallor you're ever likely to see outside a mortuary. He could have fitted the description of death warmed up but a more accurate description would have been death partly defrosted. Two other women may have had similar complexions, but had been to the Barbara Cartland school of make up and wore the results of this and several rounds of plastic surgery to disguise any actual facial characteristics. All of them probably resented nothing more than the vagaries of life reducing them to travelling on buses. Oh cruel fate to mete out such punishment.

Arriving in Beverly Hills we headed for the prestigious shopping district of Rodeo Drive where our first stop was the Martin Lawrence Art Gallery, our aim being to look at art rather than to buy anything. As you would expect the Martin Lawrence Art Gallery has very little in common with a second hand record shop on Melrose Avenue, but it did share one distinguishing feature, which was that casual browsing seems to be impossible. We had been inside but a few moments when we were accosted and asked what we were interested in. I tried the just browsing option, but it didn't register. There were two follow up courses of action we could have taken. The first and logical one would have been to leave, accepting that this was not a gallery for looking at art and you should only be there if you are buying. The second was to lie and make something up. We took this option and for the next hour we didn't just lie, we invented and inhabited an almost entirely fake world far removed from anywhere we lived.

The building up of this façade was not deliberate, it was just that at each stage of the story, just as we believed we had done enough to prove our fake credentials, they forced us to raise our game by showing an interest in our life that was as unbelievable as the life itself. We started with the simple claim that we were interested in collecting Andy Warhol, largely because a couple of pieces of his work were downstairs in the gallery. We hoped this would be enough for a safe passage around, but no, we were probed a little further with "which pieces in particular?" and "did we have any of his work already?" We were then invited to have a look around while the assistant got together some information on their collection.

We hoped that the time taken to assemble the information would be long enough for us to look and leave, but it wasn't. We hardly saw anything before we were probed further on our art collecting strategy. A few random answers later and we were a couple who had suddenly come into a bit of money and were looking to invest in art. But we didn't just want to invest, we wanted something that would fit with the design of our house, complimenting it rather than looking out of place. Yes, art was an investment, but we weren't just looking for something that was going to increase in value, it had to be something we liked.

Brochures for their forthcoming auction were bought out. I made an attempt to end the charade by honestly saying that we would have left LA before it took place. "Not to worry, you can put in an absentee bid," we were told, and the absentee bid process was then explained to us. This at least provided us with a guarantee that we would not have to admit to being fakes who had no money and couldn't afford to buy anything. As a result, we started looking with relish at the brochures for four upcoming auctions, discussing our imaginary budget of up to twenty thousand pounds – "is that forty thousand dollars?" we asked, as if we didn't know – and debating whether we would be better to go with one or two big pieces or a number of smaller items that would make our collection bigger and provide greater insurance against price fluctuations. We found that fluctuations weren't really things to worry about with Warhol, if the economy is good Warhol prices remain good, and the faking continued.

We took time to express a genuine, if unfulfillable, interest in the work of Philippe Bertho, an artist Martin Lawrence were exclusively representing, and whose work mixes pop art stylings with illusions of space and size, creating imaginative large canvases that look like they should be classics. His work was not included in the auctions, apparently because it gets snapped up so quickly by particular collectors that it wouldn't be right to do so. We took details of some of his pieces and, having exchanged e-mail addresses, finally left with auction brochures to consider what absentee bids to go for. A week or so later we got an e-mail enquiring whether we would like to make any bids for later auctions, noting we'd not bid in the first one, and we managed to stay on their e-mail list for a fair few months before they finally gave up on us. Bless them.

Leaving the gallery, we avoided further shops we knew were out of our price range - in case of another ambush by enthusiastic assistants - and concentrated on a few more impersonal looking places, before having lunch in one of the many cafes lining the nearby streets and taking a bus trip along Santa Monica Boulevard which, predictably enough, took us into Santa Monica.

Santa Monica Boulevard is the end of Route 66. Travelling along the last part of the road made it feel as if we had done what we originally intended. Even if we had missed large parts of it, were now in a bus not a car, and had never been on a Harley Davidson, I felt no qualms in completing my set of photos and adding one of me at the end of the road to go with the ones of me at the start and middle of it. The actual end of the road is uncertain and is not marked by one of the usual Route 66 signs. The bronze plaque that marks a possible end isn't even on the road, and we had to ask at a tourist information office before we found it some distance away from the end of the Boulevard in Palisades Park. Photo's completed we could see Santa Monica.

Santa Monica is a city in its own right, the beach is separated from most of the town by a freeway, and the large Third Street Promenade is the centre of a big non-mall shopping area. The promenade is pedestrian only and has the usual collection of street entertainers in the evening and at weekends. It could be like Brighton, only far more upmarket, far more plush and far more exclusive, which means it isn't like Brighton at all.

Far bigger than Redondo or Hermosa Beach, it also lacks their intimacy and character. That said we still spent several very enjoyable hours there. We walked down the Santa Monica Pier, the sign at the entrance claiming to be another world famous landmark in an exaggerating slightly kind of way. We bought Route 66 postcards and souvenirs from a old shop, and then we headed down the beach and back across the freeway for a meal at Buca di Beppo's Italian restaurant, an old low-beamed building where the walk to the table took us through a smaller room that had a bust of the head of Pope John Paul II in the centre of its one table for no apparent reason. We decided not to ask why it was there. After the meal we went to Ye Olde Kings Head, between Ocean Avenue and Second Street. Unsurprisingly it was an English Bar done out in the quaint old London pub style you find only in American films set in Old London, and not in Wetherspoon's pub down high streets in New London. The only similarities with a real London pub were the menus and the live Premiership football matches. For that reason it was so much better than the real thing, and a pub I wished my local looked like.

On the way back, we failed to spot where we had got on the bus in the morning and eventually, somewhere way out to the east of our hotel, decided we must have missed the stop. We left the bus to walk down a lesser known part of West Hollywood, passing some rather iffy looking diners and a few liquor stores and takeaways before a taxi passed and took us along a route where places worth seeing alternated with an equal number of places worth avoiding. Finally back at the hotel we relaxed once again at the bar, which tonight stayed open much later but still closed before we would have liked it to.

September 21. Universal Studios is the world's largest working studio and the biggest tourist attraction in LA. You can't really come to LA and not see it, so we bowed to the inevitable and saw it. On arrival we took the Universal Studios Tour, a kind of monorail tour where you can see sets from classic films and current TV shows, alongside special effects such as Jaws emerging from the water, flash floods, collapsing bridges, and Godzilla doing something Godzilla like. If you get a seat on the left hand side it's a great tour with endless photo opportunities. If you get a seat on the right hand side it's a good tour and you take endless photos of people's heads.

The tour also goes past the studios used for filming indoor scenes. On that day, we were told, CSI and Desperate Housewives were both filming so "you might just see your favourite star." You might also see a pig flying, and it not be the result of a special effect. The studios, which look like massive aircraft hangers, are all closed up and the stars stay on the inside where you can't go. When you think about it this is understandable. After all, in the middle of a murder investigation, if you heard a tour bus announcing "over there you can see Grisham and his colleagues," it would ruin the illusion somewhat.

After the tour, we walked round the rest of the attractions making sure we seized every naff photo opportunity going. I had my picture taken with my head in a shark's mouth, Shrek befriended us both and Liz became the unknown fourth astronaut in the Apollo 13 mission. The absence of any children didn't stop us going to the Shrek adventure or the performing animals show, where a variety of performing dogs, birds, chimps and monkeys gave a performance that put Peers Mutville's Comix Dog Show at the Illinois State Fair to shame.

Trying to be more adult, we looked for a ride with a few thrills, but not so many as to be truly daring. We settled on Jurassic Park, a ride where the 'thrills' came from special effects along the way and an eighty-four foot drop at the end. As we climbed up slowly to the start of the vast drop I braced myself for a scary adrenaline bursting surge into the water, and then discovered that eighty-four feet really isn't that long a distance. Even the most frightened person can only manage a couple of "oh fucks" in the time it takes to travel that length on a fairground ride.

Feeling emboldened I wanted to try Revenge of the Mummy which sounded like it definitely wasn't for wimps. Sadly all of the rides were starting to close so we took the tour round the special effects and sound stages where, much to my disappointment, I was not chosen to get lost, killed, or generally make a fool of myself to assist a demonstration of how things work in TV and film land.

With the attractions closing, it was back to the entrance to the studios where shops, cinemas, restaurants and, as you would expect, a Hard Rock Cafe all stayed open for another couple of hours.

The gift shops sell a vast amount of movie star toys, all of which fall unashamedly on the wrong side of tacky. I picked up a poseable Elvis, circa Jailhouse Rock, which came with a leaflet telling me how to bend him into classic Elvis poses. No historical figure is too grand to be turned into a cheap gift. Pope John Paul II makes an appearance – Pope Benedict probably doesn't have a friendly enough face to put on a toy – and so does Jesus, complete with his own miracle kit to give you the chance to turn water into wine - without producing any alcohol - and feed five thousand - loaves and fishes not supplied. In one of the few examples of understatement in Hollywood, the inscription on the box said of Jesus, 'views of who he was have varied over time, but everyone agrees he must have been a pretty special man.' I'm not sure this would appease anyone offended at turning the Messiah into a cheap toy.

We got back to Sunset Boulevard and walked past the Viper Room, where big queues of darkly clad twenty somethings gathered outside even though it wasn't even nine and the club wasn't going to open for a few hours yet. After a meal in Cravings, a French Restaurant next to a strip of designer shops and boutiques, we went into the BOA lounge, a swanky bar in the Grafton Hotel on the other side of the Strip from the Hyatt.

BOA is a bar that has reserved signs on tables that no one has reserved, possibly in case anyone sufficiently well known, rich, or both, drops in unexpectedly for a drink. Not that they would walk in unannounced, they get others to do this, which probably explained the number of unknowns who came in by themselves, surveyed the seating, looked at the clientele and left. I imagined them all reporting back to their superstar bosses who then decided if this was the bar they wanted to go into that evening.

Responsibility for deciding who was deemed suitable to take the reserved tables seemed to rest with the bar manageress. A group of young Chinese had been given tables by a member of the bar staff, and were politely moved away when the manageress saw them, even though the tables stayed empty for a long time until another group of people who met her requirements finally arrived. We had no idea who they were and, on the basis that no one checked the bar out shortly before their arrival, figured that, at most, they were up and coming B listers, while there conversation suggested they were musicians, lucky enough to be out on a night when no A listers were expected.

We stayed for a few drinks, abandoning plans to go to the House of Blues which was either closed or having a private party, but either way was out of bounds for the general public, and returned to the Hyatt as the bar was closing and another evening was drawing to a close. At least it was in the Hyatt, down the road at the Viper Room the night was still in full flow. Oh to be an LA goth.

September 22. They celebrate any ex-president in America. It doesn't matter whether they were magnificent historical figures like Lincoln, dangerous figures of fun like Reagan, or have legacies overshadowed by blow jobs like Clinton, they are all celebrated without exception. Even the one ex-president you might legitimately expect to be the exception isn't, and in Yorba Linda, California you can visit the Richard Nixon Library and Birthplace. The flyer in our hotel promised 'A dramatic roller coaster ride through a half century of California, U.S and world history. Just 15 minutes away from Disneyland.' The last sentence could relate either to the location or the subject matter. We passed on the chance of going so I can't say which.

In the afternoon, we took the Dearly Departed Tour of scandal and celebrity deaths sights. The tour bus was a dark black van, sadly not a hearse. Blue Oyster Cult's Don't Fear the Reaper was playing as we boarded, the opening strains creating a suitably dark and gothic ambience that the rest of the song just about maintained, before being succeeded by the theme from Six Feet Under, followed by the jovial tones of a tour guide who, while undoubtedly revelling in the macabre, neither looked or sounded like a man fixated with death. Which was just as well as a black clad goth running a tour round death sites would probably be a bit too much on a Friday afternoon.

The name of the tour was a slight misnomer. It wasn't entirely devoted to death and scandal, we passed the Cunninghams house from Happy Days - even the exterior wasn't shot in Milwaukee - the school yard used for Rydell High in Grease, and Matt Le Blanc's former apartment block, which was used as his home in Joey. The apartment block actually was a scene that covered both scandal and death, the scandal being that the show was made in the first place, the death being the effect it had on Le Blanc's career.

The tour guide had an almost encyclopaedic knowledge of deaths and conspiracy theories. His knowledge of the weird and suspicious was pretty much unequalled. No opportunity for an alternative explanation went unmissed as we passed the motel where Sam Cooke was shot dead, in what may or may not have been a straightforward case of self defence, and the sight of the real Black Dahlia murder, which may or may not have been committed by someone known to the police.

The scandal sites included the place where Hugh Grant picked up Divine Brown, and the place where the LAPD caught them, as well as the small news stand where Paris Hilton bought all the copies of her porn tape so that people would have to buy the official version later.

Leaving no opportunity unmissed there was only one logical stop for a comfort break, the public toilets in the Will Rogers Memorial Park, where George Michael sought a different type of comfort on April 7, 1998. For fans of cockney rhyming slang the toilets are made by Armitage Shanks, while for double entendre enthusiasts the sign by the sink says 'if towel not available, please turn knob' an instruction George presumably misunderstood. When you see the real toilets you realise that George took more than a bit of artistic licence when he recreated the moment in the video for Outside. There are no plush mirrored walls and nothing else remotely glamorous about them. They reminded me more of the toilets at the back of Walsall bus station than the ones used in the video.

The tour concluded back where it began, with Say Goodbye to Hollywood playing as we left the bus. Next on our itinerary was an evening at Warner Studios to watch the filming of Two and a Half Men.

The show has been America's top comedy for several years. Charlie Sheen plays a bachelor who enjoys womanising, drinking and gambling. Hard to see where he gets the inspiration for that part from. His character's name is Charlie Harper. It seems to be a common trait in American sitcoms for the lead character and the actor playing them to share the same first name. Whether this is because of vanity, or because producers worry they'll forget to answer to a different name, is unknown.

Time was running tight so we caught a taxi over to the studios. Finding the Warner complex was easy, finding the actual studios was far harder as the staff in the admin block seemed to have no idea what we were talking about, and reacted as if it was the first time they had heard that programmes were filmed there. If Warners have attempted to link job objectives to the fundamental purpose of their company, they haven't succeeded. Eventually we found someone with a vague knowledge of what we were talking about, and they directed us to the queue for the bus to the studio.

We made it to the queue with just over two hours to go before the show started. Any later and the chances are we would have missed it as they issue more tickets than there are seats. A string of buses turned up to take the audience to the studio. We got on one of the last ones. The crowd behind us stretched a long way down the road, meaning most of them would leave disappointed.

Filming a half-hour comedy takes about three hours. After the audience has finally been seated, the person who provides most of the evening's entertainment enters. This isn't the star of the show, it's the warm up man. Our warm up man introduced himself and then an un-aired completed episode was shown to get us in the mood before he returned.

The show was filmed scene by scene. In between each scene small set changes were completed quickly, and a whole host of producers and directors crowded at the front of the stage, studying every scene from as many different angles as possible, scrutinising what had just been filmed. This took an eternity and normally resulted in the conclusion that at least one retake was needed, so that a line could be said in a different way, or the timing of an entrance or exit could be altered by a fraction of time so small that no watch could measure it.

While all of this was going on the warm up man periodically got us to give the stars a round of applause for nothing more than being there and being famous, and warded off audience fatigue so that we would laugh as loud and as long each and every time we heard the same joke. He decided audience participation was the best way to do this, and ran a string of competitions for a key to a glass case with a twenty-dollar note locked inside it. Thanks to this, on September 22, 2006 I became a Hollywood star, albeit for slightly less time than the fifteen minutes Andy Warhol believed we are all entitled to.

He asked if there were people who were not from America, so my hand went up, along with two Germans, a Chinese man and another English couple. We made our way to the front of the stage. Our task was to sing a song that represented our country. The man from the first English couple went first. He launched into a stiff upper lipped chorus of God Save the Queen. Building on the patriotism, the first German went for Deutschland Uber Alles, and the second went for something similarly nationalistic, and then the microphone was handed to me and Liz.

Asked now to think of a classic British song I would name Bohemian Rhapsody, She Loves You, I Can't Get no Satisfaction, or, because of its all conquering radio presence, Black Horse and the Cherry Tree. But the old adage that it always easier to think of these things when you're not in a TV studio held true, and the only songs that came to mind while the others were singing were the Sex Pistols version of God Save the Queen - an ironic counterbalance to the other version, but possibly not a vote winner - and Wannabe by The Spice Girls. In the absence of any further inspiration, we launched into a spirited rendition of Wannabe. Somewhere after the first couple of lines, Liz's mind reached the end of what she could remember and her dignity reached the end of what it could bear. My mind and dignity knew no boundaries, and I made it through a verse and a chorus before finally ceasing.

I could have stopped there confident of getting the audience vote, but when the warm up asked me to sing it again, but a little less restrained this time, the showman in me once more pushed aside the shy reserved man, and my best Spice Girl impression came out complete with limited choreography, pointing at carefully chosen audience members, none of whom I wanted to be my lover. I won the audience vote, and returned to my seat with high fives from distant relatives of stars in the front row and other less well-acquainted people a bit further back. My time as audience star turn lasted about ten minutes until, in the next break between scenes, a woman married for thirty-eight years happily confessed to an audience of strangers that she'd had no romance for years, and continually missed the joke in a 'what hand is the tissue in' magic trick - the joke was that the tissue had been thrown over the warm up man's shoulder. She was the hero now, and my decline was complete when my key didn't open the glass cabinet, and the copy of the script I wanted went to a woman who had left her aged granny at home alone in New York to come to the show. Abuse of the elderly had never been so profitable.

At ten o'clock the filming of 'Apologies for the Frivolity', the sixth episode of the fourth season of the show, came to an end. Charlie Harper ended the show by going to bed with a woman even after he finally realised what everyone else had spotted from the start, which was that she was a younger version of his mother in almost every respect. It's true that there aren't too many plot variations in Two and a

Half Men, but this episode, like most of them, was excellently scripted and superbly acted. It didn't feel as if the filming had taken as long as it had, which is always a sign of a good evening's entertainment. We left the studio and managed to get a passing taxi with surprising ease. We went down to Mel's Drive-in for a last meal on the Strip, before heading back to our room to spend an hour arranging and rearranging three suitcases and a bag to comply with the fifty pounds per item of luggage limit on the LA to Seattle train. A feat of engineering made irrelevant the next day when they never even weighed them.

27 – San Francisco

September 23. The train to San Francisco takes twelve hours. It leaves just after nine in the morning and arrives just after nine in the evening. San Francisco isn't the final stop either, as almost a day after it leaves LA it makes it to its final stop in Seattle. The prospect of spending twelve hours on a British train fills me with dread, mainly because I don't know any British train journeys that are meant to last that long. Twelve hours on a train from LA to San Francisco is a different prospect entirely, however, as the American commitment to comfort and customer service really come to the fore on the west coast train line.

Rather than a cramped sweaty train where seats are at a premium and a good meal is defined as Shepherds Pie in a tin tray, they offer double decker trains where the seats are spacious and you can not only recline in your seat, but can also do it without crushing the legs of the person behind you, before heading to the dining carriage to make a reservation for the evening's a'la carte menu. And it doesn't stop there either, just for good measure there is also an observation carriage where you can take in panoramic views across the coastline to one side and the countryside to the other, while a guy from National Parks and Museums walks along showing photographs and chatting about the history of some of the places en-route. I have to admit, he may have just been a man who couldn't leave his work behind, rather than an Amtrak employee, but either way he was a good addition to the journey.

Not that providing this level of service doesn't require a certain level of co-operation that some passengers find hard to give. The train guard, who bore a startling resemblance to TV's Trisha Goddard, both in looks and attitude, ruled the train in a ruthless manner allocating seats to passengers and making sure they were under no illusion that they could sit anywhere else. She placed cards along the aisle by allocated seats, and stern words and questioning followed for anyone found in a seat without a card. A few people tried to ruin her meticulous planning, but no one succeeded.

Sadly however this meant that we had no option but to put up with the family from hell in the group of seats to the front and side of us. They consisted of three generations of family members starting with the father, a man in his mid-fifties who had either watched too many episodes of the Sopranos or was a former member of the Mafia, and was recounting his life and fond recollections of what he had threatened to do to people who had disrespected him. Given that he seemed to have no redeeming feature whatsoever it was easy to see why a lot of people would disrespect him, and therefore why he had a lot of stories to tell.

After the father, came the son. He had his own coping mechanism when it came to dealing with his father, or anyone else in his entourage for that matter. He slept, only rising from his slumbers when the train pulled into a major station and he could gather the family together to go outside for a cigarette break.

At this point, I should break away from describing the family to mention Amtrak's cigarette breaks. As in the UK you can't smoke on trains but, unlike the UK, Amtrak appears to recognise the inhumanity of making smokers travel for twelve hours without the chance to light up, and factors in breaks for cigarettes at large stations. This may be less about smokers rights and more about the risk of smokers heading to the toilets and setting off the sprinkler systems, but either way fag breaks exist. The only member of the family - which also included mother, daughter-in-law and young granddaughter - who never went out for a smoke was the granddaughter. She looked about eight, so was probably a couple of years away from being a twenty a day girl.

She had other bad habits, however, in particular the desire to constantly change seats - ignoring the ruling of the train guard - and in each new seat decide she was going to sleep and close the curtains. As she was particularly fond of the seat opposite us, this meant our view of the countryside repeatedly shrank or disappeared entirely. Every time she woke up and moved away I crossed over and reopened the curtains, then twenty or so minutes later she'd return and the view would disappear again. The occasional scowl in her direction would make her pause mid-pull, but it was only a temporary reprieve and, eventually, I took what was the glaringly obvious solution, and walked down to the no reservation needed observation carriage with almost floor to ceiling windows, no baggage racks to shrink the view, and no curtains that could be pulled by annoying children.

The first stop, a couple of hours into the journey, was Santa Barbara. Santa Barbara looks a nice place from a train window, a bit Mexicanish with a good stretch of beach to one side and a national forest to the other. From there we moved away from the coastline, and the Sierra Madre Mountains came into view across to the east, an impressive sight, but one that didn't seem unusual on this journey. The next major stop was San Luis Obispo. The line becomes single track after that stop and there was a delayed train coming in the opposite direction, so we ended up staying long enough for the smokers to need another pack of cigarettes before we moved off again.

We were joined at this stop by a man, his wife and his two oxygen tanks. They took the seats much beloved by the curtain pulling grand daughter, which pleased us no end. We guessed the oxygen tanks belonged to the man as he was clearly out of breath from the walk up the stairs. Our guess was confirmed as we left the station and, with the help of his wife, he connected one of the oxygen tanks to his nostrils and his breathing steadied. It crossed my mind that this may send out a deterrent message to the sleeping man and his family about the dangers of smoking. I'm not a smoker myself, but if I was I think I'd take needing tubes up my nose as a sign I should stop. Clearly he didn't, and the next time the train stopped, he took out the tubes and became one of the first people to head downstairs, showing a vigour you wouldn't usually associate with a man who needed regular breathing support.

We got chatting to him and his wife as we passed more scenery and he took on the role of tour guide, telling us about where we were passing until it got too dark to make anything out. We went down to the dining carriage with them for our evening meal and over dinner learned that they were both in their early sixties and had only been married about ten years. His wife was more well travelled than he was, which seemed to be a common pattern amongst people we'd met, and for the most part they took separate holidays, too long in the tooth, and too clever, to change their routines lest it ruined a marriage founded on independence.

Whilst they lived in Sacramento, he was born in San Francisco and was still a regular visitor. He sang its praises and gave us so many recommendations of places to eat and places to see that we had no chance of remembering even half of them. Our conversation came to an end as the train pulled in to Oakland at 10:40, over an hour late. We left it and them and got the shuttle to San Francisco.

The shuttle had come as a surprise to us, we'd imagined the journey to San Francisco would be direct, but there is no direct line from Oakland to San Francisco. The shuttle therefore is a bus rather than a small train. Its departure was held up by one half of a couple who had met on the train going back to get his bag, the first flush of love and the spontaneous decision to leave the train being so strong that he forgot his personal belongings. As a result, it was after eleven o'clock when we left Oakland and nearly midnight when we made it to San Francisco. That still left enough time for more dubious joys to unfold before we went to bed for the night.

Our end destination was The Savoy Hotel on Union Square. The name implied some kind of grandeur, calling to mind the London hotel of the same name, and finding out that the shuttle would be stopping there seemed like a great stroke of luck, far better than having to get a taxi. All in all it should have been a good end to an unusual day, and indeed would have been if only all of the above hadn't turned out to be wrong. Firstly the stop wasn't in Union Square it was a couple of blocks away on an anonymous looking late night street. Secondly, our hotel also wasn't in Union Square, it was in Geary Street, three blocks away from the square in the opposite direction, leaving us five blocks away, with no taxis nearby and the prospect of having to haul three massive suitcases through the streets at half past eleven. Thankfully, on seeing our cases the shuttle driver took pity on us, put them back on board and offered to drive us direct to the hotel. This was a kind gesture, but the hidden message behind it was that we'd be unlikely to make the hotel with our lives and our bags in tact if we set off on foot. One reason for this, and one reason why the hotel claimed to be in Union Square when it wasn't, was that it was actually in the Tenderloin, a neighbourhood that boasts seven of the city's top ten violent crime spots - an achievement unsurprisingly omitted from the holiday brochures.

We pulled up at 580 Geary Street, allegedly home of The Savoy Hotel, only to find that it wasn't its home anymore. It was now home of the Hotel California. From the outside, we could only assume it had ceased to use a name associated with a prestigious brand for fear of legal action. This was not a place that oozed class. It oozed something, but it certainly wasn't class. The day before we had seen the hotel used for the cover of the Eagles album of the same name, a vast hotel with palm trees inviting you in. From that perspective the Hotel California was just as inappropriate a name as The Savoy Hotel was.

Dreading the prospect of discovering that our booking had been lost sometime around the time of the name change we stepped inside. The guy on reception, who I took for the owner, confirmed it was the same hotel and the name change occurred a month ago. He was clearly proud of his hotel and eager to please. Problem was it was difficult to see what he had to be proud about. The small lobby, and the small hotel that lay behind it, could have had the kind of charm and character larger hotels can only aspire to, but while retaining some character, any charm had long since gone.

We took the lift to the 5th floor and walked down the corridor to room 514. The room looked like it had been decorated sometime in the late sixties. This could have been because they wanted to recreate a Californian summer of love feel, but could equally have been because it had last been decorated sometime in the late sixties. The wardrobe hung together more because there was not enough space for it to fall apart than because it was well-constructed, and the small TV in the corner had a remote control that you just knew wasn't going to work the second you looked at it.

The walls were a bright yellow with a painted skirting line repeating well-known quotes about San Francisco and California. The first, courtesy of William Sarayan, read 'If you're alive in San Francisco you can't be bored, if you're not alive San Francisco will bring you to life.' The second, courtesy of Brian Wilson and Mike Love, was the slightly less prosaic 'I wish they all could be California Girls.'

In the bathroom there was a small mirror with writing underneath proclaiming 'the real star of this room.' Any guest looking at it would feel a sense of self-worth and achievement that would last until their gaze moved a couple of inches to the left or right and they surveyed the rest of the accommodation. All in all, not a good first impression.

Of course, as I remembered thinking on our first day in Montreal, a room is only a part of a hotel, and a hotel is only a part of a city, so, disappointing as the room was, we weren't going to write the remains of the evening off just yet. We went down to the hotel bar and restaurant, where I remembered that, in Montreal, the city had been as disappointing as the room on that first day, and, as a result, it came as no surprise to find the bar was closing.

The bar man suggested two other bars nearby, one next door and one over the road. We went next door. It looked alright in an upmarket yet downmarket kind of way with a DJ and a large crowd of well-off young executives trying to look as if they were slumming it before getting someone to drive them home. In that unique way that people with lots of money and no real social skills have, they were completely oblivious to everyone and getting to the bar was an impossibility as they refused to move an inch to let people through. We left and surveyed the street. Across in one direction was a bar where the people outside were all young and hyper fashionable, or stoned, or both. The taxis that were conspicuous by their absence earlier, were now out in force and racing through Geary Street to get to somewhere else so there was no chance of crossing over the road without a long walk. Instead, we headed across a smaller road to our right where we saw the inappropriately named 'Highlight Bar.'

It should have been obvious that we were not going into one of the neighbourhoods more reputable bars when I had to sidestep the arms of a small guy sat on the floor as we went in. He had been tugging aggressively at the leg of someone who had just come out, and now tried to get me in a sort of slow motion style rugby tackle by the door. Making it inside the bar, we were greeted by the smell of smoke and a strange bandit country atmosphere with a group of Mexicans and Cubans sat in the corner and two young female Malaysians behind the bar. We headed towards an alcove at the far end of the bar only to find ourselves in a backroom full of empty bottles and beer kegs with nowhere to sit. Back in the main part of the bar a table became free, but was then out of action as they mopped up the remains of something which, in spite of it looking fairly disgusting, had not been so bad as to make the previous occupants decide to move elsewhere to finish their drinks. With nowhere to sit, and safe in the knowledge that we didn't want to stay any longer, we stood at the jukebox by the poolroom, drank up and left.

We contemplated whether to head anywhere else. It was a brief contemplation. Groups of ex-hippies, homeless, stoned and drunk people on nearby roads in unfamiliar surroundings were enough to make us decide to put off further exploration till the morning. We went back to the hotel, raided the mini-bar and turned on the TV. The remote didn't work. We closed the wooden shutter blinds over the window and found that each of the slats had declared autonomy over the whole, destined never to close completely. In the bathroom, the message on the mirror greeted me ironically as I brushed my teeth.

Welcome to the Hotel California.

September 24. Started the day with a determination to like San Francisco. Headed up to Union Square for breakfast. Forty or so feet from the square, someone shouted to Liz, "white cocksucker, suck my fucking black dick." A charming introduction, guaranteed to work I'm sure. Could we wind back and start the day again maybe?

The re-started day was a mix of peaks and troughs as my initial impressions of the city were dispelled and then reinforced on a regular basis. Breakfast was at a cafe in Union Square, which looked like a cross between Piccadilly Gardens in Manchester, but without the buses, and Trafalgar Square in London, but with a lot more shops. It was an okay area, but didn't have any sense of uniqueness or individuality about it. We got tickets for a little two-stop trolley bus, having been told we couldn't get the main hop-on hop-off sightseeing bus from the square. As soon as we had parted with our money, and not a second before, we were told it was half an hour till the trolley went out. In that half hour of sitting doing nothing, the hop-on hop-off bus that doesn't stop in Union Square, pulled in and loaded up by a sign saying it did this every twenty or thirty minutes during daytime. I got a feeling it was not going to be easy to like the city.

The trolley bus was good. It took us to Portsmouth Square in Chinatown where the site of old men sit out playing Chinese Chequers was the first piece of local charm and character we had seen, and then on to Fisherman's Wharf, which for the most part resembled a typical run down northern seaside town, rather than a one-off place of beauty, until Pier 39 and the seafood restaurants around it provided a touch of individual style and a refreshing view out towards the ocean and away from the city. After that we headed to North Beach, San Francisco's Little Italy and a place where, as if desperate to mark out and preserve its territory, the Italian flag is painted on every lamppost. From there it was into Washington Square where Marilyn Monroe and Joe DiMaggio had their wedding photos taken. They didn't get married there, the church wouldn't allow it, but rather than take photos outside the anonymous city hall where the wedding was held they took them at the church after the ceremony, perhaps in the vague hope that at some point in their old age they would be sat together looking at them. A good reason to do it, even if it never happened.

Washington Square's other claim to fame is as the place where, in the first summer of love, San Franciscan hippies held a mass sit-in calling for the end of the Vietnam War. Hippies deciding to protest, but doing it by sitting down in a park on a hot day, rather than marching down busy streets holding banners, chanting anti-Government songs, and fighting with police, says more about the late sixties than any outdoor festival or song ever could

After the peak of the tour came a couple of troughs. The first was one of two trips back to Chinatown. The main Chinatown area, beyond the obligatory Dragon gate on the corner of Bush Street and Grant Avenue, was a mixture of a few shops selling Chinese goods, a lot of shops selling cheap cameras and electrical equipment, a large outdoor market, and far less restaurants than you get in your average Chinatown. The camera shops were the reason for the trip, the aim being to get a digital camera at a bargain price. We weren't sure if they sold the real thing or cheap imitations, but a quick look at boxes showed no one was selling the Olympiccs, Sonny or Pentacks varieties so we gambled on them being genuine, and prepared for the haggling we were told to expect.

Or at least we tried to prepare for the haggling, only to discover that haggling is an all together more aggressive past time in San Francisco than it is elsewhere. The shop owners and street traders seem to believe that if they offer you a good deal you can't turn it down without good reason. At the first store, I asked about one camera and, having got answers, decided to leave to look elsewhere and compare prices. The storeowner demanded to know why I was leaving, then offered me memory cards and a case for the camera at no extra cost if I bought now. This convinced me I could find something cheaper elsewhere, and eventually I extricated myself from the store and into another one where the same process began. A few stores later I gave up for the day, my desire to get a good camera put on hold by my desire to not be harassed by a succession of far from relaxed Chinese businessmen. A decided trough, and one that was followed by the subsequent search for somewhere for lunch.

The plan was to go back to North Beach, as we both knew the way there. The only problem was that we knew two completely different routes, and so eventually we found ourselves back in Fisherman's Wharf. Liz sat outside at Boudin Bakers Hall, the home of sourdough bread, while I waited an eternity in a queue before emerging with something that wasn't sourdough, at which point the wind decided it would have a laugh at the sun and made sitting outside look like a bad idea. My views of San Francisco took another step down, but then managed a few steps back up in quick succession.

The first of these came with a walk along Hyde Street Pier, stopping to look at the old boats and tall ships and taking in the view of the Golden Gate Bridge, half shrouded in fog. This was both relaxing and scenic, away from the claustrophobic atmosphere of other parts of the city. A rest in a park just off the beach was a further plus point and a superb Irish Coffee at the Buena Vista, allegedly the first place to serve Irish Coffee in America, saw the swingometer move fully on to the positive side for the first time that day.

Maintaining the away from it all mood, we avoided the crowded main streets and made our way back to the hotel via Hyde Street and Russian Hill, a nice neighbourhood on an incredibly steep hill. This means it isn't one of the regular tourist walks, and is all the better for it. We stopped at a bar and were served by a barmaid who read Camus, to herself, in between serving customers. If only all the city had been like this the rest of the day would have been good, but sadly, as we emerged out of Russian Hill, we came back towards Union Square and the cheap shops and run-down districts that reminded me there was still something about San Francisco I didn't like.

Back in the run-down hotel, the TV news represented another downturn in hope and expectation as the main local item was about the ferry service to Alcatraz. Following a tender exercise, the contract to run the ferry had been handed on to a new company, and former workers were planning to picket the ferry terminal. The picket and other teething problems meant the chances of the new contractors being able to start the service as planned were low. The new service was starting this week. If it wasn't running my chances of seeing one of the main things I wanted to see were nil. The swingometer was back in the negative area, and all that could revive it would be a good evening meal. Where better than Chinatown? I wish I knew the answer, because the experience of Chinatown in the evening suggested there had to be somewhere.

In comparison to the bustling daytime, Chinatown in the evening seemed curiously empty, and our experience at The Four Seasons Restaurant was curiously reminiscent of our experience at the Chinese restaurant in Chicago as they too seemed less than eager to bother serving anything after the main course. As we walked down the stairs on our way out we gave them a helping hand in their attempts to close for the night by turning their 'open' sign round.

Bringing a mixed day to a bad conclusion, we toyed with a drink in a couple of halfway decent looking bars but decided that as they were all suffering from Sunday night syndrome with a limited number of customers eeking out the last drink of the weekend, we'd return to the hotel to drink wine and watch the first of the new series of Desperate Housewives. We got up to the room and put the TV on just in time to hear the closing strains of the end theme tune and realise that somewhere along the way we'd got the time of it wrong. The evening ended with old episodes of Seinfeld and a bottle of wine in a cramped room in an unloved hotel. I don't really need to say where the swingometer had ended up.

September 25. Liz's birthday. Thankfully we were not going to be spending it in the Hotel California, although we were still going to be in San Francisco. As we originally thought the city would be so much bigger, with each area having so much to offer, we had booked three days in the Holiday Inn in Fisherman's Wharf to follow our two near Union Square. As it turned out, the city didn't seem so big and Fisherman's Wharf didn't seem so special, but if we had to stay in San Francisco it was a far better location than Geary Street. Our time in the city had to improve, but not without a few more things to remind me there was something I really didn't like about the place.

We started the morning with an early trip to good shops around Union Square and followed it by stopping at a Gallery with a great exhibition of photography on the Beatles. The euphoria was once again a mere passing phase as our attempt to get a taxi from the hotel to Fisherman's Wharf reinforced the impression that San Francisco is full of people who do deals and have friends, and can not be trusted in any way, shape, or form. It started just after the receptionist sent us to the bellman who checked where we were going and said he would get a relative of his with a limo to take us there. He made it sound like this was a friendly gratis gesture, rather than a costly journey across town to a hotel that you really don't need to arrive in style at, and one that we could have done for far less in a regular taxi, if only he'd got one for us.

260

On the short two mile journey the driver asked us how long we were going to be in the City and where we were going to next. We told him we were heading into the wine country. He then spent the rest of the journey trying to persuade us to hire him for a tour of wineries, promising to be cheaper than anyone else, "I'll do it for $55 an hour, others will charge you $65" he claimed, and this would have been fine were it not for the fact that we had told him we were actually staying in the wine country, not looking for a day trip. He seemed determined not to let minor details like this get in the way of business.

As we approached the Holiday Inn he told us "You'll be alright here, my brother's the porter", creating the impression that his family controlled the porter system for the cities hotels and wherever you were going another member of the family would provide the only transport you were offered.

Inside the hotel, his brother and a sidekick took our bags and told us we could go out and when we got back our room would be ready and our bags would be in it. Like a fool we believed him, and we left the hotel to get the hop-on hop-off tour bus, finding to no great surprise that you had to purchase tickets for it from street vendors who all offered what they claimed to be the best deal in the city for multiple trips. After various attempts to get us on more trips than it was possible to do in the time the tickets were valid for, they sold us a ticket for the tour we wanted and nothing else.

On the tour bus the driver informed us of just how many world firsts San Francisco claims to have, the first topless dance - Carol Doda at the Condor Club on North Beach in 1964 - the first bottomless dance - Carol again at the Condor, this time in 1969 - the first paperback book shop - the City Lights Bookstore est. 1953 - and the first Chinese Fortune Cookie. Of all of these, you would imagine that the fortune cookie would be the one most likely to be a first in America only, and yet strangely enough it is the only one that was a genuine world first, although the claims of San Francisco are open to debate with Los Angeles also claiming the title.

As well as various world firsts, San Francisco also boasts what is allegedly 'the world's most crookedest street.' Lombard Street is a narrow diagonal road down one of San Francisco's many steep hills. Because of problems with the volume of traffic, and the speed people went down the road, they redesigned it and created a zig-zag structure which means that after every two cars length the road twists and heads off in the other direction until it reaches the bottom. Most other places would have gone with speed bumps, and for that reason alone I'm tempted to accept without question that no street in the world is more crooked than Lombard Street.

After the bus tour we had Clam Chowder served in a hollowed-out round piece of sourdough bread, at the Blues Bar at the far end of Fisherman's Wharf. It was gorgeous, the bread and the chowder combining as if put together in an experiment by a mad scientist. I tried it again outside of San Francisco and it was never quite as good. If San Francisco didn't actually invent this, they certainly perfected it.

Relaxed and happy we returned to the hotel, got the keys to our room, and walked across to the neighbouring block to unpack. We opened the door and looked for the bags the porter was going to bring up. There were none to be seen. I rang the front desk and asked to speak to the porter. He told me he had never said he would bring them and wouldn't have been able to make the offer as the room wasn't ready when we checked in. For good measure he added that I was lying when I said he had offered. Somewhat confused I asked if he could bring them now. He promised to do this, and ten minutes later approximately nothing had appeared. I rang again and was told I would have to come and find the bags. I walked back to the main hotel reception and was shown to a cupboard and asked "are your bags in there?" as if him putting them there earlier that day had never happened. Half fearing that the bags would have gone the same way as his memory, I was relieved to find them where he had put them, with easy to spot labels prominently on the top.

A brief standoff followed as he looked at me and I looked at him, both of us expecting the other to pick the bags up. I won, but with each move of the bags he gave an exaggerated moan aimed at generating some form of sympathetic co-operation. Had he not called me a liar, and had it not been so over the top, he may have succeeded. Instead I took a perverse pleasure in staying with him and doing nothing as we left the reception, crossed the courtyard, and went into our block. I did give him a dollar tip but only because he stood outside our room looking like he would otherwise settle in for the night.

In the evening, we checked out various restaurants and bars before settling on McCormick and Kuletos, where I opted for Ahi Tuna, a dish that would have been sent back as undercooked anywhere other than at a Sushi Bar, or McCormick and Kuletos. Rarer than I expected it to be, it tasted great, but a couple of short hours later I found that raw fish really didn't agree with me. I held out for a while, but eventually our trip to Dirty Martinis Bar and Jazz and Blues Club was cut short as I contemplated the effect another drink would have on my ailing digestive system. We headed back to the hotel, another night in San Francisco coming to a strangely muted end.

September 26. A good way to piss off a company who have just lost the most lucrative contract they ever had is to go along to their office and ask where you have to go to now to get tickets. In this respect, the people at the Blue and Gold Ferry Company hadn't really done themselves any favours by still advertising tickets to Alcatraz at their offices at Pier 43, and consequently their staff had got very pissed off over the last twenty-four hours.

They still managed to smile when I approached them and asked the same question yet again, and they carried on smiling when they told me where to go – by which I mean they told me where to go to get tickets as opposed to where to go with my request for directions. Hornblower Cruises, the new company, were running their ferries from a makeshift office at Pier 33. From the look of the office it seemed like they had been expecting a last minute legal challenge and had decided against committing too much expenditure just in case. As it was, this hadn't happened and neither had the planned protests the day before. Instead sailings were going ahead almost as planned, the only problem was that the time needed to sell enough tickets to fill a ferry was longer than the time between each departure, so they were going out about three quarters full. People like us queuing for tickets for the following day didn't help, but they didn't stop us, probably because they guessed that they would at least have a full ferry at some time tomorrow.

We'd purchased tickets earlier for a bus tour over the Golden Gate Bridge. The bus left once a day at 12:30, but this being San Francisco there was no attempt to match the number of tickets sold to the number of seats on the bus, so some people would end up disappointed. We split our queuing duties as lunchtime approached, and Liz left to get in line for the Golden Gate bus, whilst I stayed with Alcatraz waiting and hoping that I would reach the front and be back by the bus stop for 12:30.

Miraculously I not only made it, but also had time for a leisurely stroll back, taking in the sight of a cruise ship loading up at Pier 35 as I passed. The scene could have come from a 1940s movie with the wide pavements and the roads outside the terminal full of well dressed elderly white people and their cases about to embark on a cruise. Completing the old time feel all the porters in charge of the long trolleys stacked with cases were black. One of them - who looked like he was in his fifties and had had a hard life getting that far - was even summonsed by a well-to-do woman with the words "young man" and a click of her fingers thrown in for good measure. The realisation that this type of person still existed and still took cruises was one of the biggest discoveries I had made in all the time we'd been away.

On the bus to the Golden Gate Bridge, the atmosphere and dress code were more relaxed as we headed past Fort Mason, the decommissioned military base, and stopped at the Palace of Fine Arts Exploratorium, another site that was built for a centenary celebration in 1900 and then left to stand after locals decided it was too impressive to knock down. The Exploratorium's ornate Italianate style cloisters, and columns topped off with Roman style carvings, gave it a grand old European feel that seemed totally out of place against the backdrop of most of San Francisco. But more noteworthy than the architecture was the pond, nestling in the greenery of the surrounding park, where a small unimpressive black and grey duck followed four perfect white swans as if the roles in the children's song had been reversed and the ugly duckling was just that. It was one of those sights that could make even the hardest people gush and sigh, and think of the world as a lovely place, at least for one brief moment.

After leaving the park we went across the Golden Gate Bridge, which in true San Francisco style, is not golden and doesn't have any gates. It is more of a red copper colour, the golden gate moniker coming from it being a gateway to the land where gold was discovered almost immediately after it had been bought, or taken, from unsuspecting Mexicans at a knockdown rate, according to a decidedly unpatriotic tour guide, who likened this to American attitudes towards land with oil in the middle east.

Today was one of those rare days when the bridge wasn't surrounded by fog, and from one side of it bridge you could see most of the almost nine thousand-foot long construction. From the bridge the city looked distant in spite of being so close, displaying a splendour that it struggled to display at ground level.

For all that the views across the Bridge are impressive, the thing you remember most about crossing it in an open top bus isn't the sights, it's the strength of the wind. Even on a relatively still day, it feels as if it's trying to blow off any skin that isn't tightly held on to your face. The force could probably single handedly reverse cosmetic surgery and turn tight faces back to flabby ones. But it's not just your face that you worry about, it is also almost impossible not to fear that the bus will tip over at any moment, the wind is that strong. The faint hearted and cautious on our bus would also have been worried by the tour guide talking about the 1906 earthquake and how it is commonly expected that another earthquake of such force will occur sometime soon along the San Andreas fault, simply on the grounds that they normally happen every hundred or so years. This may be true, but the largest bridge across the city was not the best place to tell people about it.

After crossing back over the bridge we took a trip round the Presidio. The Presidio is a former army base, and was the setting for the 1988 Sean Connery movie of the same name. From there we went to another place that gave its name to a movie, Pacific Heights.

Pacific Heights is one of the nicest and richest areas in the city. The parks at the top offer views out to the Bridge and Alcatraz, amongst other places. The streets on the edges of the area offer small stylish independent shops and small stylish independent restaurants, which suggest that the Pacific Heights community is fairly self-contained and don't venture out too often. It looked like a place to come back to for a great meal, which is probably why, in spite of our best intentions, we never went there again.

Back in the city, after another Clam Chowder in Sourdough bowl, we walked along the Embarcadero, the large palm lined road that circles most of the Eastern harbour. With various sculptures, and the Vaillancourt fountain opposite the ferry building, it made for a far nicer journey into the city centre than the shorter, more direct, route. Restaurants, including the obligatory Hard Rock Cafe, lined the way along with a couple of pier type cabaret theatres where long forgotten seventies stars like Thelma Houston were plying their trade in pier-type cabaret shows.

The Embarcadero Center was a less welcoming place. Four large buildings with a mixture of shops, offices and multiplex cinemas, it looked like a bit of a maze and felt as if we'd walked into it by mistake as a result of vast empty spaces and a general lack of people. We left it and went up to the Museum of Modern Art before making our way to Market Street, which resembled Oxford Street at the start and Tottenham Court Road at the end, as Department stores gave way to cheap shops and self proclaimed nude girl bars. San Francisco has a similar amount of nude girl bars on ordinary streets as New York did before it was cleaned up, and the city as a whole felt how I imagine New York did before Guilliani appeared and the regeneration started.

Outside the Virgin Megastore we stopped to listen to an unsigned band, who had been joined by a couple of panhandlers who appeared to be auditioning for the role of Bez from Happy Mondays, and actually looked like they could give him a run for his money, notwithstanding the extra years they had on him. The band were busking to get the money for the train fare up the coast to the studio where they were booked to record their first album. It would be great to feel that I was there at the start of something big, but somehow, mainly because the songs were nothing special, I don't think I was. After a short while we moved on and worked our way back towards the harbour road, stopping at the Hard Rock Cafe having decided that we could resist it no longer.

Sufficiently stuffed we left and walked back past beggars displaying either a refreshing honesty or a love of the bizarre. One had a piece of card with the words 'why lie, it's for drink' and another card read simply 'money for booze' while the man holding it told us "it's true, I'll spend every penny on it." He seemed so happy I wanted to give him money, which was probably the plan. The most bizarre sign asked for 'help for delinquent drag queen' and was held by a man who wasn't in drag. Maybe he wanted the money to get some clothes.

We went for an Irish coffee in the Buena Vista. A barman in his late fifties made several at one time, with a majestic style that would have made him look like the Tom Cruise of Irish Coffees had he been twenty years younger and a few feet shorter. We watched mesmerised, and then went back to see what new seasons were starting on TV that night. Ted Danson's Help Me Help You was opening to poor reviews, destined to be cancelled mid-season, and David E. Kelley was taking the third season of Boston Legal down the same road to self-parody that he had previously taken Ally MacBeal.

With this being probably the best day in San Francisco so far, we didn't risk ruining it by going out again. We had an early night ready for an early start on a 9:30 boat to Alcatraz.

September 27. We went for breakfast in Johnny Rockets, a small chain of diners built in a 1950s style. The décor of the restaurants include jukeboxes, chrome counters, red leather seats, and waiters and waitresses dressed in the attire of the period. The staff are known to sing and dance, twirl straws and make smiley faces with ketchup, but at half eight in the morning they didn't seem to be up to it somehow.

When we got to Pier 33 we found that for some unknown reason it had been besieged by flies, with several hundred people engaged in an unwinnable battle to swot them. From a distance it looked like some bizarre Masonic ritual or Country dance. We joined in, having no choice to do otherwise, and in between bouts of slapping ourselves got chatting to a group from Scotland who told us they were on a three week train tour to see the whole country. They were clearly very proud of themselves for seeing New York, Las Vegas, and the Grand Canyon, and, as I didn't want to sound like I was engaging in one-upmanship, I didn't say how long we'd been there and what we'd done.

The flies stayed with us on the short ferry over to Alcatraz island, AKA The Rock, and they continued to give us their undivided attention after we landed, only leaving us as we started heading up the rock into the prison itself.

We stopped to pick up leaflets and guides. They cost a dollar each and there were honesty boxes to put your dollar. Needless to say the temptation to take something without paying in a maximum security prison was too strong, and I took a guide and two leaflets with a total value of a dollar-fifty, to complete the third, and final, very petty crime of the trip, joined this time by several other felons doing exactly the same thing.

Alcatraz did not begin life as a prison, its first use was as a military fort in 1853. In 1859 it started to be used as a military prison, whilst retaining its role as a fort. It had eleven prisoners. By 1915 it ceased to be a fort and became 'Pacific branch - U.S. Disciplinary Barracks', and finally became a federal penitentiary in 1934. Robert Kennedy gave the order for its closure in 1963, the year his brother was assassinated. The only group of people to occupy the island since then were native Americans who claimed it, in the name of the 'Indians of All Tribes', in 1969, as part of a large and long lasting protest against the seizure of lands from Native Americans. The position and the history of Alcatraz made sure any occupation would gain a lot of media attention, but also rendered it unlikely to be permanent, and in June 1971 the last of the occupants left the island. The graffitied sign behind the United States Penitentiary board, reading 'Indians Welcome', remains as a marker of this phase of the islands history.

The setting of the prison, in splendid isolation on an island so close and yet so far from the city, is a large part of the reason it appears such a foreboding, unforgiving place. It has no aesthetic charms. The cells are small, the corridors have no adornments, and there is no sense of warmth in the building. Not punishment enough to subject you to confinement, the windows and the recreation yard look out onto the mainland to remind you of what you have been forced to leave behind. Prisoners did not lead pampered lives here.

While there were successful escape attempts when it was a military prison, they claim that none of the thirty-six escape attempts throughout its time as a maximum security prison succeeded. The only man known to have reached dry land was rewarded for surviving the cold, shark infested, waters by being recaptured when he arrived at the Golden Gate Bridge, nearly dead from hypothermia. Hardly the best end to such a difficult journey.

This is why I doubt they can be sure that the five escapees who were never seen again all failed in their attempts. If they got back to San Francisco unnoticed they would hardly have stood up and said, "look at me I'm here." This is not a trip over Niagara Falls in a barrel. No matter how proud you are of your achievements, you're not going to shout about it.

Inside Alcatraz I found out that Robert Stroud the 'Birdman of Alcatraz' was never known by that name during his life. He never had any birds during his time in Alcatraz, although he had canaries at Leavenworth Penitentiary, and got the rather less snazzy nickname of 'Bird Doctor of Leavenworth' as a result. It's easy to see why that one was changed for the movies.

We also got to see, and stand in, the cell where Al Capone was imprisoned for tax evasion. There is a plaque outside to confirm this, and yet, in the Tour of The Rock leaflet it says that the exact location of the cell is unknown. Maybe they should mention that to the guy who made the plaque.

After exploring pretty much everything there was on the island we went back to wait for the next ferry. The flies reappeared and stayed with us till shortly after we left Pier 33.

Back on the mainland, we went to the Musee Mecanique on Hyde Street Pier, a small museum covering the development and decline of San Francisco as a seaside town, and also home to the Amuse America collection of old penny machines and amusement arcade games. The dazzling array of seaside history ran from What the Butler Saw slide shows, old style Punch and Judy machines, and Skittles games through to the early Pacman machines that you had to sit down to play. Everything in the collection was incredibly cheap, and yet we still managed to leave with very little money. I wonder why.

After the museum we returned to the Holiday Inn for a happy hour that contravened the trade descriptions act, as a surly barmaid told us what drinks weren't included, before going on to tell us that they were out of most of the drinks that were. In the evening, we went down to Pier 39 to pick from the array of restaurants we couldn't pick from two nights previously. We choose the Franciscan Crab Restaurant. Part way through the meal, presumably due to an allergic reaction to something unknown, Liz felt a swelling in her throat, one of her eyes started to close, and the skin above it also swelled up. The rest of the meal went uneaten, and the swelling went as quickly as it came.

We headed over to the Italian part of North Beach, a short walk down lively streets in the daytime, and a long walk down anonymous streets in the evening. Many of the shops and cafes had closed for the day. We found two bars different from each other in almost every respect. The Rogue Bar had an underground feel, selling beers that looked like they were made from a home brew kit rather than a micro brewery out the back. The Washington Bar and Grill was a far swisher affair. Although it was a restaurant, there were more people sat at the bar than at any of the tables and this gave it the feel of a late night piano bar, notwithstanding the absence of a piano player. After a drink in each we headed back to Fisherman's Wharf and stopped at a small Irish bar where a would be Bob Dylan delivered songs from a wide range of artists in a way that made even the Johnny Cash classic A Boy Named Sue sound like a Dylan outtake. It somehow brought the evening, and our first stay in San Francisco, to a nice conclusion.

I'd grown to like the city more by the end of the stay, but it still paled in comparison to LA and Hollywood. After five days I was glad to be getting away. In the words of B. A. Robertson's Kool in the Kaftan "I don't want to offend thee, but San Francisco has its faults." Many a true word spoke in a three-minute pop song.

28 – Sonoma

September 28. Descriptions can be deceptive, as indeed can maps, particularly if they are the type that appear in holiday brochures. For that reason, and in spite of their close proximity to each other, we had booked two days in Sonoma Valley followed by two days in Napa Valley. We'd imagined both of them to be a long drive from San Francisco and a long drive from each other. How wrong we were. The longest drive we did before leaving Napa Valley would be little more than an hour.

Returning to the road meant getting another car. This time it was a brand new Ford Mustang. I never realised Ford made the Mustang. For some reason no one puts the word Ford in front of Mustang when they talk about them, maybe to avoid the association with such cool demons of the road as the Mondeo and the Fusion. The car had a mere six miles on the clock and looked cool with a low roof and a sleek two-door design. It was also red, a colour that would be a minus point on anything other than a Mustang or a little corvette. If only we'd had this on Route 66, I could have parked at the front of diners.

Coolness always comes at a price however, and the Mustang's design was its biggest drawback as well as its biggest draw. It had a trunk so small that trying to fit in three large cases and a small bag became a feat that required greater skills than we possessed. We struggled for ten minutes before deciding to use the back seats for the last of the cases. This proved to be a challenge akin to putting a ship into a glass bottle. It was clear that there was enough space for the case, but there was no apparent means of getting it into it. Some while later, after various contorted movements, we completed the task and road trip part two commenced with the short journey to the Lodge at Sonoma. It was so short that we drove straight past the entrance and carried on for a further couple of miles before we realised, turned round and drove back again.

The Lodge was a two-storey low-rise cantina style hotel in its own grounds about fifteen minutes walk from the centre of Sonoma. After the oppressive feel of large parts of San Francisco it was a welcome change to be back in open spaces, with clear skies and a hotel of character. The daily free wine tasting session was an added bonus.

Sonoma is a city but, even more than places like Springfield, required a large stretch of the imagination to see it as such. The centre was little more than a small network of streets built around a Plaza that resembled a village green square. Around the Plaza there were various small cafes and shops, including more than a few wine specialists, and restaurants and bars. Nothing appeared as if it was built less than a hundred years ago, and nothing was more than two storeys high. The contrast between here and nearby San Francisco was as marked as it was between Springfield and nearby Chicago, and the Mexican influence was everywhere, lending it the same laid-back atmosphere as Santa Fe.

The main draw of the place is clearly the vineyards and wineries, but there are other things to do and see including the Mission San Francisco Solana at one end of the plaza. The Mission was the twenty-first built in California, but the only one built under Mexican rule. Between its establishment in 1823 and 1832 it expanded to cover more than ten thousand acres of land. All that remains now are five rooms of the original mission, but this still serves as a good reminder of Sonoma and America's history. The old white adobe building has a basic wooden cross behind a wooden arch that supports a wrought iron bell, and looks like a simple place of worship and comfort for settlers and, as a result, is completely at odds with the average modern day Church or Cathedral.

The Mission lasted eleven years before it became the Parish Church of Sonoma in 1834. The chapel dates from that era and has a high pulpit which probably helped the Priest put the fear of God into parishioners, as much as it got over the acoustic problems that existed in the days before microphones. Outside, the nearby Vallejo's home and barracks also conjured up a bygone age, and as I looked out across the nearby hills where occasional white crosses appeared in amongst the trees, seeming to belong to nothing or no one, the whole place seemed to be part of another era.

We headed back to the lodge and went to the daily wine tasting, where people selling wine chatted enthusiastically about their wines and where people were from, happily and liberally pouring away, without seeming to mind that no one was buying anything. The relaxing day continued with drinks in the courtyard, as the sun continued to shine, and concluded with a meal in the hotel's Los Carneros Restaurant. We chose a bottle of a local rosé, which pleased the waiter as he praised our choice and told us how the owner of the winery had been a fairly large scale wine producer but had had a breakdown and sacked all his staff. He had now got a wood fire oven and started again from scratch. The waiter made it sound like any bottle of his wine they sold represented another small step on his road to recovery. We were happy to assist before retiring to a sumptuous looking bar to end the evening. Bliss.

September 29. The newspapers and TV news had been filled for two days with the saga of the alleged suicide attempt of troubled sports star Terrell Owens. Owens is destined to be the subject of a biopic, his career is littered with high profile, high fee transfers with mixed levels of success, bust-ups with former managers, and prima donna episodes too frequent to support his publicists claims that he is an innocent victim. His recent move to the Dallas Cowboys had, so far, not been one of his best. He failed to turn up for training for several weeks and had made a questionable contribution when he did appear. This had made it easy for an apparent bad reaction to prescription medicine to be turned into a desperate suicide attempt. The denials that were now coming out sounded as if he was just embarrassed that the attempt had failed. America's obsession with sports and scandal meant that the story would not go away, and Arnold Schwarzenegger signing into law the US's first cap on greenhouse gases got relegated to page five in his own state as a result. Lest anyone spots an opportunity for moralising, even though the cap followed some apparently nifty footwork by Tony Blair, in the UK it probably didn't even make the first half of the paper.

Not that Terrell, Arnie or Tony were of any real interest to us today, we were heading into the valley for a $69 five hour, five winery, tasting session with all wine included. The tour guide was a lady called Linda, who, whilst being a far better guide than the limo guy in San Francisco was likely to have been, still tried to sell us things we didn't want. She told us she was also a realtor - an estate agent in English terms - and gave us her card in case anyone wanted property in any of the areas she was going to take us too. It was not likely. The largest group on the tour - Patty, Kathy, Katie, Chris and Paige - were on their yearly girls outing for Paige's birthday. Paige was twenty-eight and about ten years younger than the rest of her friends. Their previous annual expeditions had taken them to places such as Napa Valley and San Francisco. As they lived in nearby Sacramento, it is fair to say that the purpose of their outings was not travelling and sightseeing, and certainly not property buying. They sang, joke, chatted, got drunk, and made the other people on the tour - a respectable looking couple from Ontario - so embarrassed that they stood at the opposite end of the bars, or in different rooms, until the afternoon when a few glasses of wine made them more amenable.

Our first stop was at the Kunde Estate Winery where we got a cave tour as well as a tasting. The caves, carved out of volcanic rock nestling behind the winery, stretch back for thirty-two thousand feet underneath fields where the vines are grown. They provide the ideal conditions for fermenting the wines without having to rely on air conditioning. They also draw in more customers than anything above ground would do, and in an area with this much competition that can't be bad. The owners clearly understand this, and so to add to the experience have a tasting room carved into the rocks, furnished with handcrafted tables and benches made from timber from an old barn that used to be on the site. Throw in free tastings, and they're on to a definite winner.

Our second stop was the Ledson Winery. Set in several acres of grounds, and with a sixteen thousand square foot French-Normandy style building, known locally as Ledson Castle, this clearly wasn't a small-scale wine maker. Ledson is a lifestyle not a brand, as was illustrated by their luxury hotel in the centre of Sonoma. At the castle they had four regal looking tasting bars where we drank another four small samples before buying lunch from their gourmet market and eating it amongst the oak trees that formed the picnic area. We then left the opulence behind and headed for more simple surroundings, and some simple people, at the St Francis Winery.

The people were a badly dressed Californian husband and wife who claimed to be psychics, and appeared to have stepped in from another place in history. They turned their attention to us after an attempt at courting Patty and her friends proved fruitless. The wife complemented Liz on her layered clothes, which were actually a T shirt, top and small coat, before going on to say that she herself had no sense of fashion and was styled by her husband. His multi-coloured shirt and her striped dress suggested he didn't have much of a clue either.

When it came to the kind of insights you might expect from two psychics, they weren't much better. The husband told me, "Patty's an alpha male, do you know what I mean?" I answered, in all honesty, "no, I'm sorry, I don't," and he explained that "in lay mans terms, it means you'd be okay with her if you weren't already sorted."

He then told me he could guess my middle name. Hardly in the top ten impressive things a psychic can do, I thought, but I decided to let him try anyway, mainly as I didn't seem to have any choice in the matter. His first few guesses were way off the mark. I gave him the starting initial, both to help him and to stop the agony carrying on any longer than necessary. He made several more wrong guesses. I could take no more, and gave him the answer.

I guessed his name at the first attempt, mainly because he had practically said it a couple of seconds earlier. I tried to tell him this, thinking it may be of some comfort when he was contemplating his own failures. He would have none of it, "You're psychic yourself," was his explanation. He then tried to gain some advantage out of this, by saying, "I knew that you were." He hadn't told me this earlier, however, and I hadn't guessed that he thought it, so, on balance, whichever way you look at it, he was wrong.

Even without psychic skills I knew it would be a bad move to take up his offer of going on to another vineyard with them, so we declined, explaining that we had to stick with the tour. They thanked us for visiting and for boosting the American economy.

Back on the tour bus I told Patty she was apparently up for it. She told me she knew this, not because she was psychic, but because he had already told her, and didn't take her walking away as evidence to the contrary.

By the time we got back to the hotel we'd tasted somewhere between twenty five and thirty wines and in truth the distinctions were getting harder to note as they all started to blend into one. Not that this put us off going to the tasting in the hotel and having another three or four small glasses of red. While none of the glasses equated to anything close to a pub-sized drink, the cumulative effect was more than enough to bring an end to any ambitious plans we had for the evening. We went back to our room for coffee and then fell asleep. When we woke, the furthest we wanted to walk was across the road where, conveniently enough, there was an Italian restaurant.

We crossed the dark deserted road and walked down the dark deserted sidewalk, which in some places was part of the road and in other places was part of a grassy verge, but in no place was a pavement as we knew it. At the end of it there were a couple of stores that were closed for the night, and the Sonoma Traintown Railroad, a vintage children's fairground, with a model railway, miniature pond, and miniature zoo with miniature animals, that was there for no apparent reason. There was also Pizzeria Capri, which had about five or six people in it, and proved itself to be the quintessential roadside restaurant, with food that was basic but good, and a waitress who wanted to know where we were from and what we were doing, but never said that we had seen more of her country than she had. Walking back from the restaurant and, staggering back into the lodge, reminded me of something from Sideways, and as scenes from that film go, it was a better one to imitate than the one where they crash the car to cover up an indiscretion on a stag weekend.

29 – Napa Valley

September 30. A couple of times in San Francisco I'd thought that concluding the holiday in LA would have been better than the anticlimax that seemed to follow. This feeling had disappeared in Sonoma and I was determined to make the most out of our last week. All of which made it a shame that the Marriott Napa Hotel was such a monumental disappointment. Four miles out of central Napa, all that was nearby was a Starbucks, a Laundromat, a petrol station and a take away, all of which looked like they'd been part of a cinema and shopping complex which had otherwise mysteriously disappeared. Added to that, compared to the Lodge at Sonoma, the Marriott was stuffy with no outside courtyards, and our room looked out over the car park. What more could we fail to want?

We had lunch in the hotel, there being no alternative, and briefly explored the surrounding area before going to central Napa in the evening. Napa's centre is bigger than Sonoma's, it reaches the size of a medium town rather than a village green. It still doesn't quite make it to city size however, and once we'd walked through it once and come back to where we'd started, it seemed to have shrunk. Going down the main street a second time it seemed smaller still. If we'd walked up and down it all night, it would probably have consisted of nothing more than a house by the time we'd left.

While it is small, what there is of it is lively. A bit like Redondo beach it's clearly a place where there is money, and where no one seems to need or want to earn any more, so instead they open up bars and restaurants where they can relax and be laid-back.

The best of the bars was the Bounty Hunter, which had a full range of wines, a large collection of continental beers and an eclectic mix of food thrown in for good measure. We started and ended the evening there, in between visits heading down the shrinking main street to

276

Ristorante Allegria where we sat out under umbrellas eating excellent food and drinking superb wine. All was well with the world apart from only having one more week to go, and a faceless hotel to go back to.

October 1. We thought we'd had a good meal the night before, but it was nothing in comparison to the fare that Jim and Judy, our tour buddies for the day, had had that same night at their son's wedding. The wedding meal had been held in an exclusive restaurant in an exclusive castle. It was a nine-course affair with a different wine to accompany each course, and in case that wasn't impressive enough, the restaurant was rated as one of the four best restaurants in the world, or at least it was according to Judy, who also wanted us to know that in this instance the world did not just mean the US. She did this by saying the words "not just the US" and putting a particularly strong emphasis on them, just in case we didn't get it. Better still, for the recently retired Jim and Judy, the bill for all this had been paid for by the bride's mother. If I ever have a son, I hope he meets a woman with a mother like her.

They told us this while we waited for the tour round the Napa wineries to start. There was time for us to hear this, and many other stories, because the concierge had told us the tour bus would be here long before it was ever scheduled to appear. As well as meaning we found out about the lives of Jim and Judy, this also meant we found out that Jim was a man for whom patience didn't come easy but insults did, as he continually confronted the concierge, venting his spleen and bemoaning the incompetence that had led to him being there half an hour before he needed to be. Judy informed us that it wasn't just the tour incident that had done for Jim's relationship with the concierge, he had a problem in general with him. Jim clarified what the problem was by telling us that the concierge was an asshole.

For a while, this description could equally have applied to Jim. Asked to describe Jim's physical appearance, apart from saying old and cranky, the only distinguishing feature to spring to mind would be one long grey hair that protruded from his neck just above his shirtline. It was too high to be the start of chest hair, and too low to have once been the end of a beard. When Jim was irritating me, the hair irritated me, and all I could find myself thinking was why the hell didn't he cut it, rather than leave it there, long and alone in ridiculous isolation. I probably missed some of Jim's more enlightening observations whilst I fixated on that hair.

Shortly after the bus arrived, Jim's quarrelousness was joined by a welcome sense of self-awareness and self-deprecation. He knew he could be irritating, but also knew how to laugh at himself and, as a result, he ceased to be an asshole. Sadly, the same could not be said of the tour guide who on arrival was an asshole, at the end was an asshole, and at all times in-between was an asshole.

In stark contrast to the slick professionalism of Linda in Sonoma, his was a low budget experience. Linda offered a set itinerary, free drinks at selected venues, and an inclusive lunch in the grand settings of Ledson Castle. He told us we could go anywhere we wanted to go - missing the obvious fact that we were on the tour because none of us knew the area - and lunch consisted of sandwiches and a free drink from a small deli whose owner he knew.

The offer of free drinks with lunch extended only to cold ones. We decided to hang the expense and get coffees at a dollar each, and then drank them at the back of the bus like schoolchildren on a day trip. The sandwiches were kept by the guide until a later stop at a small winery with a little garden. Getting a glass of wine to drink with them required a level of negotiating more often associated with trying to secure the release of hostages or getting a decent pay rise for a low paid worker.

We had told the guide that, rather than tell him particular places to go, we wanted him to follow a general principle which was to go where we could taste wine for free, as we'd imagined that part of the vast fee we had paid was meant to be for wine tasting, rather than for his banter and bus alone. He agreed to this but, rather than Linda's carefully selected pre-booked appointments, the wineries he took us to were ones that he had managed to collect sufficient free drink coupons from the local papers to get a few drinks from. At every stop he tried his best to ingratiate himself with the staff but it was clear that they couldn't really give a toss, even if he did come in on a weekly basis. Normally I would have felt sorry for him, but there was just something about him which made it easy to see why he wasn't treated like the valued customer he should have been.

Finding out that he was married came as something of a surprise. He was about fifty, so was clearly old enough, but he looked and sounded like he still lived at home. When he said his wife was a Thai bride and explained how the marriage had come about, it started to make more sense. He had met her in America in 2000, and after 9/11 had got worried about what America might do to foreigners, even though she was not, to use his term, "strictly illegal". He didn't elaborate on what this meant, or on what sort of halfway house exists between strictly illegal and strictly legal, but my guess was that, if there was one, she was probably on the wrong side of it for US immigration purposes.

Fearing her deportation, he proposed to her and, in a conclusion that is probably even less surprising than the ending of an episode of Columbo or a Benjamin Kunkel novel, she accepted. They married a week later and, a short while after, went to live in Thailand, using his words again, "to escape the war." This was presumably the war in Afghanistan, which wasn't taking place in America and didn't feature anyone who looked even vaguely Thai as an enemy. He didn't elaborate on the sense of fear for his Bride's safety that the war engendered in him, but he did tell us that they hadn't managed to escape it in Thailand, and so came back to America a year later and eventually, after several trips back to the US embassy in Thailand, got permission for her son from an earlier relationship, and her mother, to join them.

A true love story for the gullible. Not that it was just us who thought so, as Judy provided the most perceptive, succinct, observation of the day when she said, "I think he's a bit of a fantasist."

We bonded with Jim and Judy after the shaky start. It didn't matter that we'd only just met them and would probably never see them again, we could take the piss like long lost friends, and laugh when Jim revealed himself to be a lightweight in comparison to Judy, switching to water, as the excesses of last nights wine caught up with him, whilst she drank everything that came her way.

The tour ended at 4:30. As we got back to our room we found the cleaner was also there, so we went for a walk around the area, only to discover it contained even less than we'd expected, and made the decision to return to the centre of Napa that evening an easy one to take. We headed back to the Bounty Hunter where we discovered that the main courses, or at least the Salmon Salad and something close to Sausage and Mash, were as good as the wines and beers. On the way in, our taxi driver told us he was a musician and had been playing in town the night before with an R'n'B band at a bar that had been too busy to get into. Today it was emptier, possibly because it was a Sunday, and possibly because the band playing were a kind of sub-Nirvana tribute band whose less than cheery collection of songs really didn't create an inviting atmosphere. As a result, and with a long drive to Lake Tahoe ahead of us, we retired to the hotel with a bottle of wine from Sonoma to accompany the latest new TV shows. Calista Flockhart's comeback in Brothers and Sisters was on. I thought it looked like a curious mix of a daytime soap and Desperate Housewives and wouldn't make it onto anything other than a satellite channel in the UK. As further proof that I am the last person who should be in charge of getting US programmes for British TV, it made it on to Channel 4.

As always when you want to get to sleep early, we were far too awake and alert and ended up watching TV late into the evening and early into the next morning. We discovered we had been sharing the road with Oprah Winfrey and Gayle, her chef, for several weeks. They had been taking the route from LA to New York, but the main differences between their journey and ours was that they were going from west to east, and were being filmed as they went. We watched as they stopped in Sedona and Durango and wondered whether our paths had crossed at some point on some Interstate or in some sleepy town. We decided that, as we had never seen a large van with a production crew, they probably hadn't.

The last thing I remember watching was an advert for a sleeping solution. As with most adverts for tablets or health products in America, a list of possible side effects were read out at the end. The side effects almost always include something at odds with the fundamental purpose of the product. For example, we had seen adverts for anti-depressants that had the possible side effect of a higher risk of suicide, and adverts for hair restorer tablets that could cause an inability to keep an erection - so even if your full head of hair did lead to women finding you attractive, you wouldn't reap the benefits. The side effects of the sleeping solution included the possibility of making you drowsy. I would have thought that mere drowsiness would have been a sign that the product wasn't working, not that it was doing something unintended.

With that thought, and without a sleeping solution, I finally went to sleep.

30 – Lake Tahoe

October 2. The big breaking political scandal concerned Mark Foley, a Florida congressman, who was Chairman of the House Caucus on missing and exploited children, and who, in a country that allegedly doesn't do irony, had been sending explicit e-mails to a fifteen-year-old intern. As the scandal unfolded, more recipients of unwanted e-mails came forward, questions were asked over just how many other Republican congressmen were aware of Foley's interest in young males, and Foley disappeared, pretty much confirming that most of the rumours were true.

On the main morning news spokesmen for the Republicans and Democrats avoided serious discussion on how to prevent Paedophiles becoming congressman, let alone congressmen heading up committees to protect exploited children, and instead traded insults and competed to see who could list the largest number of dodgy politicians. The Republicans pointed out the numbers of scandals Democrat congressmen were currently involved in and, just in case anyone wasn't aware of who and what they were, listed them all. Sadly for them they dropped their guard by saying Foley was the only Republican caught in a scandal. With this the Democrat spokesman laughed before reeling off a list of names that sounded like a verse of Billy Joel's We Didn't Start the Fire, and then laughed again. And thus the news item ended without one single mention of the fifteen-year-old, but with proof that the issue is no longer convincing the public that politicians aren't corrupt, but convincing them that the other side is worse.

Rather than dwell on what this said about the state of the world, we went for breakfast in Starbucks where the scalding heat of the ciabattas destroyed our tastebuds and prevented us from discovering how truly lacking in taste they were. At least the coffees were sufficiently lacking in heat to act as some form of coolant.

After two destinations that were ridiculously close to each other and to San Francisco, we were now moving on to the first of two places that were ludicrously remote from each other and several hundred miles away from San Francisco. First up was the one hundred and sixty-odd mile drive to Lake Tahoe. The drive took us into the pleasantly titled Eldorado National Forest, which runs parallel to the ominously titled Desolation Valley Wilderness Area, a name that doesn't entice speculative visitors.

Driving through the forest, fog descended turning the scenic nothingness of the landscape into pure nothingness and carrying with it the fear that, at an elevation of seven thousand feet, we would have some serious and unexpected drops, along with some serious and unexpected sheer rock faces, to contend with. Occasionally the fog lifted, and then promptly descended again, until it eventually cleared to reveal the lake ahead of, and several thousand feet beneath, us. Our destination was now in sight. Whilst the view was stunning, it was tinged with sadness, as we reached the town and realised, for the first time we could remember, that we had driven more than three hours without hearing Black Horse and the Cherry Tree. A part of our holiday had come to an end.

We drove past a few motels and diners and turned off towards the South Lake Tahoe Best Western Station House, only a few hundred yards from lakeshore beach. From the outside it had a slightly rundown, down at home feel to it. The large numbers of bright purple chairs dotted around outside the chalet/cabin style rooms added to this, while a small swimming pool, positioned at the edge of the car park with no noticeable views out to anything, completed the picture. It wasn't a bad motel, it definitely had some charm to it, but something about it added to the emerging feeling that we were reaching the end of the trip, a feeling that grew as the day progressed.

Strolling into town we looked up at the main ski slope, and found out that from this week the cable car to the top of the slope was closed till Thursdays, as we were now 'out of season'. It seems there are two seasons in South Lake Tahoe. In the summer it draws in boating enthusiasts and general holidaymakers. In the winter it is a popular ski resort. On a Monday in October it is neither. From the point of being able to get to the beach, which belongs to one of the many boating clubs in the area and is out of bounds during the summer, this is a good thing. From most other points, it isn't.

As well as having two seasons, South Lake Tahoe is also split between two states, California and Nevada. As casinos aren't legal in California, the exact point where California ends and Nevada begins is easy to spot even without the aid of any 'welcome to Nevada' road signs. The Californian side is like a smaller, less quaint version of Sedona with motels, a Marriott timeshare with restaurants, cinema and designer shops, a couple of small out of town shopping malls, and wide streets with two or three bars and two or three diners. The Nevada side begins with Harrah's on one side of the road, the Hard Rock Cafe on the other, and a quarter of a mile of other casinos stretching beyond them.

Compared to Vegas it is decidedly small time. For all the over the top extravagance of Vegas, the casinos and city have a certain energy and allure. The same can not be said of the Lake Tahoe casinos. They don't have a vast array of theme cafes and bars, they don't have sideshow attractions, they don't have as many people in them, and the people they do have don't carry the same misplaced air of hope and optimism. I didn't see a craps table to try and recreate my feat of gambling brilliance, and even the swirling monotony of the music from the slot machines sounded different, if it was there at all. There was evening entertainment, but it wasn't Cirque de Soleil or Celine Dion. In South Lake Tahoe it was chicken in a basket cabaret stars of yesteryear.

Case in point was Harrah's where we got our first and only sighting of the holiday phenomenon that is the Drifters on tour. The Drifters at their height consisted of four, maybe five members. At least one of them is now dead, and another – Ben E King – has probably not performed with the group since he began a solo career with no one to stand by him. In spite of the therefore limited number of Drifters in existence, the band still manage to appear simultaneously all over European resorts with a presence that suggests either cloning of soul bands has begun, or that at least some of the so-called Drifters never appeared with any of the original band. It would have been interesting to see the American variety of Drifters, but this being an out of season Monday in October, it was not to be - the entertainment was reserved for weekends.

We walked to the beach and idled away the remains of the afternoon on the swings and slides, with no one around to tell us we were too old to use them. In the evening we headed back into town for a meal in Cecil's, a place that promised much but, ultimately, turned out to be a cross between a glossy fast food joint and a British Home Stores Restaurant. We then looked for a bar.

It being the start of the week, and out of season, the bars were quiet, with atmospheres that encouraged melancholic reflection. It occurred to me that however you choose to live your life, you are governed by the working week. This means that places are neglected half the time, and swamped the other half. Weekend visitors go away thinking a place is crowded and wishing there were slightly less people about, whilst in the week the bar owners close early for lack of trade. If you observed it from the outside you would think it was illogical, but we accept it as inevitable, and consequently on the 2nd of October 2006, I couldn't get on a cable car, or see the Drifters, and felt like a man who was being told it was time to go home even though I wanted to stay away.

In spite of this we didn't drown our sorrows to any great extent. We planned out the next day and decided on a boat trip on the lake, hoping against hope that they were still running.

October 3. We looked through leaflets for boat tours. We spotted a few and also thought we'd found a bus that would take us to them. Sadly the routes of the buses said more about the decline of culture, and lack of appreciation of natural wonders, than I had thought possible. In a place where a vast lake sits amongst mountains and canyons, the only bus we could get took people less that one mile down the road to dark casinos, without any windows or views.

Consequently, we took the car and drove to the Tahoe Keys Marina where the day long cruise with full meals and complimentary drinks had just left for the day. Luckily for us, this wasn't the cruise we wanted. We wanted the slightly shorter, slightly faster, more enthralling, no meals, journey offered by the Safari Rose Boat tour. Unluckily for us, it was not running on account of it being out of season.

There was a still shorter trip leaving from Zephyr Cove on the Nevada side of the lake. We rang to check if it was running and to book tickets. We got an answering machine telling us it would run if there were enough people and asking us to leave our number and say how many of us there were. Tempting as it was to say twenty and then pretend others had dropped out along the way we decided against this. We left our details and headed in the other direction to do a bit more sight seeing while we waited for a call back. We stopped at the Lakeside Marina where our luck improved as we booked on the Tahoe

Queen along with every one else foolish enough to holiday out of season. There were quite a few of us.

The trip lasted a couple of hours, and was truly a wonderful experience. As we pulled away from the shoreline I looked out in all directions. Way across to the east I could see where the lake ended, but ahead to the north at first there was nothing but water, miles of clear blue lake slowly opening out in front of us, until eventually we could see across to the trees, rocks and parched land that frames it. Everything seemed splendid and isolated, even though we were on a boat with more than a hundred people intent on blocking our view or pushing past to get a photograph.

We crossed over towards Emerald Bay a small bay which has only one building - Vikingsholm - a thirty-eight room mansion, which is almost impossible to reach other than by private boat, and looks like the sort of place where an eccentric old lady would invite people for a weekend and kill them off one by one. Less sinister, but equally bizarre was Fanette Island, which would be little more than a rock were it not for the fact that Lora Josephine Knight, the original owner of Vikingsholm, built a tea house on it for herself and her friends. They had to be transported to the island by motorboat, and once they got there there was nothing to do but drink tea. I wondered how many of her friends asked her just to put the kettle on in the main house.

Although the tour covered little more than a small corner of the Lake, the views out and the remoteness of the location made it seem like we had seen so much more. We arrived back feeling relaxed and refreshed, the impending end of the holiday receding from consciousness once more. We had lunch at the Riva Grille on the lake and headed back towards the hotel and the shops feeling again that this was how we lived and this was our world.

Later that afternoon I wondered back down to the beach, camera in hand and observed another part of the lake and an early sunset, taking photos as the sun came down to set the seal on the day. If only there had been an equally beautiful destination to go for a romantic meal the day would have been perfect. Sadly, we went to Appleby's. Not that Appleby's was bad, the quality of the food was surprisingly good for what was essentially the American equivalent of a Little Chef, but cut it any way you want, as romantic meals go it was not in the same league as the CN tower looking out across Toronto, or the restaurant at the edge of the Grand Canyon on your birthday. On the other hand, it still beat the pants off Cecil's, which was good, if not hard to do.

October 4. The day began with breakfast with Bonnie, which isn't a couch based TV show on a local cable channel. Bonnie was the waitress that morning at the South Lake Tahoe Best Western Station House. By the looks of her, she had also been the waitress at the South Lake Tahoe Best Western Station House for many previous decades worth of mornings.

While she was, and hopefully still is, a wonderfully friendly and contented lady enjoying life with an ease we could all benefit from, at first appearance, in silhouette from the other end of the restaurant, we thought a small monkey or ape was going to be serving us as something dressed in black, and walking in a strange slightly bow legged way, headed towards us. She looked eighty at least. The only non black item of clothing she wore was an old style red hat that looked like it came from the deep south around the time when slavery was fashionable. She introduced herself as Bonnie, the hostess with the mostess, and asked us where we were from. We told her we were from England and she told us how she served three hundred or four hundred English people a year, as if she was trying to keep count, and knew all about the English tea that we liked.

The previous day, tea had been served with everything you could imagine you may need except for a cup. Today, the full breakfast included enough items to be re-named the 'so full it could give you a coronary' breakfast, but came with no fork. We pointed this out, and Bonnie reacted as if we had stumbled on a private joke where the staff would always leave out one key item and see how customers reacted. Either that or it was just a coincidence and all the staff were nearing senility and incompetence. I hoped that wasn't the case.

There was something about Bonnie that you would not find in your average hotel waitress, she displayed a charm and attitude that seemed to be formed from years of happy service in a time when this was a career, rather than a short term job for low paid foreign workers. Whilst it seemed cruel that she was still being made to carry hot breakfast plates at her age, I imagined it would be crueller on Bonnie if they tried to stop her. We said goodbye at the end of the breakfast and she wished us well on our travels.

Liz packed while I went to the reception to check the route. I imagined reception would do the usual reception type thing, and key a few details on to a computer to produce directions to take us to where we were staying. Instead, the receptionist got out a map, and then another map, and looked at them with an intensity that suggested she had never realised the world stretched beyond the edge of town. I decided to go on the Internet while she studied them. A couple of minutes later, as she started to mark out a route, keeping one finger on the final destination to make sure she didn't forget it, I had a full set of printed directions, and we were on our way to Yosemite.

31 – Yosemite National Park

We headed across the state line into Nevada and through some small towns and confusing road signs before picking up Interstate 395 and starting a scenic ride through the desert. The small towns of Walker and Bridgeport were the only places to intrude upon the desert terrain. Both seemed aware of their place as intruders, and came and went quickly in as quiet and unassuming a way as possible. We had got blasé about views after three months travelling, and recent scenery had not been of quite the same standard as Oklahoma, New Mexico and Arizona, but as we drove along the 395 further into Yosemite, this was about to change as we reached Mono Lake. Clint Eastwood's High Plains Drifter was filmed at and around the Lake but that is just a minor detail. The lake is among the oldest in North America. It is believed to have formed at least 760,000 years ago, and is possibly a remnant of a larger and even older lake that once covered a large part of Nevada and Utah. The sight of the lake itself wouldn't be enough to take your breath away, but add in the surrounding rock structures, and the absence of almost anything else, and you are left gasping. Mono Lake is in a geologically active area at the north end of a volcanic chain stretching ten miles north to south and topping nine thousand feet. The Bodie Hills to the north and the Cowtrack Mountains to the east are remnants of an earlier volcanic era that predated the existence of the lake by hundreds of thousands of years. The Mono Craters, which stretch to the south, erupted more recently in geological time, but still hundreds or thousands of years ago in our time. The whole lot combined to create a surreal colour scheme and rock structure that could only be artificially created by using every lens and filter available and putting them together in previously unconsidered combinations.

Even this however paled in comparison to the view that greeted us as we turned off Interstate 395 and on to State Highway 120. A black rock mountain rose up out of the ground, dominating the entire skyline. Its size, textures, steep face, and occasional unnatural white flecks that could have been snow, added to the effect, and announced the last stage of the drive into Yosemite. We entered the park, passing through Tuolumne Meadows, stopping at most of the stopping points along the way, and looking out on vast monolithic rocks and mountains, with sheer faces dropping down to lakes, rivers and creeks. Closer inspection revealed people climbing up the rocks, showing a level of courage I could never hope to attain, and, taking in the view, it was clear that, once again, we were in an America that had been left alone to nature and, once again, I felt completely insignificant in the grand scheme of things.

Driving out of the Park and on to Cedar Lodge on Highway 140 the surroundings remained impressive notwithstanding the sudden intrusion of a treatment works and some rather ugly parts of a university as the directions took us down a spur road for no apparent reason. Getting back on the right road we found Cedar Lodge about fifteen miles outside of Yosemite. Our room was a typical lodge room, the entrance was direct from the car park, and it had two double beds with a black and white picture of a scene from Yosemite over each of them. It was basic accommodation, a place for the hardy traveller who wants somewhere to sleep, eat and drink. There was nowhere to walk to and nowhere to sit and enjoy the views. There were also lots of warnings about bears and the dangers of eating food outside. There are a lot of bears in the area, and while every activity is potentially dangerous, eating food outside carries the highest risk. Leaving food in your car is also a no-no, as it attracts bears to your room, so carrying hot food back later that evening left us worrying that a group of hungry bears were following us, a fear not eased by the large numbers of bear statues, dark and convincing enough to make the wary traveller do at least one double take.

The Lodge boasted a couple of places to eat. The first was a diner with fifties and Elvis themes to it for reasons that weren't explained. The second was the grandly titled Emerald Dining Room, which couldn't fail to not live up to its name. After checking in, we tried the dining room, but were told it wasn't open yet, so we headed for the diner which turned out to be in the same small building but through a door at the other side. We went in and were greeted by the man from the dining room, emerging from the opposite side of the same long bar we'd just seen him at. He didn't seem to see anything odd about saying hello to us again so soon after saying goodbye. On reflection, this spoke volumes about the people round this way.

We ate bacon cheeseburgers which, consisting of more than one type of meat as well another dairy product, was one of the more imaginative items on the menu. We drove off towards the Yosemite View Lodge, on the edge of the park, which seemed to be bigger when we passed it earlier, but on return offered little more than the Cedar Lodge. With darkness fast approaching we realised there was little to do that evening. We headed along to a small group of houses with a post office for Liz's obligatory card to her sister, and then drove back. As the nearest towns were at least thirty miles on from the lodge, down roads that you wouldn't want to drive along in the dark, we decided to have a night in. On TV there were warnings of rain and snow. The last few days had been full of similar predictions that temperatures would drop, snows would fall and anyone driving would need to take their chains, but so far it seemed each day had been warmer than the last. We hoped and perhaps expected that today's forecasts would be equally way off the mark. With ridiculous predictability they turned out to be almost entirely accurate, and I woke up early the following morning to discover that, with consummate timing, the rain had arrived, and it was foggy over the mountains.

October 5. Liz had had trouble sleeping following the discovery of a 'giant' beetle in the bathroom in the very early hours of the morning. I use inverted commas as the beetle was an inch long at most. The beetle had not been the only scary thing for her, although it was the only one that was real. The absence of nothing but the front door between us and the outside world, and the outside world consisting of forests and trees and the birds and creatures that live in them, had combined to make a feeling that we were under attack. In this frame of mind a smoke detector and a green light, which reflected off a mirror to a spot on the wall, came together in a sinister way and, rather than the harmless light of a smoke detector, appeared as some kind of glow worm or other unnatural inhabitant. As a result from 4:30 Liz was awake and reading a book, too scared to sleep. She stayed awake until she was too tired to be scared, while I gradually woke up and became too awake to sleep at around 7:35.

I walked to the lodge reception, used the Internet, and then went back to the room. The rain was slowing and the fog was lifting, but this, almost literally, turned out to be a false dawn. The drive into Yosemite saw the rain increasing and by the time we parked it was as heavy as ever. We took the visitor shuttle bus from Yosemite Valley, where the Awahnee Hotel announced itself as a place we knew nothing about but would have been far better to stay at than an anonymous roadside lodge thirty miles away.

I was determined to get off the bus and explore the park in spite of the rain, but Liz's enthusiasm for the rugged outdoor life lasted only till the first hop off the bus at the, in the circumstances, inappropriately named Happy Isles. When we reached Mirror Lake, the next place I deemed worthy of exploring, Liz stayed on the bus.

Full of the pioneer spirit I followed the signs to the lake, one and a half miles off the bus route. Seeing two roads, one of which was fairly wide and flat, and the other more of a dirt track, I decided to take the dirt track on the grounds that the smallest least explored route would have to be the one for the hardy adventurer. As I headed off further into the unknown I began to question my assumptions, particularly as I trudged past an inordinately large amount of what I hoped was horse manure, seeing as how the alternative was that it came from the bears we'd spent an evening trying to avoid. I couldn't turn back of course, I was on a mission to get to Mirror Lake, it was a once in a lifetime opportunity, and rain, mud and an increasing worry that I was going the wrong way could not deter me.

Eventually in the distance I saw the larger road that I hadn't taken, so I knew I was somewhere in the right area. I climbed up some rocky steps and walked through another muddy piece of horse dung covered path before completing my mission by arriving at Mirror Lake, a stretch of water that provides mirror reflections of Tenaya Canyon and the Half Dome, the most prominent landmark in the park. It was then that I found out that Mirror Lake dries up before the end of summer. There is no water and no reflected views in early October. Instead there was a dry mass of sand. It still looked eerily impressive with the parched land surrounded by trees and hills, and the Half Dome, visible in the near distance, hinting at what could have been. That said, even though I will always remember walking across what should have been the lake, I would still rather have seen it in springtime.

My next stop was Yosemite Falls. Yosemite Falls is also a seasonal site. In spring when the heat starts to rise, the snows of the high country begin to thaw and as they thaw they turn to water and thunder down the mountains making for spectacular viewing. As the summer progresses, and more of the snow thaws, the falls become less spectacular and by early autumn they slow to a trickle.

I made it to the stopping point for the lower falls. Even on one of the wettest days of the year, there was nothing to be seen. I decided not to head off down the long walk to the centre of the falls.

After further walks in the rain, I rejoined Liz back at the car. The road to Glacier Point, in the west of Yosemite, normally only closes from late fall to late spring when the wintry conditions make it impassable, but fog, rain and fear of snow meant it was closed today and sights that didn't lose any of their beauty in the late summer were off the itinerary. There was not much else that could be explored. Overall, I felt I'd achieved something by seeing as much of the park as I had done, but it was not the natural unspoilt experience I had hoped for, where I could relax and let my senses revel in their surroundings with no effort on my part. Yosemite has great views, an awesome panorama with a wider variety of sights than even the Grand Canyon, but a wet day in October turns a great experience into a rewarding but altogether different one.

As we drove out of Yosemite it finally began to stop raining, but we don't feel confident enough to turn round and try it again. Instead we headed to Mariposa, a small town about fifty or so miles out of Yosemite, and the first town on State Highway 140. The main junction at the entrance to the town had the usual array of Burger Kings and other fast food places, but beyond this was a charming little town which had its heyday in the 1849 goldrush, explaining why the other highway running through it was Highway 49.

We stopped for lunch at the excellent Miners Restaurant, an old style restaurant which we imagined, given its name and the history of the area, would have a mining theme, and yet bizarrely had a small rail track running round inside it, and no mining instruments whatsoever. Turns out that Mariposa had a second miniature boom after the gold rush when the railroad ran through it, cutting the time it took to get to Yosemite. That boom ended in 1917 when trains started running direct from San Francisco, and the only surviving remnant of the era is the inside of the Miners Restaurant, which presumably at the time was a surviving remnant of mining history, and would have to change its name again if there was ever another boom period for Mariposa County.

At its peak, Mariposa County was the largest county in California covering approximately 30,000 square miles, nearly 160 years later it covers a more modest 1,455 square miles, but the town still boasts an excellent family run hotel and a host of small shops, restaurants and bars that retain the original atmosphere of the place. It also boasts the oldest County Courthouse in continuous use west of the Rockies. Built in 1854, it heard some of the most celebrated cases in US mining law, and is on the National Register of Historic Places, preserved as a shrine to justice in California. The Courtroom remains how it has always been, with beams held together with pine pegs, and strengthened by mortise and tendon joints, with no nails to be seen. Even the clock, added in 1866, remains hand wound, and the court has no jury room, meaning jurors consider cases in the jury box just like they do in the best old movies.

It's not as impressive as Yosemite of course, but it, and the rest of Mariposa, was well worth a visit, even if it did take a morning of unceasing rain and the absence of anything else between it and Yosemite to get us there.

Back at the lodge we had fish and chips in the Emerald Dining Room, washed down with several bottles of beer and wine. There was a pool table in the corner, which said a lot about the kind of dining room this was, and a group of seasoned travellers played pool and drank lager from pitchers looking every inch like the people the lodge was made for. I kind of envied them, but mainly because I fancied a game of pool.

Back in the room Liz was the tired one tonight and I was the one who couldn't get to sleep, although not for fear of smoke detecting glow-worms.

On late night news there were a number of items that said things about the American way of life. First up was an item about re-virgining, the latest trend in designer operations, where people spend thousands to regain their virginity only so they can lose it again shortly afterwards as a wedding anniversary or valentines day gift. You can't help thinking it is a lot to spend for a few weeks anticipation and a few minutes pleasure. The only thing that could make it a bigger waste of money would be if the husband paid and there was an argument about the cost which meant the wife refused to have sex. The next item was news that Mark Foley had emerged from hiding and gone straight to rehab to deal with a drink problem, which perhaps wasn't the main problem he needed help for. After that came a story about overcrowding at Fresno County Jail. Nothing unusual in that, but the accompanying picture of prisoners in black and white jail suits, like the ones in MGM classics but without the arrows, struck me as very old fashioned in a developed criminal justice system. Finally, while Arnold Schwarzenneger was saying that Mexicans should follow his example by losing their allegiances to the old country and fully embracing life as Americans, the Amish community, who resisted most parts of modern day America, had been rocked by a school shooting spree.

It all combined to create a picture of America as a larger than life, stranger than fiction, kind of place, boasting a variety of traditions, people and places, disparate but united by common themes. It's fascinating and versatile in a way that no other country can be, simply because no other country is large enough to contain so many differences. I wanted to stay. Approaching our last full day in the States there was so much more I wanted to do and see. Seattle was but a few days away. From there we could re-enter Canada at Vancouver. We'd make it before the roads become impassable and chains become compulsory. But it wasn't going to happen. We didn't have a few days left, the trip was at its end.

32 - San Francisco Part 2

October 6. We set off relatively early from Yosemite. First task was to check what roads were actually open, what roads you had to have to have chains for, and what chains were. The man at the lodge had the answers to all of my questions. He told me that as far as he knew the 120 was open westwards all the way, so we would be able to drive through the last bits of Yosemite. He told me that we should have chains for every road just in case we needed them, but if we had a new car we would be okay. He also told me that chains are exactly what they say they are, which is chains that you put around your tyres to provide extra grip for the road. He told me they last for about an hour and after that they have bedded themselves into the normal tyre, so not only are they useless but your tyres need replacing. I thanked him, pleased to have learned a bit more about something I knew nothing about, and equally pleased that we had a new car.

I got back to the room and only half jokingly said to Liz that we should drive to Mexico. She only half seriously dismissed the idea, but the two halves didn't make a whole and we didn't attempt to take an overdue hire car into a country they don't let you drive hire cars into.

We drove off, stopping a few times in Yosemite to get a last few photos before leaving the park and driving for what seemed like an eternity looking for somewhere to stop. The first small town we came to was Groveland, which looks every inch like a Wild West town. A one street town with shop fronts straight out of a movie. Maybe it was a movie set with nothing being filmed that day, that would explain why everywhere seemed closed.

Passing Moccasin Creek we reached a stretch of State Highway 120 where we descended six thousand feet, rose back up, and went back down again in a five mile drive round what ought to be known as corkscrew hill, as the road curled as if it were a very large corkscrew. It had a speed limit of twenty-five miles an hour, which very few people managed to travel at let alone exceed. This says all you need to know about how tight the bends were. Driving along it was as exhilarating as it was scary. Out in the distance I could see what I thought was Tulloch Lake, a vast lake with an expanse of flattish land to reassure me that there was a straight flat road to come soon. When we got down there the Lake offered up more great vistas as rock and desert met the water and stretched back against an unspoiled landscape. It was the last great bit of scenery we saw.

We stopped for something to eat in Oakdale, a place that was curiously lacking the charm of either Mariposa or Groveland. On the radio Suddenly I See had replaced Black Horse and the Cherry Tree as the new KT Tunstall song, suggesting not only that our journey was over, but that we were intruding on a different journey with a different soundtrack.

We headed on to the Interstates as the 205 and 580 led us over the San Francisco Bay Bridge and back into San Francisco. We followed signs we hoped would lead us to Fisherman's Wharf but didn't. Eventually we reached the Embarcadero and worked our way round towards the Hyatt Hotel. I returned the car and handed the keys over, then walked back to the hotel from where we went back to the Blues Bar for a last clam chowder. From one of many cheap gift shops, Liz got a card with a picture of the American flag and the words 'God Bless America'. She wrote it and sent it as the last card to her sister. We went into the city and bought the last two CDs of the trip. The first was The Killers Sam's Town, a band already bigger in the UK than America, the second was KT Tunstall's Eye to the Telescope, for obvious reasons. We then went to the new Westfield Centre Cinema where we saw The Departed, the film we'd been told about as we stood on Boston Common at the start of the movie tour, and which was on its first day of release as we were on our last day.

We walked back along the bay and stopped at Fog City Diner, a classic style diner in a great setting just back from the bay. The perfect setting for a last meal, the only let down being that both the food and the service were dreadful. From there it was back to the Buena Vista for a last one of their famous Irish Coffees, a few other drinks, and a Sour Apple Martini which proved that the Buena Vista had no speciality drinks other than Irish Coffee.

The conversation turned into a reflection on the journey, what we had found rewarding, what we had found disappointing, what we had learned about ourselves, and what we had learned about each other. Leastways I think it did, but the following morning neither of us could remember any of it, so maybe this is just what I want to believe, and, actually, all we had done was engage in the sort of gibberish babble you expect from two people who had drunk too much on their last night in a foreign country.

For what it's worth, I had discovered that it was wrong to think of America as one country, just as it would be wrong to think of Europe as one country. I felt I knew so much more about the place than when I arrived, but also that I was leaving with a far greater amount to left to discover.

On a personal level, I knew that there was something about travelling that appealed to me, and that even when you pull into another town that may look the same as so many others there is still much to discover thanks to the people and the history that made it. Most of the places we went to are places I'll probably never return to, and some of them were places that you really shouldn't go out of your way to see, but, as part of a bigger journey, each of them played their part in shaping our experience. The experience was now at its end, but the memory of it would remain.

October 7. I woke up at half past seven, in spite of not getting to sleep till two. I pretended to myself that being awake was a good thing, it would help me sleep on the plane and avoid excessive jet lag. The reality was that I couldn't have got back to sleep anyway.

With nothing else to do I began to look for somewhere to stay on our first night back. I ended up booking the Travelodge.

I contemplated my quest to unearth the next US band to make it big in the UK. Would any of the CDs I'd bought get in the charts back home? Had I bought The Fray, who had the Cable Car Song on constant rotation in the last few weeks of the trip, and got a UK top twenty single with it in 2007, the answer would have been yes. As it was, I may have been better off trying to spot the next big book as Gary Shteyngart's Absurdistan, a book I bought in San Francisco, got five star reviews on its British launch in 2007, whilst my CD purchases went unnoticed.

One thing I had managed to do while were away, was to stick to my commitment to go to hotel gyms regularly. On the last morning, I managed a near continuous half-hour on the treadmill, and promised myself I'd keep this up when I got home. I managed this until some time around January 1, 2007. My other promise of attempting to run the marathon in 2008 was forgotten around the same time.

The last thing we bought in America was a small suitcase. We got it after breakfast and took it to our room where we began to re-organise our belongings to make sure we were observing all weight limits and didn't have the heaviest single piece of hand luggage ever assembled. Large amounts of unworn clothes, that had moved up and down suitcases without ever coming out, finally saw daylight as various jars, cups, glasses, and books got re-packed. When everything was fully and finally in place, we rang downstairs to get the cases taken down.

The concierge had told us to get a taxi at twelve for a flight at four. It turned out this had nothing to do with the need to get to the airport early, it was simply the hotel checkout time which suggested they were not keen on having our bags, or us, there any longer than necessary. The taxi turned up and the taxi driver drove along the bay, past all the bits we'd been to and on to a part we'd never seen and looked like it might have been worth going to. At the airport he unloaded our cases and dropped them off on the kerbside.

As he drove off I realised our one bag of hand luggage remained on the passenger seat where he had put it. Thankfully he returned with it just as I got through to the hotel to ask them to get him to turn round. As we got to the front of the check-in and were asked whether anyone could have tampered with our bags since we packed them, the obvious answer was "yes," but yes was also the inconvenient answer that would have meant getting all our stuff out and facing a long interrogation and a lecture on the importance of security and personal vigilance in our troubled times. I said "no," and then watched as the bag went through the scanner and a couple of security guards looked at it with great interest.

Then they told me to stand away and not to even think of touching the scanner or anything near it. Then they said they were going to investigate the bag for something amiss they had spotted. Visions of a future in Guantanamo Bay, protesting my innocence, went past my eyes while I looked on wondering just what was inside the bag and cursing my look for getting a taxi driven by a terrorist.

I watched them go through the entire bag and not spot anything. This did not mean the search was over and I was free to go. They told me there was something there, and I was going nowhere till it was found. I would have been impressed with the dexterity of the taxi driver in concealing something so well and so quickly had it not been for the fear of what was about to be found. The search continued with side pockets being checked and then suddenly just as I was about to say "can I speak to the British Ambassador, I want to change my earlier answer" they carefully pulled something out of a part of the bag I'd long since forgotten existed.

It was an anti-mosquito spray that had completed the entire journey undisturbed. More importantly it was ours and could not explode. While we knew we were in for a stern lecture about asking for clear bags for liquids, we were relieved that this was all we had to come. We accepted it willingly with smiles that suggested we were truly insane.

The next couple of hours passed slowly. We had lunch, made phone calls to use up the remaining call credit, and sat and waited. And waited, and waited some more until finally it was time to get on the plane. There was a slight delay to the take off, but all too soon we were taxiing to the runway and an air hostess was telling us what to do in the unfortunate event that we should crash land in the Atlantic - pray that god exists and hope for a miracle, or put life jackets on and head for an exit into a mass of water - and then we were flying over America, heading back towards the Atlantic, and home.

The initial fascination with the views and the places we might be flying over faded around the time the food came round, but a few hours later it returned and I looked down wandering which of these places we'd driven through. From the window behind me it was still clear daylight, in front of me there was more cloud cover and it was starting to get darker. It was like looking at a different time zone, mainly because that's probably what it was. After a while I could see the sun start to set behind me, while in front of me there was nothing but the skyline of clouds as the sun disappeared. Next time I looked behind me the sky was a mixture of blues, whites and oranges as the sun and the clouds came together to bring in the evening somewhere, while somewhere else in front of me it had already come in and the sky consisted only of two different shades of blue with a thin orange line dividing them. Then the line disappeared and left just a dark sky. I watched as the same dark sky descended behind me and then pulled the blinds down. I had no idea where I was, or whether, in whatever place was immediately below, it was the evening or almost the next day. At some point October 7 became October 8 although it is entirely possible that I was never anywhere at the time this happened, and I reached the next day without the last one ending.

With the view gone and night all round, I read a book and played endless games of Tetris until suddenly England was coming back into view.

October 8. The journey was almost over. I remembered everything we had done, three short months flashing before my eyes. Now it was no more. However long you spend away, as the plane touches down, it always seems shorter than it was. I wondered how I would feel if we had been away for the year we originally planned. Would I feel more like it was time to come back, or would it feel that there was no longer anywhere to come back to, and I was returning to somewhere I'd almost forgotten. Would it seem like the start of a new adventure or the end of an era. I tend to think it would be the latter. That's how it felt that day. We had done something we'd never done before, and could never do in the same way again. We could do similar journeys, but they wouldn't be the same, simply because they wouldn't be the first one. Not that this makes it any less likely that I won't attempt to recreate the moment the next time I get the chance, of course.

We landed at twenty past ten, got off the plane, collected our bags and waited for a friend to turn up with my car.

He turned up at the time I asked him to, which would have been excellent if my assumptions of how late the plane would be and how long it would take to get the bags had been right. As it was it turned out I was wrong on both counts, so we sat in the airport drinking tea and coffee. I turned on my mobile and found I had eight messages from all the time we'd been away. Four weren't even for me.

My apprehension at having to drive on the left for the first time in three months was not quite on the same scale as my apprehension at having to drive on the right for the first time ever had been, but I was still nervous when I got in the car and pulled out of the airport. I got to the first roundabout and guessed correctly which way to go. Nothing to it, I thought. I reached the first set of traffic lights, and left the engine idling until they changed to green. I went to pull forward and immediately stalled the engine. Driving a manual again wasn't so easy.

After stalling a couple more times, and having one or two uncertain moments about what side of the road I should be on, we arrived in

Kingston. We had a Sunday roast with Yorkshire pudding and Bisto browned, seasoned and thickened gravy in a pub called The Oak. It was as far away from an American meal as you could get. We checked into the Travelodge, where there was no Internet, one double bed, a small TV, and very little room - all at a price that would have been excessive if it had been in dollars let alone pounds. It was as far away from an American hotel as you could get. Welcome home.

In the evening, before the desire to sleep overtook us completely, we went to the Druids, a pub as opposed to a group of people with strange hats and ancient traditions. Music was playing on a random basis. Four or five songs in, there was a familiar count, an equally familiar 'woo, hoo' refrain, and a guitar strum arriving as Black Horse and the Cherry Tree unexpectedly came over the speakers as if it was playing for us alone. I closed my eyes and was back on Route 66, hoping that one day I would open them and find myself there again.

THE END

Author's note

Since completing this book, most of the artists I bought CDs by have remained unknown in the UK. However at the start of 2009 Eyes of the Night, a track from the Starlight Mints album Drowaton, was used as the introductory music to the ITV programme Demons.

Woody Allen's Scoop, whilst still not getting a theatrical release in the UK, was shown on BBC2 for the first time on February 7, 2009. I missed it, as I only noticed it was on twenty minutes before it finished. One day I'll get to see it…maybe.

Every road trip has to have a soundtrack, and the full list of songs, good or bad, that came to define this one are; KT Tunstall, Black Horse And The Cherry Tree; Snow Patrol, Chasing Cars; Rhianna, SOS; Gnarls Barkley, Crazy; Shakira, Hips Don't Lie; John Mayer, Waiting On The World To Change; The Killers, When You Were Young; Keane, Is It Any Wonder?; Nelly Furtado, Promiscuous; Natasha Bedingfield, Unwritten; Corinne Bailey Rae, Put Your Records On; The Fray, Over My Head (The Cable Car Song); Justin Timberlake, Sexyback; Pearl Jam, Last Kiss; Barenaked Ladies' If I Had a Million Dollars; something by Nickelback that wasn't Rockstar; and last, and by all means least, Blue October, Hate Me Today. That may explain why I bought a lot of CDs.

My thanks go to Howard Ripley for the many long hours he spent on the front and back cover designs, to Eddie Coleman for letting me know I was capable of being a travel writer, and, most of all, to Liz for coming with me on the journey and enduring my constant companionship for three months. I should also like to thank the long-forgotten property boom that helped to fund the journey via the sale of my flat. May it rest in peace.

I hope you've enjoyed reading the book. If you did, let me know via the NoLogoPublications website (NoLogoPublications.co.uk).

Lightning Source UK Ltd.
Milton Keynes UK
26 August 2010
159033UK00002B/137/P